Market Risk Management

⊙ GARP | Global Association of Risk Professionals

Second edition published in the United States of America by the
Global Association of Risk Professionals

111 Town Square Place, 14th Floor
Jersey City, NJ, 07310, USA
Tel: +1 201.719.7210 • Fax: +1 201.222.5022

2nd Floor, Bengal Wing
9A Devonshire Square
London EC2M 4YN, UK
Tel: +44 (0) 20 7397 9630 • Fax: +44 (0) 20 7626 9300
Website: www.garp.org

© Global Association of Risk Professionals, 2015

All rights reserved. No part of this publication may be reproduced, stored in a retrieval system, or transmitted, in any form or by any means, electronic, mechanical, photocopying, recording, scanning or otherwise, without the prior permission in writing of the Global Association of Risk Professionals, or as expressly permitted by law, or under the terms agreed with the appropriate reprographics rights organization.

Inquiries concerning reproduction outside the scope of the above should be sent to the Global Association of Risk Professionals, at the address above.

You must not circulate this book in any other binding or cover and you must impose the same condition on any acquirer.

The Global Association of Risk Professionals has made every effort to ensure that at the time of writing the contents of this study text are accurate, but neither the Global Association of Risk Professionals nor its directors or employees shall be under any liability whatsoever for any inaccurate or misleading information this work could contain.

ISBN:978-1-933861-05-0

Printed in the United States of America

*This book is dedicated to GARP's Board of Trustees,
without whose support and dedication
to developing the profession of risk management
this book would not have been necessary or possible,
and to the Association's volunteers, representing thousands
of organizations around the globe, who work on
committees and share practical experiences in numerous
global forums and in other ways, and whose goal is
to create a culture of risk awareness.*

Contents

Introduction xiii

Acknowledgements xv

Introduction to Market Risk Management xvi

Chapter 1
Introduction to Bank Risk Management 1
  1.1   Bank Risk Management 2
  1.1.1   Identifying Risk 4
  1.1.2   Measuring Risk 5
  1.1.3   Monitoring Risk 6
  1.1.4   Reporting Risk 6
  1.2   Risk Classification and Objectives of Risk Management 7
  1.3   Risk Management Failures 8
  1.3.1   Consequences of the Failure to Manage Risk 10
  1.3.2   The Cost of Risk Management Failure 12
  1.4   Organizational Structure of Risk Management in Banks 13
  1.5   What is Market Risk? 14
  1.5.1   Foreign Exchange Risk 14
  1.5.2   Interest Rate Risk 14
  1.5.3   Equity Price Risk 15
  1.5.4   Commodity Price Risk 15
  1.5.5   Credit Price Risk 15
  1.5.6   Implied Volatility Price Risk 15
  1.5.7   Implied Correlation Risk 16
  1.6   Summary 17

Chapter 2
Foreign Exchange Markets, Instruments, and Risks 19
2.1 The Foreign Exchange Market 20
2.2 Spot Foreign Exchange Transactions 22
2.2.1 Exchange Rates for Major Currencies 23
2.2.2 Drivers of Foreign Exchange Rates 24
2.2.3 Bank Trading in Foreign Exchange Markets 27
2.3 Forward Foreign Exchange Transactions 28
2.3.1 Currency Forward Contract Pricing 28
2.3.2 Risks in Foreign Exchange Forwards 29
2.3.3 Foreign Exchange Swaps 30
2.4 Currency Futures 31
2.4.1 Futures Contract Features 32
2.4.2 Differences Between Forward and Futures 32
2.5 Currency Swaps 33
2.6 Currency Options 34
2.6.1 Market Option Pricing Dynamics 35
2.6.2 Quantification of Option Price Dynamics 37
2.6.3 Risks in Option Trading 38
2.6.4 Execution Risk 41
2.7 Exotic Options 42
2.7.1 Types of Exotic Options 42
2.7.2 Risks in Trading Exotic Options 44
2.8 A Nested Risk Model for FX Instruments 44
2.9 Summary 45

Chapter 3
Interest Rate Markets, Instruments, and Risks 49
3.1 The Importance of Fixed Income Instruments 50
3.2 Cash Fixed Income Instruments 51
3.2.1 Loans and Deposits on the Interbank Market 51
3.2.2 Loans to Customers 53
3.2.3 Bonds 55
3.2.4 Bond Classifications 55
3.3 Pricing Cash Fixed Income Instruments 57
3.3.1 Yield Curves 57

3.3.2	Theories of the Term Structure of Interest Rates	60
3.3.3	Drivers of Interest Rates	61
3.3.4	Drivers of Credit Spreads	62
3.4	Price Risk In Cash Fixed Income Instruments	63
3.4.1	Present Value of a Basis Point (PVBP/PV01)	63
3.4.2	Modified Duration and Macaulay Duration	63
3.4.3	Convexity	65
3.4.4	Nonparallel Shifts in the Yield Curve	65
3.4.5	Floating Rate Risk	66
3.4.6	Bond Risk and Bank Balance Sheets	68
3.4.7	Overview of Bank Interest Rate Risk Management	68
3.5	Fixed Income Derivatives	69
3.5.1	Forward Rate Agreements	69
3.5.2	Interest Rate Swaps	69
3.5.3	Currency Swaps	71
3.5.4	Interest Rate Swap Valuation and Risks	72
3.6	Options and Exotic Fixed Income Instruments	73
3.6.1	Caps and Floors	73
3.6.2	Exotics	73
3.6.3	Structured Debt, CDO, and CDO-squared	75
3.7	Fixed Income Risk Map	75
3.8	Summary	77

Chapter 4
Equity and Commodity Markets, Instruments, and Risks ... 79

4.1	Equity	80
4.1.1	Equity Cash Instruments	81
4.1.2	Drivers of Equity Values	83
4.2	Equity Derivatives	86
4.2.1	Individual Equity Forwards and Futures	86
4.2.2	Equity Index Futures	88
4.2.3	Equity Swaps	88
4.2.4	Equity Options	89
4.2.5	Equity Exotics	90
4.3	Commodities	90
4.3.1	Overview	90

4.3.2	Commodity Cash Instruments	91
4.3.3	Physical Commodity Risk Drivers	93
4.4	Commodity Derivative Instruments	93
4.4.1	Commodity Forwards	93
4.4.2	Commodity Options	96
4.4.3	Commodity Derivative Risks	98
4.5	Credit	101
4.5.1	Credit Instruments	102
4.5.2	Credit Derivatives	103
4.6	Risk Maps	105
4.7	Summary	107

Chapter 5
The Risk Measurement Process ... 111

5.1	Value-at-Risk (VAR)	112
5.1.1	Definitions	112
5.1.2	Parametric VaR and the Normal Distribution	112
5.1.3	VaR Conversions and Conventions	114
5.1.4	Estimating the VaR From Historical Data	115
5.2	Critiques of VAR	117
5.2.1	Constant Parameters	117
5.2.2	Normality of Returns	118
5.2.3	Equal Weighting of Historical Data	120
5.2.4	Forward-Looking Volatilities	123
5.2.5	Other Volatility Forecasting Methods	124
5.3	Nonparametric Methods and Historical Simulation	124
5.4	VaR for Multiple Factors	125
5.4.1	Correlation and Covariance Definition	126
5.4.2	The VaR of a Two-Asset Portfolio	127
5.4.3	Bucketing with Correlation	128
5.4.4	Criticisms of Correlation as a Measure of Interrelationships	129
5.4.5	Historical Simulation and Correlation	130
5.5	Position Mapping and Aggregation	130
5.5.1	Bucketing and Mapping Plain Vanilla Positions	130
5.5.2	Conversion of Option Positions	133
5.6	The Daily VaR Process	136
5.7	Quality Control in VAR	137

5.8	Alternatives to VaR in Light of the Financial Crisis	138
5.8.1	Expected Shortfall	140
5.9	Basel III Treatment of Market Risk	141
5.9.1	Stressed VaR	144
5.9.2	Incremental Risk Charge	145
5.9.3	Comprehensive Risk Measure	145
5.9.4	Credit Valuation Adjustment	146
5.10	Summary	147

Chapter 6
Risks in Bank Trading Strategies 151

6.1	Overview of Bank Trading Activities	151
6.1.1	Development of Trading Activities	152
6.1.2	Position Management and Hedging	154
6.1.3	New Product Development	155
6.2	Bank Trading Strategies	157
6.2.1	Basic Trading Strategies	157
6.2.2	Leverage in Trading	160
6.2.3	Carry Trades	162
6.2.4	Trading Through Clearinghouses	163
6.2.5	OTC Clearinghouses	164
6.3	External Risks in Bank Trading	165
6.3.1	Market Liquidity and Depth	166
6.3.2	Market Behavior	167
6.3.3	Trading Style	169
6.3.4	Margin Requirements	169
6.3.5	Basis Trading	170
6.3.6	Option Hedging Risks	171
6.3.7	Failure of Trading Controls	172
6.3.8	Mark-to-Market Process	173
6.3.9	Problems with the Mark-to-Market Process	174
6.4	Managing Market Risk	174
6.4.1	Portfolio Diversification Approach	174
6.4.2	Hedging Approach	175
6.4.3	Synthetic Portfolio Approach	176
6.5	Summary	177

Chapter 7
Market Risk Organization and Reporting 179
- 7.1 Components of Market Risk 180
- 7.2 Governance of Market Risk 181
- 7.2.1 Objectives 181
- 7.2.2 Organization 183
- 7.2.3 Risk Classification 184
- 7.3 Tools Used to Measure Market Risk 185
- 7.3.1 Non-statistical Risk Measures 185
- 7.3.2 Value-at-Risk 187
- 7.3.3 JPM's Value-at-Risk Report for 2013 189
- 7.3.4 VaR Backtesting 190
- 7.3.5 Debit Valuation Adjustment (DVA) 191
- 7.3.6 Loss Advisories and Drawdowns 192
- 7.3.7 Economic Value Stress Testing 192
- 7.3.8 Earnings-at-Risk Stress Testing 192
- 7.3.9 Risk Identification for Large Exposures (RIFLE) 193
- 7.4 Risk Monitoring and Control 193
- 7.4.1 Limits 193
- 7.4.2 Qualitative Review 193
- 7.4.3 Model Review 194
- 7.5 Uses and Users of Market Risk Reports 195
- 7.6 Summary 198

Glossary 199

Index 217

Introduction

The global financial crisis of 2007-2009 has made financial institutions even more aware of their responsibility for managing risks. In the wake of the spectacular, unprecedented, and fundamental transformation of the global financial infrastructure that has followed the crisis, the responsibility of risk managers has changed. At financial institutions worldwide, banks and regulators increasingly rely on the skills, knowledge, and integrity of risk managers to pilot the transformation financial system with improved risk management policies, practices, and systems.

As risk management has moved to the forefront of banking, risk managers are becoming increasingly visible, important, and trusted at banks. This evolution is driven both by banks themselves and by bank supervisors. Banks are increasingly sensitive to the role of risk management in making decisions. Supervisors have come to recognize that better understanding of risk management principles and practices is vital, not only for the success of individual banks, but also for the safety and soundness of the global financial infrastructure.

As a result, bank supervisors have refined regulations that were outlined by the Basel Committee on Banking Supervision in the International Convergence of Capital Measurement and Capital Standards, also known as the Basel II Accord. The changes to Basel II, and new regulations that form the Basel III Accord, reflect the new financial world order, codifying the risk management practices of many highly regarded banks. While this book does not specifically address the Basel II or Basel III Accords, it does reflect the principles and practices—both qualitative and quantitative—that they embrace.

Market Risk Management is part of the GARP Financial Risk and Regulation (FRR) Risk Series that offers a qualitative introduction to banking risks, risk management, and the international risk-based regulation of banks. The goal of Market Risk Management and other related volumes in this series is to ensure that the reader develops a deep understanding of the qualitative aspects of a typical large bank's risk management activities, including risk assessment, measurement, modeling, and management, across the trading and banking books.

Taken as a whole, the GARP FRR Series—Market Risk Management, Credit Risk Management, Operational Risk Management, and Asset and

Liability Risk Management—enhances the understanding of specific risks and shows the right questions to ask when qualitatively analyzing the risks of financial instruments or assets. These books create a broad understanding of the key risks banks face and how these risks can be best managed.

Understanding the specific sources of risks is essential in the management process of measuring, monitoring, and managing risk. The material is presented in a user-friendly format enabling readers to understand the key qualitative risk factors and how they drive bank risk management. Each book contains numerous examples of actual financial events, as well as case studies, diagrams, and tables that explain these complex relationships. Overall, these volumes foster a better understanding of why and how financial risks emerge and how these risks can impact individual financial assets, financial institutions, financial systems, and ultimately, the global financial infrastructure.

Students who successfully complete market, credit, operational, and asset and liability risk management readings will gain a broad understanding of how the various risks reinforce each other. Such students are strongly encouraged to sit for GARP's International Certificate in Financial Risk and Regulation, an integrated look at the chief risks financial institutions face and how to best manage them. To complete the program, students may decide to take a certification exam.

These readings contain several technical terms used in banking and risk management. While the material requires a fundamental understanding of finance and banking, the intended readers are not practicing risk managers but bankers who want to have a better understanding of the qualitative factors affecting risks and who have familiarity with fundamental banking and finance concepts. This study text has adopted the standard codes used by banks throughout the world to identify currencies for the purposes of trading, settlement, and the displaying of market prices. The codes, set by the International Organization for Standardization (ISO), avoid the confusion that could result from many currencies having similar names. For example, the text uses USD for the US dollar, GBP for the British pound, EUR for the euro, and JPY for the Japanese yen.

Acknowledgements

Market Risk Management, a volume in the GARP Financial Risk and Regulation series, has been developed, and now revised, under the auspices of the Banking Risk and Regulation Committee at GARP who guided and reviewed the work of the contributing authors.

The Committee would like to thank David C. Shimko, Ph.D., Peter Went, Ph.D., Amanda Neff, Graeme Skelly, Christian Thornæs, Andrew Cunningham and other members of GARP for their contributions to this latest edition.

Introduction to Market Risk Management

Market Risk Management, a volume in the GARP FRR Series, focuses on market risk management practices at global financial institutions. It consists of two parts. The first part of the book focuses on market risk of financial instruments by addressing risk identification, risk measurement, and risk mitigation practices. The readings introduce various financial instruments in increasing order of complexity, from cash instruments such as foreign exchange to sophisticated commodity instruments. Throughout the readings, the focus is on understanding the risks of these instruments from a qualitative perspective. The second part of the book focuses on market risk measurement and management, and discusses the use of Value-at-Risk (VaR) to manage market risk, including stress testing and scenario analysis.

CHAPTER 1

Introduction to Bank Risk Management

In Foundations of Banking Risk (FBR) we studied the fundamentals of banks, bank products, and bank functions, exploring bank risk management in detail, both in theory and practice, with an emphasis on the latter. In this volume, we first discuss the sources of market risk in all of a bank's market and product areas. In the next three volumes, we address asset-liability management (ALM) risk—including the relation of bank risk management practices to bank regulatory requirements under Basel II and III—credit risk, and operational risk. We conclude by discussing risk integration, bank capital, and the establishment of a risk management culture.[1]

Because we separate bank risk management practices and bank risk regulation in this volume, we are able to focus on financial risk concepts that are relevant for many firms as well as banks. Hence, this book is useful for a broad set of financial executives; Risk managers at life insurance companies, asset management firms, and other financial services firms will find much of

---

1   The definitions of risks and risk management in financial services and banking have wide ranging interpretations. For instance, according to one of the regulators of banks in the United States—the Office of the Comptroller of the Currency—banks face credit risk, interest rate risk, operational risk, liquidity risk, price risk, compliance risk, foreign exchange risk, strategic risk, and reputational risk. Other bank regulators may put the risks in different order or label them differently. Typically, bank failures are due to credit risk coupled with liquidity problems; historically, banking crises have been due to credit risk and foreign exchange risk.

the material in this volume to be relevant for their companies, even if they are not banks.

Financial Risk and Regulation (FRR) is designed as a comprehensive, qualitative approach to understanding bank risk management. FRR deliberately avoids complex mathematical analysis and derivations, though basic calculations are covered to help the student understand the mathematical foundations of pricing and risk concepts necessary for bank risk management. For those interested in delving deeper into the mathematics, there are numerous books available that address quantitative approaches to financial risk management.[2]

On completion of this chapter, the reader will have an improved understanding of:

- Bank risk management functions
- Identifying, measuring, monitoring and reporting risk
- The types and classes of risks banks face
- The objectives of risk management
- Important financial institution failures and the consequences of failure to manage risk
- The five classes of market risk

Later chapters apply these general concepts in bank markets, products, and management. Students reading this volume are expected to know the basic functions of banks and bank products, and to have some exposure to the capital markets. This material is covered, for example, in FBR, the companion introductory volume to this one. FBR, however, is not strictly needed for students to complete this program. Moreover, students are not expected to have advanced knowledge of bank product pricing, financial mathematics, or statistics. The material this book, while not quantitative, is demanding and comprehensive. Thus, this book can serve as a foundation for further, technically advanced studies in financial risk management, or as a platform to understand the key concepts of financial risk management.

1.1 Bank Risk Management

The term "risk management" is used in many different ways. In a bank, everyone is a type of risk manager. Senior management strives to maximize returns while keeping risks at an appropriate level. Bank treasury personnel

---

[2] One recent example is Steven Allen, *Financial Risk Management: A Practitioner's Guide to Managing Market and Credit Risk*, 2nd ed. (New York: Wiley & Sons, 2013).

monitor the risk of the bank's loan portfolio and may manage interest rate risk using interest rate swaps, derivatives, or other risk management tools. There are risk managers that seek to mitigate the risk of default by employing sophisticated credit default swaps and other credit derivatives that shift the risk of default from the bank to others,[3] or by simply selling loans to other banks to reduce the risk in the bank's loan portfolio. Even the security guard at a local bank branch is a risk manager, since his purpose is to protect the bank in some measure against unruly customer behavior or other threats to the bank branch.

In this volume, when we speak of risk managers, we are referring specifically to the people who are responsible for identifying, measuring, monitoring, and reporting risk. Risk managers are also responsible for ensuring a bank's compliance with risk regulations. Ironically, risk managers usually do not directly manage risk, rather, they provide the information that allows business managers to manage risk. For the purposes of this program, these risks include market risk, credit risk, and operational risk, all defined in Section 1.2. In some banks, risk managers also have the authority to make transaction decisions in emergency situations, but normally risk management personnel only have the power to assess risk and to recommend management action.

While many nonbank firms worry about having sufficient capital and available liquidity to fund their operations, banks generally see risk as a greater concern than the level of cash accessible to the bank. Provided normal conditions prevail, banks can expect to raise additional cash by offering deposits at competitive rates and conditions, acquiring deposits from the interbank market, borrowing from their central bank, or borrowing from each other. Therefore, while corporations focus on return on cash investment (ROI) as an indicator of performance, banks tend to focus on return-on-risk measures, such as risk-adjusted return on capital (RAROC). Clearly, risks can have impact on cash requirements, but if cash is in ready supply, risk

---

3 While most banks do not use derivatives to manage their risks, the number of banks that have integrated derivatives in their risk management toolkit has increased dramatically. For instance, according to statistical information compiled by the OCC, at the end of 1995, there were 549 US commercial banks that reported derivatives exposures with a notional exposure of roughly USD 17 trillion (OCC's Quarterly Report on Bank Derivatives Activities, Fourth quarter 1995). At the end of June 2009, there were 1,100 banks that reported derivatives exposures with a notional exposure of more than USD 203 trillion and by the end of September 2014 1,389 and USD 239 trillion (OCC's Quarterly Report on Bank Trading and Derivatives Activities Third Quarter 2014.) At the end of 1995 and again 19 years later, in 2014, the largest 25 US commercial banks accounted for more than 97% of all derivatives exposures. In 2014 this had grown to 99.8%, when the top 4 banks took 92.6%. Internationally, data released by the Basel Committee for Banking Supervision reveal similar trends.

matters more than the cash. This is because, for a bank, risk capacity is constrained more than cash availability. RAROC and the computation of the measure are covered at length in Chapter 4 of the Asset and Liability Risk Management book in the GARP FRR Series.

For the purposes of this introduction, we can say that a bank focuses on risk because of both business and regulatory considerations. It must choose a portfolio of business activities that maximizes its return in light of a regulatory or internally prescribed maximum risk level. Because it will not enjoy the benefits of a diversified business portfolio, it cannot allocate all of its capital to the most profitable business. While a bank's more profitable businesses tend to get greater allocations of risk capital to foster growth and increase financial performance of the bank, the benefits of over-investing in any business must always be balanced against the cost of the lack of diversification.

1.1.1 Identifying Risk

Risk is defined as anything that can cause an adverse outcome for a bank. Sometimes risks are obvious. Foreign exchange rate or interest rate changes, for example, directly impact bank products and clients and thus banks. Other risks are less obvious. For example, if the government of Turkey decides to make the Turkish lira inconvertible, disallowing its conversion into any other currency, the effect on a European bank with trading operations in Turkey may not be clear. Sudden inconvertibility may trigger a sequence of events affecting a bank in an unexpected way, such as terminating trades with Turkish banks and being unable to collect on the value of those terminated trades.

Whatever the source, risk managers are responsible for identifying material risks to the bank. Because a risk manager is not necessarily an expert in every one of the bank's products or businesses, this responsibility is normally shared with the bank's business units. In this case, the risk manager is expected to work with the business units to design, develop, and apply a common framework to continually identify new specific business risks that have not yet been identified and to propose possible mitigation techniques.

EXAMPLE

Before the start of the global financial crisis in 2007, and the subsequent credit crisis of 2008, bank risk managers would have been aware of many risks in their bank's collateralized debt obligation (CDO) portfolio, as would the traders managing those portfolios. They would have built mathematical models to assess the risk, but because the models used data from the past to determine risk estimates for the future, it is likely these models were unable to foresee a massive increase in default correlations across US subprime loans, or to assign a high enough likelihood to this event that it would be material. Some banks may have had supplemental reports or stress tests that could have indicated large looming risks, but it is possible that management did not act upon the warnings. While some analysts blame risk managers for failing to measure the potential risks of the crisis, others blame the business managers for failing to act on the risk information they had.

1.1.2 Measuring Risk

Measuring risk is one of the risk manager's most difficult tasks. The risk management department is tasked with building mathematical models that describe the risks inherent in every transaction the bank undertakes. In the loan portfolio, for example, these are the probability of default, the loss given default, and correlations among borrowers relating to joint default. In the trading portfolio, these are risks related to the fluctuations in prices of all the securities and contracts in the bank's portfolio. When dealing with operational risks, the risks stem from failed procedures and processes.

Why is risk measurement so difficult? Risk measurement attempts to look into the future to assess potential risks, but of course, the future cannot be known. Therefore, most risk models use past price and market data to estimate likely future risks. The logic of this may seem perverse: it is much like driving a car down a curvy mountain road by constantly looking at the rearview mirror—we know how the road looked behind us, but we do not know what is coming around the next bend. Anyone who uses historical risk information as the sole forecasting input to a risk model is bound to make grave errors in risk assessment, and therefore investment strategy. No rational investor should rely only on past returns to predict future returns, or use only past risks to predict future risks.

The only realistic alternative to backward-looking risk assessment is a set of forward-looking scenarios generated by bank experts—scenarios that describe what the financial environment may look like in the future by anticipating the effect of each scenario on the bank. Because scenarios are based on the imagination of bank executives and risk managers, they cannot be expected to encompass all possible outcomes. Without any historical precedent, singular events such as the attacks of September 11 on New York, for example, could not have reasonably been foreseen. Even if a historical precedent had been identified, assessing the probabilities and impacts of a repeated event would be close to impossible. Clearly, historical analysis, while it forms the basis for risk measurement in most banks, should not be relied on as the only indicator of future risk.

1.1.3 Monitoring Risk

Some risks are measured by models and updated on a daily basis. For example, banks normally produce daily reports to estimate market risks in all of their trading departments. Other risks change over time without having an impact on reported risk—the risk exposures communicated to senior management, regulators, and those responsible for managing these risks. For example, if a risk manager sees that a particular trading group has a lot more trading activity than usual, it is his or her job to find out the reason for the increased volume: the business unit may simply be responding to an increase in market opportunities and/or changing its trading strategy from buy-and-hold to capturing short-term gains, typically a riskier strategy.

Monitoring risk requires attention to material changes in risk reports, business units, and the markets that affect a bank's portfolio. If a previously unidentified material risk arises, such as the failure of a major counterparty in the marketplace, the risk manager must report the new risk and find a means to measure and track it so that management can make timely decisions based on accurate information. When risks change materially, management must decide if the bank should bear the increased risk or if it would be more appropriate to mitigate the risk by hedging or by closing out trading positions.

1.1.4 Reporting Risk

Reporting risk refers to all communications of the risk management department to outside groups. These outside groups include not only senior management, but also the board of directors, credit rating agencies, equity analysts, lenders, trading counterparties, banking regulators, and shareholders. In Chapter 7, we will look at JPMorgan Chase's reporting of its risks to shareholders as a comprehensive example.

Some reporting is automated, and some may be performed by other bank departments outside of risk management. Other types of reporting are highly customized to ensure the right information reaches the right parties.

1.2 Risk Classification and Objectives of Risk Management

Banks face numerous risks, which are normally divided into three main categories: market risk, credit risk, and operational risk. Market risk derives from changes in the value of traded securities or contracts held by the bank. It represents the risk of a loss due to adverse movements in the bank's trading book. Trading losses affect reported bank earnings immediately, as the trading portfolio is regularly "marked to market."[4] For some banks, this is their largest risk factor.

Other banks see credit as their largest risk. These banks tend to be regional banks that have more lending than trading activities. Credit risk in the banking book comes from the possibility of borrowers defaulting on their loans. In the trading book, credit risk comes from the possibility of trading counterparties defaulting on their obligations to the bank. While market risk is the risk of a loss, credit risk is the risk that an asset or a gain cannot be realized due to lack of performance by a counterparty to a loan or a trade.

A third risk, operational risk, is usually considered smaller than market and credit risk, but one operational risk event can destroy a bank. Operational risk refers to failures of people, processes, and systems, such as trading errors, "rogue" traders, bad credit screening systems, and faulty procedures for identifying potential incidents of money laundering.

Another risk, asset-liability management (ALM) risk, is a subset of market risk, but is restricted to the banking portfolio, i.e., the loans the bank makes, its long-term bond positions, and derivative hedges against those two. ALM risk is measured in the same way as market risk, but, unlike trading losses, fluctuations in the value of the banking portfolio do not affect reported bank earnings, because the banking portfolio is not marked to market.

In this volume, we focus on the management and reporting of market risk, ALM risk, credit risk, and operational risk. Clearly, there are other risks, such as regulatory, political, legal, or environmental risks that can affect a bank profoundly, but these are not a part of the daily function of the risk management department and are managed by other departments, such as compliance, human resources, and corporate counsel. These risks are

---

4   Marked-to-market accounting records the value of balance-sheet exposures that reflects observed or market prices. Pending regulatory, accounting, and reporting changes in the recognition of value fluctuations are expected to have a direct effect not only on the reported—accounting—earnings of the bank, but also on the bank's required level of capital.

nevertheless extremely important to senior managers and other stakeholders of the bank.

The objectives of the risk management department are to provide timely and accurate risk information to the bank's decision makers, but the risk managers do not usually make trading decisions for the banks. Thus, the objectives of risk management are compliance, risk control, portfolio management, communication, and planning.

Examples of risk-management needs include:

1. Compliance-driven needs: reporting risks to bank regulators and maintaining sufficient capital relative to those risks to cover adverse outcomes.
2. Control-driven needs: minimizing controllable adverse outcomes for the bank, such as loan fraud.
3. Portfolio-driven needs: allocating the bank's risk-taking capacity to activities that will have the greatest collective positive benefit to the bank.
4. Communication needs: disclosing internal reports in order to help ratings agencies and trading counterparties assess a bank's creditworthiness, and to inform other stakeholders of a bank's risks.
5. Planning needs: assisting a bank in planning contingent actions as adverse events occur.

1.3 Risk Management Failures

Regrettably, banking institutions fail. Fitch Ratings reported in its sample of 1,768 banks over 17 years (1990-2006) that there were 117 bank failures in 101 countries. Of these, 105 received liquidity support from their governments or third parties and 12 defaulted on their financial obligations.[5] In 2007 and 2008, many more banks failed or were consolidated into larger banks. Hence, more than default alone, bank failure must be considered the result of a combination of liquidity shortfall, default, reorganization, and even severe drops in market value.[6] Moreover, as bank failures are typically concentrated in times of severe economic distress, there is a cyclical component to the phenomenon of bank failures: banks are more likely to fail

---

5   Ian Linnell, *Fitch Ratings Bank Study: Transition and Failure 1990-2006* (New York: Fitch Ratings, 2007).
6   To compare, during the savings and loans (thrift or S&L) crisis, between 1985 and 1994, almost 1,200 banks failed in the United States. During the worst year of that crisis, 1988, more than 200 banks failed in one single year.

during periods of economic distress when credit and other losses accumulate and capital and other reserves are inadequate to sustain a bank's long-term survival.

Recall that risk managers are primarily concerned with market, credit, or operational risk. The "Wheel of Misfortune" published by SunGard Corporation lists a few top failures in these categories that were considered notable at the time[7]:

Bank/Institution	Amount Lost	Cause	Risk Type
Bank of Credit and Commerce International (BCCI)	USD 10 Bn	General Fraud	Operational (4)
Bankers Trust	<USD 100 Mn	Lawsuits Trading	Operational (2)
Barings Bank	USD 1 Bn	Losses Trading	Market/Operational (3)
Lehman Brothers	USD 65 Bn	Leverage	Liquidity (1)
Long Term Capital Management (LTCM)	USD 3.6 Bn	Spread widening	Market/Liquidity (2)

Note: the numbers in parentheses correspond to Professor Stulz's classifications (see below).

FIGURE 1.1 Top Bank and Financial Firm Losses

The SunGard website offers case studies of these and other risk management debacles. BCCI's failure can be linked to a lack of monitoring for fraud risk and deliberate manipulation of risk controls. Bankers Trust's failures can be linked to a failure to take counterparty legal risks into account in the sales and contracting processes. Barings Bank's failure came directly as a result of one particular trader's losses in the Singapore office, in conjunction with false risk reporting to senior management. Finally, LTCM, not a bank but an asset manager, failed due to a combination of market risk and high leverage. It is unclear whether the risk models underestimated the risk or whether the risk was known, but LTCM suffered a scenario that was very unlikely to occur. The former would be a risk management failure, while the latter would not. LTCM provided the first example of an unregulated entity causing a systemic problem. All banks are moving their proprietary trading into unregulated fund management entities as a result of recent banking regulation.

---

7 James Lam, *Enterprise Risk Management: From Incentives to Controls*. (New York: Wiley Finance, 2014)

In a 2008 paper,[8] René Stulz, Professor of Finance at The Ohio State University, presents a typology of possible risk management failures:

1. Failure to accurately measure known risks
2. Failure to take risks into account
3. Failure in communicating the risks to top management
4. Failure in monitoring risks
5. Failure in managing risks
6. Failure to use appropriate risk metrics

Of these possible risk management failures, risk managers are strictly responsible for items 1, 3, 4, and 6. Responsibility for taking risks into account (2) is shared with the business units, and the act of initiating risk management recommendations (5) is usually designated to the business unit, except for certain emergency situations.

1.3.1 Consequences of the Failure to Manage Risk

If a bank fails to manage its risks, the results may be immaterial, catastrophic, or anywhere in between. In some cases, for example, an unrecognized risk can actually benefit a bank, such as when an error is made by a trading counterparty in a confirmation that benefits a bank. Unfortunately, most risks have more downside than upside potential. In some cases, the bank may have a drop in its equity value due to trading losses or the perception of mismanagement; or the bank may see a drop in its credit rating, making it more difficult to initiate customer business. In extreme cases, a regulator may revoke a bank's license, put a bank into receivership, or force the bank to merge with another. In the worst case, a bank may simply be allowed to fail, causing the bank to default on its obligations.[9]

The impact of bank failure cannot be overstated. Employees are likely to see bonuses disappear, to be made redundant by new managers and owners, or to lose their jobs along with the value of any bank shares they may own. The impact on lenders and counterparties is usually a partial or delayed payout on their claims. Shareholders normally lose everything, or nearly everything. Customers may face delays in having their claims processed and

---

8   Stulz, Rene M. "Risk Management Failures: What are They and When Do They Happen?" (Fisher College of Business Working Paper No. 2008-03-017, October 2008.) Available at SSRN: http://ssrn.com/abstract=1278073
9   Regulators also allow banks to fail to send a signal to other banks that they will not always be rescued. This signal is important because it discourages banks from taking excessive risks. The failure of Lehman Brothers in September 2008 is a good example.

paid, even if the claims are guaranteed. Depositors can lose their savings to the extent they are uninsured.

In normal years, the failure of a single bank can have systemic repercussions, affecting the banking industry worldwide. The famous 1974 Herstatt Bank failure, for example, led to a currency crisis because of the inability of a single bank to pay out on its currency trades, thereby causing a catastrophic—albeit brief—systemic risk to the entire banking system. The events of 2008 underscored the fact that systemic risks can be much worse. If most major banks invest in the same assets, and the asset class fails, we can expect a reduction in earnings and market value for all banks and simultaneously experience a massive liquidity crisis (because of the inability of any banks to supply capital at any price). The events of 2008 caused bank regulators to focus more on correlated risks across banks, and not just individual bank risks in isolation.

So, what happened to the financial institutions mentioned in SunGard's case studies? Quickly, here are their stories[10]:

BCCI
When BCCI's problems were uncovered in the 1991 probe, regulators in seven countries moved quickly to take over the bank's branches. On July 5, offices in the UK, US, France, Spain, Switzerland, Luxembourg, and the Cayman Islands were seized, and the bank's business activities were frozen. BCCI's assets were ultimately liquidated, and a pool was established to reimburse depositors who had lost their funds when the bank was shut down.

Bankers Trust
In October 1994, Procter and Gamble Co. (P&G) sued Bankers Trust for USD 195 million, alleging that the bank had misled P&G as to the suitability of an interest rate swap. In December of the same year, Bankers Trust agreed to pay a fine of USD 10 million over allegations that it willfully gave Gibson Greetings inaccurate values for its derivatives portfolio.

In October 1995, P&G added civil racketeering charges to its suit, which would have allowed the company to seek triple damages. In January 1996, Bankers Trust settled with Air Products and Chemicals, Inc. for USD 67 million in connection with interest rate swaps the company entered into with the bank. In May 1996, P&G agreed to pay USD 35 million of the USD

---

10 Other case studies from GARP's website: http://www.garp.org/media/673455/measurementandmanagementoffinancialriskacasestudyapproach-chumo_072911.pdf

195 million it owed Bankers Trust and to forgo between USD 5 and USD 14 million in gains on a separate contract.

Barings Bank
On February 23, 1995, at the close of trading, a Barings error account contained 55,399 Nikkei contracts expiring in March and 5,640 contracts expiring in June. As of February 25, these contracts showed a loss of JPY 59 billion on Simex. The next day, Barings' Board met to discuss a hastily prepared analysis of the fraudulent transactions recorded in Account 88888. In March 1995, the Dutch Bank ING agreed to purchase Barings for GBP 1 and assume all of its liabilities.

LTCM
On September 23, 1998, the Federal Reserve Bank of New York, acting to prevent a potential systemic meltdown, organized a rescue package under which a consortium of leading investment and commercial banks, including LTCM's major creditors, injected USD 3.6 bn into the fund and took over its management in exchange for 90% of LTCM's equity.

Lehman Brothers
On September 15, 2008 Lehman Brothers Inc (LBI) filed for bankruptcy, following a weekend where Merrill Lynch had been instructed to find a buyer for the over-leveraged LBI. Merrill Lynch was known to be next in line for collapse and bail-out in the liquidity challenged pre-crash US investment bank sector and ended up selling itself to the buyer (Bank of America) instead. LBI had used an accounting device called Repo 105 to mask the true risk and liquidity positions in its business for the three quarters prior to its failure. LBI ran out of sufficient collateral to raise cash. The fall of LBI was the largest US corporate bankruptcy in history with USD 613 billion in debt.

1.3.2 The Cost of Risk Management Failure

Of these five institutions, Bankers Trust was the only one that survived immediate failure; it was acquired by Deutsche Bank in 1999, mostly on the strength of Alex Brown, its brokerage business. The reputational risk of the many derivative-trading lawsuits harmed the bank's business activity and its share price, making it an easier acquisition target. In the cases of BCCI, Barings, and Lehman, risk management failures led to the near-immediate acquisition, restructuring, and disappearance of those financial institutions.

When systemic risk becomes a threat, the public at large, as well as stakeholders, feels the impact of the dissolution of financial institutions. The events of 2008 have added a long list of banks and financial institutions to the list of failed institutions. Some of these banks were reorganized, others were sold, many were put into receivership, others were taken over by governments and nationalized, and a few were allowed to fail.

1.4 Organizational Structure of Risk Management in Banks

The structure of the risk management department is considered in more depth in Chapter 7. However, it is helpful to know how risk management fits into the overall bank organization.

The "front office" describes the business units of the bank. Examples are the foreign exchange trading desk or the corporate advisory function. Banks may have dozens of different front office units responsible for trading, customer services, retail functions, and other bank products.

For example, recently, the front office functions at JPM Chase were as follows (with each function being broken down into further subgroups):

- Investment banking
- Consumer financial services
- Small-business and commercial banking
- Asset and wealth management
- Private equity

The "back office" describes the operational functions of the bank, such as check clearing, payment collections, trade confirmations, and other clerical functions necessary for the smooth functioning of the bank.

The "middle office" refers to risk management. Ideally the middle office operates independently from the front and back offices, with separate reporting lines to senior management. The middle office normally runs parallel to the front office, except that risk positions often report to the heads of market risk, credit risk, and/or operational risk management (for larger banks). Those group heads then report to the Chief Risk Officer, who is responsible for all risk communications to senior management and other stakeholders. Financial reporting can also, in some cases, be considered part of the middle office.

1.5 What is Market Risk?

Market risk, generically, is the risk of loss on a position in a financial instrument due to adverse changes in the market price of that instrument. Some market risks are direct: the primary market price change is realized on a 1:1 basis in the position value. This is common for all cash markets, i.e., markets for bonds, equities, and commodities. Other market risks are indirect: the price of the financial asset is derived from another, underlying, market, usually in some ratio that is not necessarily 1:1. This is common for all derivatives markets.

Any trader/investor who is "long" the market, i.e., owning/holding the market-risky asset, is at risk of falling prices, while any trader/investor who is "short" the market, i.e., having sold a borrowed asset, is at risk of rising prices.

1.5.1 Foreign Exchange Risk

Foreign exchange risk is unique insofar as a long position in one currency necessitates a short position in the other. In other words, the trader/investor is long one currency and short another at the same time. Losses occur when the long currency position falls in value, but can also occur if the short currency rises in value. This may sound confusing, but remember that the two currencies rise or fall relative to each other.

1.5.2 Interest Rate Risk

When a trader/investor lends (borrows) money or any other financial instrument, a rate of interest will be received (paid). It follows that changes in this rate of interest will have an impact on the financial result for the trader/investor.

A trader who is long a fixed coupon bond will find that other investors are more willing to buy the bond if interest rates fall. The more that interest rates fall, the more the bond rises in value. Conversely, if interest rates rise, fixed coupon bonds lose value, as fewer and fewer investors are interested in buying the bond, with its now "low" coupon rate. A trader who is short a fixed coupon bond will gain if interest rates rise and lose if they fall.

However, the situation is different for owners of floating rate notes (FRNs). When interest rates start to rise, owners of FRNs find that their bond's coupon rises accordingly. When interest rates fall, FRN interest rates fall as well. The interest rate on an FRN will therefore always be in line with market As a result, the price of an FRN will hold relatively steady at around 100% of the face value of the note.

1.5.3 Equity Price Risk

Traders/investors with a long position in equities find that their Profit and Loss (P/L) is tied directly to the direction of equity market movements. When equity prices go up, long positions gain; when they go down, long positions lose. A short position in equity will gain value when the stock price goes down and, conversely, lose value when it goes up.

1.5.4 Commodity Price Risk

Commodities display identical characteristics to equity when it comes to P/L. A long position in a specific commodity will lose value if the commodity price goes down, but gain if it goes up. Conversely, a short position in a commodity will gain value when the commodity price goes down and lose if it goes up.

1.5.5 Credit Price Risk

Credit price risk is a relatively new form of market risk, compared to those mentioned above. While credit risk is normally classified as default risk (and treated separately in the Credit Risk Management book in this series), credit price risk is a market risk. More specifically, it is the risk that the market price for a particular credit instrument will change for reasons other than default and cause a gain (loss) as a result.

When the credit instrument is a corporate bond it is important to know why its price has changed. If the bond price has changed as a result of interest rate changes, then the bond investor has been subject to interest rate risk. If, however, the bond price changes as a result of a change in its credit spread, then the investor has been subject to credit price risk.

1.5.6 Implied Volatility Price Risk

Many traders/investors consider implied volatility to be a separate asset/risk class. Most financial instruments, whether cash or derivative, are not subject to price changes as volatility changes. Options, however, explicitly change value as implied volatility changes. A long position in an option (calls or puts) will increase in value if volatility increases and decrease in value if volatility decreases. The opposite is true for the short option position: the value increases as volatility decreases and, conversely, the value decreasing as volatility increases.

Some options, notably in the exotic options, can have unusual and unexpected reactions to volatility changes, but the majority of options behave as described.

1.5.7 Implied Correlation Risk

When two separately traded assets display similar characteristics in relation to market price changes, they are positively correlated. The extreme of this phenomenon is perfect positive correlation, or a correlation of 1. Financial assets whose prices seem unconnected to one another are said to have low correlation, the extreme of which is zero correlation.

Negative correlation occurs when the price of one financial asset goes up and another goes down—or vice versa—as a result of the same market influence. The extreme of this phenomenon is perfect negative correlation, or a correlation of –1. This is rarely found in financial markets, although highly sought after, as a long position in each of two assets that are highly negatively correlated reduces the overall market risk of the portfolio dramatically. In practical terms, volatility is one of few traded assets that is negatively correlated with most other market risks, making volatility swaps very attractive as tools to reduce portfolio market risk exposures.

Correlation risk is, by extension, a portfolio risk that manifests across multiple, interconnected assets. Basket, index, and other portfolio products are subject to correlation risk. Being long correlation means gaining value when correlation increases and losing value when it decreases. Being short correlation is the exact opposite.

For example, the volatility of a stock index can never be more than the weighted average of the constituent volatilities, but it is usually lower than that. A profitable trade, which is long correlation, would go long index volatility and short constituent volatility, with rising correlation. This trade would lose value if correlation decreased instead. This type of trade is referred to as a dispersion trade.

Most banks are long credit correlation risk in their loan portfolios. Good credit portfolio management, i.e., diversification, helps to minimize this correlation.

While it is relatively simple to identify market risk losses for single positions in financial instruments, as described above, it quickly becomes complicated to aggregate market risks across an entire portfolio, especially for portfolios of compound market risks, such as, for example, foreign exchange options on currencies where there is a known correlation between the currency and the local equity market. In this case, a portfolio of options would simultaneously be subject to foreign exchange risk, interest rate risk, volatility risk, and equity risk, as well as the correlation risk between each of these risks.

1.6 Summary

This chapter establishes a framework for risk identification, assessment, and management that will be described in detail in coming chapters.

Bank Risk Management
- Every bank employee is a risk manager. Our focus, however, is on those who are responsible for identifying, measuring, monitoring, and reporting risk.
- Ironically, bank risk managers do not usually manage risk except in extreme situations, that is, they are not typically the risk-management decision makers.
- Risk identification is achieved by risk managers in concert with bank business groups; not all risks are obvious.
- Risk measurement is the risk manager's most difficult task.
- If models rely solely on past data, they can only provide a partial assessment of future risks.
- Many risks are monitored on a daily basis; some are reported less frequently.
- The goal of risk management is not necessarily to eliminate risk, but to help the bank determine the optimal way to take risk in order to maximize its returns relative to risk taken.

Risk Classification and the Objectives of Risk Management
- Risks are often divided into market risk (price risk), credit risk (customer or counterparty performance risk), and operational risk (people, processes, and systems).
- A fourth risk, asset-liability management, is a subset of market risk applied to the banking book.
- The objectives of risk management are compliance, risk control, portfolio management, communication, and planning.

Risk Management Failures
- Much can be learned about risk management by studying its failures.
- Failures can be caused by the failure to accurately measure known risks, to take risks into account, to communicate, monitor, and manage risks, and to use appropriate risk metrics.
- The rate of bank failure is very high (6.6% in one study by Fitch), but since most banks are rescued by third parties before defaulting on their obligations, the public is not greatly affected by this.
- BCCI, Bankers Trust, Barings Bank, and Lehman were all examples of banks that failed in part due to risk management oversights. There are many more examples.

Organizational Structure of Risk Management in Banks
- Bank functions can be divided into a front office (business lines), middle office (risk and financial reporting) and back office (clerical, payments management, documents).
- Risk functions of the middle office report to a Chief Risk Officer.
- Best practice calls for independence of the risk management function from the main business lines of the bank.

Five Classes of Market Risk
- There are generally five types of market risk: interest rate risk, FX risk, commodity price risk, equity price risk, and credit price risk.
- There are two additional types of market risk: volatility price risk and correlation price risk. These are relevant to pricing certain instruments, specifically options and index products.
- Many financial instruments are subject to several of these risks concurrently.

CHAPTER 2

Foreign Exchange Markets, Instruments and Risks

This chapter expands on the introductory treatment of traded foreign exchange (FX or forex) instruments given in FBR book. Most traded financial instruments can be classified by market and type. Market instruments include currency, interest rates, equity, and commodities. Types of instruments include cash (or spot), forward/futures, swaps, options, and exotics. This chapter discusses all instrument classifications for the foreign exchange market. The FX market is used to introduce market risks in this volume because most large, internationally active banks have significant exposure to foreign exchange trading and the financial instruments in the FX markets. While many smaller banks are active in the FX markets—buying and selling foreign currency to provide services for their clients—it is the large global banks such as HSBC, Citibank, and Deutsche, with their widespread branch networks and well-established international linkages, who play a significant, if not dominating role, in the foreign exchange markets. Also, many of the instruments used in the FX markets have risk profiles that resemble instruments used in other markets.

With this chapter as background, the student can readily explore more sophisticated financial instruments used in the interest rate, equity, and commodity markets. The chapter does not cover more advanced issues such as complex valuation formulas. The emphasis is on understanding the primary traded FX products and their risks. In later chapters, the discussions of these risks will lay the groundwork for more intense analysis and discussion of complex risks and risk management practices.

On completion of this chapter, the reader will have an improved understanding of:

- Cash foreign exchange market transactions
- Cash instrument value and risk drivers
- FX forward instruments
- Differences between forwards and futures contracts
- Currency swaps
- Risk drivers in forward markets
- Option instruments
- Exotics
- Risk factors for options and exotics

This chapter sets the framework for the chapters that follow. Chapters 3 and 4 explore the other major bank markets using the same transaction type structure.

2.1 The Foreign Exchange Market

Trading instruments come in many types and "flavors." The common products, in terms of volume, are the main instruments traded globally; they are commonly called "plain vanilla" products because they are relatively straightforward with no added complexities. However, for every standard product there is also likely to be a complex version. What is more, new products are continually being developed to meet customer demand. For all the instruments discussed below, the main currencies traded are the US dollar (USD), euro (EUR), Japanese yen (JPY) and the British pound (GBP). Other currencies discussed in this section are the Swiss franc (CHF), the Canadian dollar (CAD), the Australian dollar (AUD), and the Hong Kong dollar (HKD). The principles discussed in this chapter apply to any freely traded currency.

Innovation in the financial markets is expanding the number of financial instruments traded in order to fit the needs of market participants. As the financial markets adopt new instruments, old instruments that no longer meet participants' needs are abandoned.

All financial products and instruments, however complicated, can be modeled by combinations of positions in simpler instruments. The risk of the simpler instruments provides a clue to the risk of the complex product. Also, any pricing model for a product gives us clues to understanding the risks of the product. Any input to the pricing model that can fluctuate is called a risk factor. For bonds, for example, market interest rates are a risk factor. Exchange rates in forward and futures contracts, typically determined by market interest rates and inflation differentials (as will be explained more fully below) are considered risk factors. The importance of any risk factor can be determined by measuring its effects on the instrument's pricing.

The definitions of the various instruments provided throughout the rest of this chapter describe the risks generated by each instrument, regardless of the underlying currency. However, all instruments valued in a currency other than a bank's reporting currency will generate foreign exchange risk for the bank. Even if the values of those instruments do not change in foreign currency terms, those values change in domestic currency terms.

A bank's risk management problems are large and complex, and it is difficult to tackle them all at once. We begin by focusing on the FX markets first, for several reasons:

- Foreign exchange is a large part of trading activity for many banks
- Global volumes of foreign exchange trading are high
- The foreign exchange market is geographically diverse and trades 24 hours per day, except weekends
- The foreign exchange market is considered the most liquid in the world
- Foreign equity, fixed income, and commodity markets create foreign exchange opportunities and challenges for banks

Foreign Exchange Trading and Market Trading Activity
According to the Bank for International Settlements,[11] the average daily trading in global foreign exchange markets was about USD 5.3 trillion in 2013. Trading in the world's main financial markets accounted for the vast majority of this total, as follows:[12]

- USD 2.0 trillion in spot transactions
- USD 0.7 trillion in outright forwards
- USD 2.2 trillion in foreign exchange swaps
- USD 0.4 trillion in FX options and long-term currency swaps

---

11 "Foreign exchange and derivatives market activity in 2013," Triennial Central Bank Survey (September 2013), Bank for International Settlements. http://www.bis.org/publ/rpfx13fx.pdf
12 Notes: Options are not reported separately.

The most widely traded currencies, in terms of market share and as of April 2013, were the USD (87% market share), the EUR (37%), the JPY (23%), and the GBP (11.8%). No other single currency had more than an 8% share of the traded market.[13] When trading activity is recorded in foreign exchange, it is recorded twice, as it is a simultaneous purchase of one currency and a sale of another. Because each currency trade is recorded twice, the total percentages add up to 200%, not 100%. Therefore, these four currencies account for 155% out of 200% of trading volume, or more than three quarters of all bank trading in FX.

The most active banks in the foreign exchange market can be determined from survey data.[14] In May 2014, Citibank accounted for 16.04% of foreign exchange trading by banks, Deutsche Bank 15.67%, Barclays Capital 10.91%, UBS AG 10.88%, and HSBC 7.12%. No other single bank was responsible for more than 5% in trading volume.

In the United States, during the third quarter 2014, foreign exchange derivative contracts accounted for approximately 14.4% of all derivatives transactions. Although approximately 12% of all US commercial banks engage in derivatives trading, these transactions occurred mainly between a few large internationally active banks, where the risks are also concentrated.[15]

2.2 Spot Foreign Exchange Transactions

The market for spot transactions is perhaps the most liquid market in the world. In the spot foreign exchange market, one currency is exchanged for another.

EXAMPLE

On behalf of a client, a German bank needs to buy JPY. The German bank sells EUR and, in exchange for the EUR, buys JPY.

---

13   Triennial Bank Survey, 2013
14   Euromoney FX survey FX Poll 2014: The Euromoney FX survey is the largest global poll of foreign exchange service providers, see http://www.bloomberg.com/news/articles/2014-05-08/deutsche-bank-currency-crown-lost-to-citigroup-on-volatility-1-
15   OCC's Quarterly Report on Bank Trading and Derivatives Activities Third Quarter 2014, available at http://www.occ.gov/topics/capital-markets/financial-markets/trading/derivatives/dq314.pdf. Note that "most derivatives activity in the US banking system continues to be dominated by a small group of large financial institutions. Four large commercial banks represent 92.6% of the total banking industry notional amounts and 85.9% of industry net current credit exposure."

Spot transactions generate foreign exchange risk, since the relative value of the two currencies in the spot transaction may change. By convention, spot foreign exchange transactions are exchanged two business days in the future, which is known as the spot date. The two-day timeframe came into practice when settlement instructions between banks were transmitted by telegraph and banks needed two days to ensure that instructions could be issued and acted upon. Although settlement is now carried out electronically, the two-day settlement rule remains.

2.2.1 Exchange Rates for Major Currencies

Foreign exchange rates change constantly, but a snapshot of prices at a point in time is useful to show reporting conventions and pricing relationships. As an example, the spot exchange rates for eight major world currencies are shown below. At that time, it would have cost HKD 7.7514 to buy USD 1, or CAD 1.0942 to buy USD 1.

	USD	GBP	CAD	EUR	JPY	HKD
USD		1.6388	0.9139	1.2921	0.0092	0.129
GBP	0.6102		0.5576	0.7884	0.0056	0.0787
CAD	1.0942	1.7931		1.4138	0.01	0.1411
EUR	0.7739	1.2683	0.7072		0.0071	0.0998
JPY	108.64	178.03	99.28	140.37		14.01
HKD	7.7514	12.703	7.084	10.016	0.0713	

FIGURE 2.1 Exchange Rates for Major Currencies, September 2014

Similarly, if USD 1.00 were converted to HKD 7.7514, and HKD 7.7514 were converted to CAD 1.0937 (= 0.1411 x 7.7514), and that were converted to USD, that result would be roughly USD 1 as well. In reality, FX rates are not perfectly aligned (note the 5 pip[16] difference above), so a "round-trip" USD-HKD-CAD-USD as illustrated would appear to open up an arbitrage opportunity. Arbitrage is a risk-free trading strategy that generates a positive profit. Arbitrage will not take place, however, if the estimated profit is not sufficient to cover transaction cost.

---

16 A pip is a market term used in foreign exchange trading to denote the smallest price change under normal market conditions, for example for USDCHF it is 0.0001, but for USDJPY it is 0.01

2.2.2 Drivers of Foreign Exchange Rates

Banks often engage in significant foreign exchange transaction activity, and the risks of those transactions are fairly well understood. Broadly speaking, foreign exchange rates are driven by economic factors, international political factors, and market psychology. To understand the economic forces affecting exchange rates, it is best to think of currency itself as a product. For example, if a Hong Kong investor sees USD 1 as a product, its price in HKD is 7.75; the product has value because it can be used to purchase other goods and services, or earn USD returns on investment.

Under this paradigm, the USD strengthens—its price in HKD rises—whenever the global demand for USD increases. The USD will strengthen if one or more of the following events occur (a similar logic can be applied to any currency; this is just an example).

Ironically, a strong currency discourages demand for US exports by making US goods more expensive abroad. This in turn reduces the demand for US goods and USD, having a weakening effect on the currency. Because of this natural balance in the system, exchange rates are expected to trade in a natural range, based on purchasing power parity (PPP). PPP is an economic theory that postulates that an identical basket of goods should be priced the same in any given country, ignoring transaction costs.

In practice, foreign exchange rates differ substantially from rates implied by PPP. There are multiple reasons why, most having to do with transaction costs. For example, tariffs limit international trade and impact import and export prices, as do taxes and other transaction costs. Other factors include differences in supply, demand, and consumption patterns, which may lead to different price levels in different countries, skewing the implied exchange rates of PPP. When exchange rates fall outside normal ranges and float freely, or are managed by a central bank or similar entity, speculators and central banks will often take positions anticipating corrections to normal levels.

EXAMPLE

An intriguing and increasingly popular approach to quantify PPP and to use it as an indicator of future long-term changes in exchange rates is the Big Mac Index created by The Economist magazine.[17]

The Big Mac Index, or "Burgernomics," builds on the PPP. It argues that the same basket of goods—in this case a Big Mac—should cost the same all around the world. While in the short run, there might be differences in the purchasing power of two currencies, in the long run the equilibrium implied by the purchasing power differentials should prevail. McDonald's sells the Big Mac in about 120 countries; it has identical ingredients anywhere it is sold, making the cost of the product comparable across different countries. The PPP-implied price of a Big Mac determines what its value should be in the long run. If there are deviations from the PPP, the currency is either under- or overvalued relative to the USD, which is at the base of "Burgernomics."

---

17   http://www.economist.com/content/big-mac-index

January 22, 2015	Currency	Local Price	Dollar Rate	Dollar Price	Implied PPP Rate	Over(+)/ Under(-) Valued by
United States	USD	4.79	1.00	4.79	1.00	0.0%
Australia	AUD	5.3	1.23	4.32	1.11	-9.8%
Britain	GBP	2.89	0.66	4.37	0.60	-8.8%
China	CNY	17.2	6.21	2.77	3.59	-42.2%
Euro area	EUR	3.68	0.86	4.26	0.77	-11.0%
Hong Kong	HKD	18.8	7.75	2.43	3.92	-49.4%
Hungary	HUF	860	271.39	3.17	179.54	-33.8%
India	INR	116.25	61.62	1.89	24.27	-60.6%
Indonesia	IDR	27939	12480.0	2.24	5832.78	-53.3%
Japan	JPY	370	117.77	3.14	77.24	-34.4%
Mexico	MXN	49	14.63	3.35	10.23	-30.1%
New Zealand	NZD	5.9	1.31	4.49	1.23	-6.2%
Norway	NOK	48	7.62	6.30	10.02	31.5%
Russia	RUB	89	65.23	1.36	18.58	-71.5%
Singapore	SGD	4.7	1.33	3.53	0.98	-26.4%
South Africa	ZAR	25.5	11.48	2.22	5.32	-53.6%
South Korea	KRW	4100	1083.30	3.78	855.95	-21.0%
Sweden	SEK	40.7	8.19	4.97	8.50	3.7%
Switzerland	CHF	6.5	0.86	7.54	1.36	57.5%

FIGURE 2.2 Big Mac Index according to The Economist, on January 22, 2015, prices and exchange rates.

In the Euro zone, the cost of a Big Mac is EUR 3.68, while in the US it is USD 4.79. Thus the PPP implied by Big Mac is 3.68/4.79 = 0.77. On that day, the exchange rate between EUR and USD was 0.86, implying that (according to this PPP relationship) the EUR is 11% overvalued compared to the USD. This suggests that the EUR will decline in value against the USD, and consequently the USD would increase in value against the EUR. As shown in the table, the CHF is most overvalued relative to the USD, while the USD is most overvalued relative to the RUB (Russian ruble).

2.2.3 Bank Trading in Foreign Exchange Markets

Spot Trading
Banks may trade currencies to meet customer demands, but they may also take positions on expected future demands based on an understanding of their own transaction flow. While customers have demands for spot currency to meet their foreign exchange liquidity needs, most speculative trading is done in the foreign exchange forward markets—buying at dates further into the future than the spot date, mainly as a result of the much lower transaction and operational costs compared to those for spot instruments.

Derivatives Trading
As banks and exchanges have sought to create innovative products for their customers and reduce their trading costs, derivatives have grown to become a major constituent of trading over the last 20 years. Derivatives include forward contracts, futures contracts, swaps, options, and exotics. The term "derivative" takes its name from the fact that the value of a derivative instrument "derives" from the value of its underlying cash instrument. The underlying instrument can also be a derivative, such as an option on futures contracts.

Some derivatives are traded on futures exchanges and others are traded on the over-the-counter (OTC) market. The OTC market is where banks trade directly with each other and their customers. There are many types of "exotic" derivatives that have a combination of risk and payment profiles. However, almost all of them can be approximated by combinations of simpler, "plain vanilla," products for the purposes of valuation and risk assessment.

Usually, derivative trading is more cost-efficient than spot trading. Banks use derivatives in foreign exchange for both speculative and market-making purposes. Speculative profits are based on the changes in value of the contracts. Market-making profits come from the spread banks charge their customers in the form of a bid-offer spread on foreign exchange transactions.

Corporate customers use foreign exchange derivatives to lock in the value of foreign-denominated current or future receivables and payables. They will use forwards to lock in the value of foreign security issuances, asset purchases, and asset sales. In brief, forwards, futures, options, and swaps are valuable hedging instruments for corporations.

Asset management customers speculate in currencies, but they can also use foreign exchange derivatives to eliminate exchange risk on foreign asset holdings. This generally allows the asset manager to hedge an unknown foreign exchange risk in order to take more precise, intentional risks in the development of portfolio strategy.

2.3 Forward Foreign Exchange Transactions

Forward foreign exchange transactions are for exchange at an agreed upon date later than the spot date. For example, a US company needs to pay JPY 100 million for a shipment of Japanese goods that is due in three months. To lock in the USD cost of the shipment, the company agrees with its bank to buy JPY 100 million at the current forward rate for three months, which is 100. This fixes the cost of the shipment at USD 1 million at an exchange rate of 100 USD/JPY. In three months' time the company pays USD 1 million to the bank and receives JPY 100 million, which it pays to its supplier.

2.3.1 Currency Forward Contract Pricing

The forward market usually trades maturities for up to one year, although some banks quote prices for longer periods.

Forward exchange transactions create both exchange rate and interest rate risk. This is because, in combination with the current spot rate, the forward rate is determined by the relative level of the interest rates between the two currencies. The following example describes how forward exchange rates are determined by spot rates and interest rate differentials.

EXAMPLE

A Japanese bank could agree to buy one Australian dollar (AUD) for 66.22 JPY today, or it could buy the AUD one year from today. The price one year from today—the forward price—can be precisely determined by this formula:

$$\text{Forward Price of AUD in JPY} = \text{Spot Price of AUD in JPY} \times \frac{(1 + JPY\ Interest\ Rate)^t}{(1 + AUD\ Interest\ Rate)^t}$$

In this equation, t represents time to transaction (one year in this case); the Japanese one-year, risk-free interest rate is 0.50% and the Australian one-year, risk-free interest rate is 3.41%. Therefore the forward price for transacting one year from today is 64.36 JPY per AUD. The forward price is lower than the spot price, reflecting the implicit expectation that the AUD will devalue relative to the JPY.

$$\text{Forward Price of AUD in JPY} = 66.22 \times \frac{(1+0.005)^t}{(1+0.0341)t} = \frac{AUD}{JPY\ 64.36}$$

The pricing relationship described above is particularly strong, since any deviation from the theoretical price will create an arbitrage opportunity for the bank. Arbitrage is a risk-free trading strategy that generates a positive profit. The arbitrage-based pricing equation fits market prices extremely well. In this case, given the efficiency of the FX markets, banks can perform the implied arbitrage strategy. The arbitrage is to short the currency that is expected to decrease in value in the future and buy it back at the lower price. In the above example, the actual spot rate is 66.22 AUD/JPY, but the future exchange rate implied by the relationship is 64.36 AUD/JPY. To deliver AUD in one year: borrow in JPY, paying the JPY interest rate, and use the loan proceeds to purchase the AUD today, depositing the AUD in an AUD account earning AUD interest rates. The net forward price, the price agreed to be paid in the future, reflects the interest earned on the AUD account and the financing costs paid in JPY. The next example illustrates how the arbitrage transaction might work.

EXAMPLE

Suppose a bank tried to follow this exact arbitrage strategy (described in the last paragraph). The bank will short (borrow and sell) JPY today and will need to buy it back one year from today. To do this, it will need to have AUD 1,000 one year from today (to buy back the JPY and close its short position). It will purchase AUD today and deposit it in an AUD account where it earns the AUD risk-free rate of 3.41%, so the bank needs to purchase AUD 967.02 (= AUD 1000/1.0341) today in order to have AUD 1,000 one year from today. To buy the AUD 967.02, the bank borrows and sells JPY today; at the spot exchange rate of 66.22 AUD/JPY, it needs to borrow JPY 64,036 to buy AUD 967.02. The bank will also need to cover the interest on the JPY loan, which will be JPY 64,036 × 0.0050 = JPY 320, so the total repayment amount would be JPY 64,356 (= JPY 64,036 + JPY 320). Thus, one year from today the AUD 1,000 will have to purchase JPY 64,356. Or, one year from now, AUD 1 will buy JPY 64.356. This is the exact forward exchange rate we calculated above. There is no arbitrage profit unless there is a change in the expected AUD or JPY risk-free rate, or in the forward AUD/JPY foreign exchange rate.

2.3.2 Risks in Foreign Exchange Forwards

In practice, short-term forward price fluctuations are driven by changes in the spot rate, as most risk-free interest rate differentials are small, and the effect of compounding is small for short time periods. In risk models, therefore, forward pricing risk can be approximated by a small adjustment to spot exchange rate risk. Spot risk is assessed from historical data, so the same risk measure can be applied to forward prices.

EXAMPLE

The CAD/USD exchange rate may typically change 3% in a quarter, while the spread between USD and CAD interest rates may typically change by 1% (annualized) in a quarter. At the provided sample exchange rate of 0.9139 and an assumed interest differential of zero, a net change of 1% in interest rates will affect three-month forward prices by 0.00228 (= 0.9139 × 0.01 × 3/12), whereas a 3% spot exchange rate change will change the forward price by 3%, or 0.02742 (= 0.9139 × 0.03). Therefore, the risk due to spot price changes is 12 times greater than the risk due to interest rate changes.

For longer-term forward contracts, this simplification may not work. The risks in forward prices can be seen directly from the equation above. Foreign exchange positions are sensitive not only to the spot exchange rate, but also the relative level and movement of interest rates of both countries. Forward transactions have all the risk of spot transactions, plus the explicit risk of fluctuating interest rates in the two relevant currencies.

2.3.3 Foreign Exchange Swaps

The term "swap" has several meanings that can confuse students new to capital markets. In foreign exchange markets, there are two types of swaps:

- a forex swap is a combination of a spot trade and a single forward trade
- a currency swap is a combination of several forward trades

This section considers simple forward transactions, so it is appropriate to consider forex swaps here and currency swaps later.

A foreign exchange rate swap (or forex swap) is a combination of a spot and a forward transaction. The two parties simultaneously execute a spot transaction at the spot rate and a forward transaction at the forward rate for the same principal amount of base currency. The forex swap is a common short-term transaction, normally used for funding foreign currency balances, for currency speculation, or for hedging various currency positions. The difference in the two exchange rates represents the differential between the interest rates of the two currencies for the period of the deal. Foreign exchange rate swaps generate interest rate risk, as shown in this example, just like simple forward transactions do, but they have less exchange rate risk.

EXAMPLE

A bank could buy USD and sell JPY for the 90-day forward rate of JPY 99.5 to USD 1, or 99.5 USD/JPY. Alternatively it could buy USD at the spot rate of 100 USD/JPY.

If a bank bought USD 10 million and sold short JPY 1,000 million for delivery on the spot date, and held the currency position for 90 days, the bank would need to borrow JPY 1,000 million and lend USD 10 million for 90 days.

If the rate for the USD is 3% and for JPY is 1%, the interest flows would be:

JPY 2,500,000 paid   (1,000,000,000 × .01 × 90/360)
USD 75,000 received   (10,000,000 × .03 × 90/360)

After 90 days the bank's position would be:

"long" USD 10,075,000 and "short" JPY 1,002,500,000.

By dividing the JPY position by the USD position an effective exchange rate of 99.5 USD/JPY is obtained: USD 10,075,000/JPY 1,002,500,000 = 0.01 (rounded) or 99.50 USD/JPY.

This is the forward rate the bank could have charged instead of entering into a spot foreign exchange transaction together with a loan and a deposit.

The forward price is calculated from the interest rate differential to ensure that there are no arbitrage opportunities in the market (see Section 2.3.1). Therefore the forward price is sensitive to any changes in either interest rate.

2.4 Currency Futures

While most banks focus their foreign exchange trading on the large and liquid interbank market, this market is not available to smaller banks and bank customers. For this reason, an alternative trading vehicle, the currency futures contract, was created in 1972 by the International Monetary Market (IMM), now a part of the Chicago Mercantile Exchange (CME).[18] Currency futures contracts are traded at two other major exchanges, the Euronext-Liffe exchange and the Tokyo Futures Exchange.[19]

---

[18] See www.CMEgroup.com
[19] This is a highly introductory treatment of futures. For an advanced text see, for example, Robert W. Kolb and James A. Overdahl. *Futures, Options, and Swaps.* 5th ed. (New York: Wiley-Blackwell, 2007).

2.4.1 Futures Contract Features

A futures contract is a standardized, exchange-traded forward contract with unique institutional features. Futures contracts are traded on exchanges, which act as clearing-houses for all trade counterparties. This means that the clearinghouse is the seller to all buyers and the buyer to all sellers. In a clearinghouse system, therefore, traders are not exposed to the credit risk of numerous counterparties, but only to the credit risk of the clearinghouse itself. This risk is usually minimal because the clearinghouse has the backing of its members and access to various reserves and other support systems to guarantee its performance as the counterparty to both buyers and sellers. There are futures contracts for most cash instruments, including currencies, bonds, equity indices, and commodities.

In general, futures contracts have the following features:

- exchange traded
- fixed amount per contract
- fixed dates for delivery
- standardized delivery conditions
- daily margin calls[20]

Futures contracts are subject to the same risks as the underlying instrument, with additional interest rate risk due to the future delivery date.

Currency exchange futures trades are a fraction of interbank trades. For example, in the second quarter of 2008, over USD 100 billion per day of notional currency volume was traded on the IMM,[21] roughly 20% of the volume of outright forward contracts traded on the interbank market.

2.4.2 Differences Between Forward and Futures

Futures contracts are standardized and traded on exchanges. Forward contracts trade over-the-counter, and are often negotiated to meet the specific needs of the buyers and sellers. Because there is no clearinghouse between two OTC counterparties, each must accept the other's risk of failing to perform, or require contract terms to mitigate default risk, such as

---

20   Futures margin requirements generally consist of an initial margin, or deposit, to guarantee performance, followed by a maintenance margin, which updates based on market conditions.
21   2015 FX Product Guide, CME Group, December 2014, http://www.cmegroup.com/trading/fx/files/2015-product-guide-and-calendar-fx-products.pdf

collecting collateral from the losing party in a forward contract. To mitigate the potential impact of non-performance in an OTC transaction, several exchanges and other organizations have created clearing and settlement systems to manage OTC trades.

Because of counterparty risk and margining considerations, the pricing of futures contracts will differ only slightly from that of forward contracts. Nevertheless, the same general formula will apply: the exchange rate of the currency futures contract is approximately equal to the current spot rate increased by the interest rate differential over the life of the futures contract.

2.5 Currency Swaps

A currency swap contains three elements:

- An initial currency exchange
- Periodic exchange of interest payments in different currencies
- A final currency exchange

Therefore, it can be seen as a foreign exchange swap with interest payments, or as a sequence of forward interest rate and currency transactions. To see why this is the case, consider the following transaction, where a European corporation borrows EUR from its local bank:

FIGURE 2.3 Foreign Exchange Swap with Interest Payments

If for some reason, the company decides it wants to borrow USD instead, it could pay off the local loan and get a loan denominated in USD, but that would probably be expensive (at least incurring transaction costs). As an alternative, the company may change its risk profile by entering into a currency swap with a trading bank, as in Figure 2.4.

FIGURE 2.4 Currency Swap with a Trading Bank

In this transaction, the payments of loan proceeds, interest payments, and final principal payment on the EUR exactly match, so the corporation has no exposure to EUR. On a net basis, however, the corporation now receives the loan proceeds in USD, pays interest in USD, and repays the final principal in USD. The currency swap transaction has completely transformed the company's EUR risk into USD risk, without affecting the original loan transaction.

The exchange of the loan proceeds and the final principal payment work like a forex swap: the interim interest payments are usually linked to local floating rate indices, such as LIBOR and EURIBOR. Once the corporation has converted its EUR exposure into USD exposure, it may further decide to swap its floating interest rate risk for fixed rates using a USD interest rate swap. USD interest rate swaps are discussed in more detail in Chapter 3.

2.6 Currency Options

An option contract gives the buyer the right, but not the obligation, to buy or sell an underlying contract at an agreed price. This means that the underlying transaction will only be executed if the rate is favorable to the option buyer. The option buyer can never lose more than the premium paid. The seller has an open-ended risk on the contract and receives a premium in compensation. Options can be created on almost any cash or derivative instrument; there are even options on options.[22]

The key terms used to describe options are:

- Underlying: The underlying contract or asset that may be bought or sold at the discretion of the option owner
- Call: A call option gives the option buyer the right to buy the underlying instrument
- Put: A put option gives the option buyer the right to sell the underlying instrument
- Premium: Sum paid by the buyer to the seller
- Strike price or exercise price: Price at which the underlying transaction will be executed if the option is exercised
- Exercise: The buyer "exercises" the option to enter into the underlying contract
- Expiry date or expiration date: The last date by which the option must be exercised

---

22   This is a highly introductory treatment of options. For an advanced text, see, for example, Robert McDonald, *Derivatives Markets,* 3rd ed. (Prentice Hall, 2012).

- American: An option that can be exercised on any date up to the expiry date
- European: An option that can only be exercised on the expiry date
- In the money: An option that would pay off if it could be exercised today
- Out of the money: An option that would not pay off if exercised today
- At the money: An option that could be in the money or out of the money with a small change in the underlying

EXAMPLE

The Chicago Mercantile Exchange IMM facilitates trading of standardized foreign currency options. The following GBP European call option quotes were valid on Dec 24, 2008 (the spot exchange rate was about USD 1.47 = GBP 1 at that time[23])

Strike	Mar 09	Jun 09
1500	0.0447	0.0688
1600	0.0150	0.0377

TABLE 3: Foreign Currency Options: GBP European Call Option Quotes

Adjusting for reporting conventions, the table shows that a call option, the right to buy GBP 1 for USD 1.50 in March 2009, was worth USD 0.0447. A similar option to buy GBP 1 for USD 1.60 in March 2009 was worth only USD 0.0150, reflecting the lower likelihood that this option will have value. Both of these options would have been more valuable if they expired in June, since the probability of the pound exceeding those levels increases as the time to maturity of the option increases.

2.6.1 Market Option Pricing Dynamics

Option values change continuously throughout any trading day. The changes reflect changes in the factors that affect option prices, such as the change in the value of the underlying, changes in the perception of future volatility, interest rates, and the passage of time. Option values can also change due to factors related to the demand for specific option instruments, or the supply of options with specific features, but these effects are typically very difficult to model.

---

23 See www.cmegroup.com for current delayed currency option quotes.

Underlying Exchange Rates
As the GBP appreciates (depreciates) relative to the USD, the right to buy GBP at a fixed USD exchange rate increases (decreases) in value. The opposite is true for an option to sell GBP. Since the underlying exchange rates change continuously, the option values change continuously as well.

Perceived Exchange Rate Volatility
As the perception of future foreign exchange volatility increases (decreases), the value of all options increases (decreases). To understand how changes in perceived volatility affect option values, study Figure 2.5. The exchange rate starts at USD 1.47 per GBP. The dashed curves show how traders think the rate might evolve in a low volatility environment, i.e., the possible trading range that is expected to expand over time. The solid curves show how this perception changes when market uncertainty increases, i.e., the forecasted trading ranges get larger. Because the call options are only valuable on exercise in the ranges between USD 1.50 and USD 1.60, the option value will clearly increase as volatility increases, as the probability the option will be exercised increases.

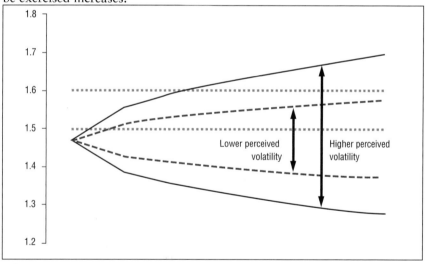

FIGURE 2.5 Perceived Exchange Rate Volatility

Future volatility of the exchange rate is unknown and changes continuously, representing a risk factor for option prices.

Interest Rates

The main drivers of currency option prices are the underlying exchange rate and the perceived future volatility of the exchange rate. A third factor that drives option values is market interest rates, but in general, interest rate effects on option prices are much smaller than the effect of the underlying asset or its perceived volatility. The only exception to this rule relates to options on bonds or options on interest rates, where interest rates also affect the value of the underlying instruments.

Time

As time passes, if nothing else changes, options lose their value. This is because in a shorter time period, under normal conditions, foreign exchange rates will be expected to vary in a slightly smaller range.

2.6.2 Quantification of Option Price Dynamics

When an option price changes, it is difficult to know exactly what part of the change is due to movement in the underlying, perceived volatility, interest rates, or simply the passage of time. To understand the effect of all the different components, it is necessary to employ a mathematical model of option price behavior.

The theory of mathematical option pricing has a long history dating to the French mathematician Louis Bachelier in 1900. Fischer Black and Myron Scholes[24] and Robert Merton[25] published seminal works in 1973. The Black-Scholes model, as it is usually called, is the most widely used model for pricing European options. Its assumptions have been adapted to price dozens of options and option-type securities. Scholes and Merton were awarded the Nobel Prize in Economics in 1997 for their work (Black had died in 1995; Nobel prizes are not awarded posthumously).

A mathematical option-pricing model can be used in several ways:

- Theoretical option price determination based on assumptions
- Implicit parameter estimate based on observed market prices
- Estimates of option-price sensitivity to parameter changes

Theoretical Option Price Determination

To determine theoretical option prices, every option model assumes a probability distribution for future prices, and some kind of financial model (such as an arbitrage model) for determining current prices. Every model

---

24   Fischer Black and Myron Scholes, "The Pricing of Options and Corporate Liabilities," *Journal of Political Economy* 81 (3) (1973): 637–654.
25   Robert C. Merton, "Theory of Rational Option Pricing," *Bell Journal of Economics and Management Science* Vol. 4, No. 1, (Spring 1973), pp. 141-183.

makes simplifying assumptions, which are best seen as approximations to the true market conditions. Nevertheless, theoretical models help banks price options, assess their risks, and trade.

Implicit Parameter Estimates
The Black-Scholes model, as an example, requires knowledge of the underlying exchange rates, the underlying interest rates, exchange rate volatility, exercise price, and time to maturity. All of these variables, except for future volatility, can be known at a point in time. Therefore, if the price of an option is known, the model can solve for the volatility that makes the model price equal to the observed market price. This number is called the implied volatility. The Black-Scholes implied volatility has become such an important part of the currency option markets that many dealers quote option prices in terms of the implied volatility rather than following the exchange conventions.

Option Price Sensitivity
Ultimately, a risk manager wants to know how changes in foreign exchange rates or perceived future volatility will affect the value of the bank's trading portfolio. To answer this question, a model produces what are known as "Greeks," i.e., Greek letters that represent the rate of change of the option price with respect to an underlying parameter or assumption. The Greeks are explained in detail in the next section.

EXAMPLE

A risk manager knows that his forward position is long GBP 1 billion, but the options portfolio decreases USD 0.50 for every USD 1 increase in his forward position. Therefore, at first approximation, his overall portfolio has the same exposure to GBP depreciation as a portfolio that is long GBP 0.5 billion. The option positions, in other words, hedge the forward position by 50%.

2.6.3 Risks in Option Trading

Currency options inherit all the risks of currency spot and forward contracts, and have some additional risks of their own. The inherent market risks can be divided into two categories: the "Greeks" and execution costs.

Foreign Exchange Markets, Instruments and Risks 39

- "Greeks" refer to the Greek letters delta, gamma, rho, and theta, and a fictitious Greek letter called vega.
- "Execution costs" refers to the costs incurred when hedging option positions, such as transaction costs and the failure to hedge in markets that move quickly.

Delta
The option delta is produced by a mathematical option-pricing model. The delta is the multiplier attached to the change in the value of the underlying that best approximates the short-term change in the value of an option (called a partial change in price because other factors affect the price as well):

Partial change in option price = Delta × Change in underlying price

The maximum likely movement of the underlying exchange rate can be specified using a risk model. Therefore, option risk can be approximated by multiplying the delta by the risk of the underlying asset. It follows, then, that deltas can be unstable.

EXAMPLE

A call option on the GBP has a delta of 0.30. This implies when the exchange rate increases by 0.01, and nothing else changes, the option value increases by 0.003. If the maximum change of the GBP is expected to be 0.20, then the maximum change of the option is estimated to be 0.06. Delta, however, does not remain constant, as gamma shows.

Gamma
Gammas are also computed from mathematical option pricing models. Gamma measures how much the delta changes when the underlying asset moves by one unit:

Partial change in delta = Gamma × Change in underlying price

Gamma represents risk in the sense that it helps to capture the nonlinear nature of option risk. Since the delta is constantly changing, this is a risk for the buyer or seller of the option.

Gamma can be used to approximate option price changes for larger movements in the underlying price. In this case, the partial change in option price can be revised:

*Partial change in option price = (Delta × Change in underlying price)
+ [½ × Gamma × (Change in underlying price)2].*

EXAMPLE

The same call option from the last example has a gamma of 1.0. This implies that when the GPB increases by 0.01, the delta of the option increases to 0.31 (= 0.30 + 0.01(1)). For a change of 0.20 in the exchange rate, we would expect the option value to change by (0.20 × 0.30) + (½ × 1 × 0.202) = 0.08. This is the delta effect (0.06) plus the gamma effect (0.02).

Vega (also sometimes called Kappa)
At a point in time, the market's assessment of volatility determines the price of the option. However, that assessment can change. For example, stock market volatility has increased dramatically since 2008. Higher volatility means the stock market will experience more fluctuations. Options will increase in value as volatility rises and fall in value as volatility falls. Hence, this is a risk factor that is unique to options.

Partial change in option price = Vega × Change in volatility

EXAMPLE

The same call option from the last example has a Vega of 0.02. This implies that when the perceived future volatility increases by 1%, the call option increases in value by 0.02.

Rho
As interest rates change, some options will rise in value and others will fall. Rather than prepare an exhaustive list, we consult a particular pricing model to determine if rho is positive or negative. If rho is positive, rising rates increase option prices. If rho is negative, rising rates decrease option prices. In sum:

Partial change in option price = Rho × Change in relevant interest rate

Theta
As time passes and an option nears exercise, the option becomes less valuable. Theta measures the expected decline in option value as one day passes, usually expressed as a positive number. Because the passage of time

is certain, this is not considered a risk factor, though it does affect the value of the option:

Partial change in option price = Theta × Change in time to maturity

As the time to maturity change is negative, the impact on option prices is always negative.

Overall, the change in option price, and therefore option risk, can be approximated by two equations:

Total Change in option price = (Delta × Change in price)
+ [½ × Gamma × (Change in price)2] + (Vega × Change in volatility)
+ (Rho × change in interest rate) + (Theta × change in time to maturity)

Partial change in delta = Gamma × Change in underlying price

Taken together, this implies that the risk model should consider changes in underlying price, volatility, and interest rates to determine option risks. The Greeks themselves are vulnerable to error if the model does not accurately represent the value or the risk of the option instrument.

EXAMPLE

The estimated impact on option prices, when the exchange rate increases by 0.20 and the perceived volatility drops by 1%, can be calculated from the previous examples. Since we calculated the impact of the 0.20 change to be 0.08, and the volatility impact to be -0.02, the option would be expected to change in value by 0.06.

2.6.4 Execution Risk

When a bank hedges its option positions, it must often use the underlying instrument to create the hedge. In the running example above, the delta of the option would be used to determine how many forward contracts to go long or short to offset the risk of the option. Because the delta changes constantly, the hedge position must be continuously modified. Every time the position is modified, transaction costs are incurred, which can present a risk factor itself. The bank must balance the benefits of perfect hedging with the transaction costs of managing the hedge.

When markets move suddenly, these strategies often fail to manage risk well. This is another type of execution risk that banks need to consider when managing their option books.

2.7 Exotic Options

Banks can trade in exotic options as well. Due to the complexity of these options, banks trading these instruments have a precise market view or they are trying to satisfy customer demands for custom-tailored options. Most of the options listed below have features in common with plain vanilla options, but in general, the pricing formulas are much more difficult. For the advanced reader, several references are available to study exotic options and their pricing.[26]

For banks trading these instruments, special care must be taken to understand the additional risks. Like plain vanilla options, these options are sensitive to volatility changes. Unlike plain vanilla options, however, these options may exhibit highly volatile valuations due to built-in option features (such as a knock-out) or due to poor model selection and design. A knock-out option may expire worthless if the price of the underlying exceeds a certain predetermined price level. Similarly, a knock-in option may only become valuable if certain price levels are exceeded before expiration. These knock-in and knock-out options are also called barrier options.

The option types discussed below are meant to be examples only. There are many different types of exotic options not mentioned here, as well as the ones that are mentioned. We will not discuss any of these options in detail, but would draw the student's attention to the fact that that each option has its own unique risks associated.

2.7.1 Types of Exotic Options

An option is path independent if its value depends only on the final price of the underlying instrument. Path-dependent options depend not only on the final price of an underlying instrument, but also on all the prices leading to the final price.

Path-Independent Options
- **Chooser Options:** The owner of the option decides if the option is a call or put option only when a predetermined date is reached. Other types of chooser options might give the buyer the right to choose the most valuable currency basket from a predetermined set.
- **Binary Options:** Binary options pay a fixed amount or the value of the underlying asset, but only when the option expires in the money. Since

---

26 See for example John Hull, *Options, Futures, and Other Derivatives*, 9th ed. Prentice Hall, 2014

a small change in the underlying can cause the binary option to be in or out of the money, this type of option is difficult to hedge.
- **Power Options:** Power options pay an amount equal to the power of the value of the underlying asset above the strike price. Like all options, the seller has the theoretical possibility of a large loss; in a power option, this loss grows at a very fast rate.
- **Basket Options:** A variation of the plain vanilla option where the underlying asset is a basket of currencies. The valuation of this kind of option is sensitive to the correlation assumption used between the currencies.
- **Exchange Options:** Exchange options give the holder the right to exchange one asset for another. All options provide the option to exchange cash for an asset or contract; because this option exchanges two assets, it is sensitive to the correlation between the two assets.
- **Extendible Options:** Extendible options allow the holder to extend the expiration date. The extension option is almost always valuable, but there may be a cost associated with extension.
- **Compound Options:** This is an option for which the underlying asset is another option. These options are generally difficult to model and therefore contain a lot of model risk.
- **Spread Options:** Spread options pay based on the difference between two underlying assets. Again, correlation is a key driver of value.

Path-Dependent Options
- **Look-Back Options:** The owner of a look-back option exercises his option at the best price achieved during the life of the option. This is generally a valuable and expensive option, and is sensitive to market manipulation that may artificially inflate or depress prices for a period of time.
- **Shout Options:** Shout options are options with two strike prices. One strike is determined when the shout option is bought, and another one is determined at the discretion of the holder. The owner "shouts" his strike price reset at any time during the life of the shout option.
- **Asian Options:** Asian options pay based on the average price of the underlying asset on a few specific dates or all dates within a pricing window. These options are used by customers that have recurring currency demands as opposed to bullet (occasional or one-time) transactions.
- **Barrier Options:** These options become active (get "knocked in") or inactive (get "knocked out") when predetermined price barriers

are reached. These options are highly prone to manipulation by the underlying market.
- **Range Options:** The range option pays out based on the difference between the maximum and minimum price of the underlying asset during the life of the option.

2.7.2 Risks in Trading Exotic Options

Exotic options combine all the risks of spot foreign exchange, forward foreign exchange, plain vanilla options, and their own unique risks. Exotic risk can be broken down into Greeks and execution risk. Because the models are customized, however, the determination of Greeks is especially vulnerable to model errors, making the trading in exotics particularly risky. Some exotics, such as knock-outs, become extremely difficult to hedge when the underlying trade nears the knock-out price.

Exotic options, however, open up a new category of risks. For example, as we saw in Chapter 1, in May 1996 Procter & Gamble (P&G) sued Bankers Trust for embedding exotic options in transactions, using the argument that P&G could not possibly have been expected to understand the risks of those instruments. In 1995, financier George Soros publicly called for a ban on barrier options. The reason was that he believed markets could be subtly manipulated to make these options knock out. Finally, many banks are simply unable to accommodate exotic options in their trading systems. At best, the risk of some exotics is approximated with other option positions, but those approximate positions do not capture the exotics' risk.

Therefore, in addition to increased model risk and hedging execution risk, exotic options create the additional risks of market manipulation, and legal, reputational, and operational risk.

2.8 A Nested Risk Model for FX Instruments

To summarize this chapter from a risk point of view, it is helpful to see how the risks in simple spot positions become embedded in forwards, options, and exotics. Similarly, the incremental risks of forwards over spot instruments become embedded in options and exotics. The analogy can be extended as shown in Figure 2.6 below.

Foreign Exchange Markets, Instruments and Risks

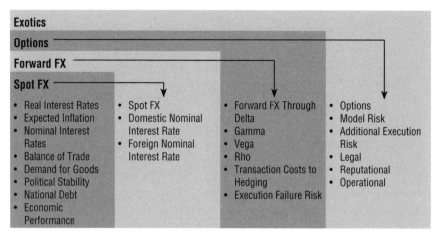

FIGURE 2.6 Risk Map for Traded Foreign Exchange Instruments

The benefit of this risk map is that it clearly shows all the risk drivers of all FX instruments. When undertaking a risk assessment, this gives a guide of how to calculate the impact of a bank's market assumptions on the risk of market instruments.

2.9 Summary

This chapter has expanded a number of introductory concepts by presenting information on foreign exchange instruments and their market risks.

The Foreign Exchange Market
- The interbank foreign exchange market is the largest and most liquid in the world, with daily volumes approaching USD 4 trillion.
- Major traded currencies are the US dollar (USD), euro (EUR), Japanese yen (JPY) and British pound (GBP).

Spot Foreign Exchange Transactions
- Spot foreign exchange transactions generate foreign exchange risk.
- Foreign exchange risk derives from economic factors, international political factors, and market psychology.
- Currency can be thought of as an economic "good" subject to supply and demand pressures.
- A currency strengthens when global demand for the currency increases.

Forward Foreign Exchange Transactions
- Banks trade forwards to speculate, make markets, and meet customer demand.
- Forward transactions enable end-users to lock in exchange rates for future foreign-denominated receipts and expenditures.
- Forward foreign exchange transactions are priced using an arbitrage relationship.
- The foreign exchange forward price expressed in domestic currency equals the spot FX rate grossed up at the difference between the domestic and foreign interest rates.
- Forward foreign exchange transactions therefore generate foreign exchange and interest rate risk.
- Foreign exchange swaps generate interest rate risk.

Currency Futures
- Futures perform the same economic function as forwards and are priced like forwards.
- Futures contracts are generally more standardized than forwards.
- Unlike forwards, all futures are marked-to-market and therefore have margining risk.
- Futures trades are cleared by clearinghouses, which have a responsibility to both the buyer and seller. This mitigates counterparty credit risk.

Currency Swaps
- Currency swaps are long-term currency contracts with periodic interest payments.
- Currency swap structure is similar to that of interest rate swaps.
- A payment of principal amounts occurs at the beginning and at the end of a currency swap.

Options
- Banks trade options both to speculate and to make markets, meeting customer demands.
- End users use options to protect their future cash positions against adverse movements, while benefiting from favorable movements.
- Option pricing models are used to value option positions; most models have some imperfections.
- Option risks include all forward risks plus additional risks.
- Additional risks arise from the "Greeks" and from execution risk associated with hedging.
- Delta measures option risk relative to the underlying instrument.

- Gamma measures changes in delta, a risk factor in hedging options.
- Vega measures changes in volatility, a risk factor for options.
- Rho measures changes in option value relative to changes in relevant interest rates.
- Theta measures the change in option value as it nears exercise.

Exotic Options
- Exotics come in a myriad of flavors.
- Exotics can be path dependent or path independent.
- Exotic risks include all the risks of options, plus additional risks of market manipulation, legal, reputational, and operational risk.

CHAPTER 3

Interest Rate Markets, Instruments and Risks

This chapter expands on the introductory treatment of fixed income instruments in the FBR book. After an introduction to interest rates, the yield curve, and the pricing of fixed income instruments derived from these rates, the chapter explores sources of risk and the impact of risk on the fixed income instruments. It is important to have read the previous chapter on foreign exchange instruments and risk, as the material here builds on the foreign exchange material.

On completion of this chapter the reader will have an improved understanding of:

- The importance of fixed income instruments to banks
- Key cash fixed income instruments
- Determinants of interest rates and the yield curve
- Sources of fixed income price risk
- Fixed income forwards and options
- Classification and risk of fixed income derivative instruments
- The basics of mortgage-backed securities and CDOs

3.1 The Importance of Fixed Income Instruments

The term fixed income instruments used to mean fixed coupon bonds and other fixed rate obligations, i.e., any promised, predetermined, future payment. Historically, the interest rate and interest payments paid on these obligations—the coupon rate—was fixed in advance and did not change. The term has now come to include instruments whose notional amount is fixed, but whose interest is computed according to an interest formula, such as LIBOR + 50 bp, (basis points, where one basis point is 1/100 of 1% or 0.01%). For the purposes of this chapter, we will focus on bonds, loans, deposits, forward rate agreements, interest rate swaps, currency swaps, options, and exotics—all sensitive to changes in the interest rates underlying these instruments.

Banks hold fixed income instruments as assets and as liabilities on their balance sheets. A bank's assets include securities it owns, loans (credits) it has extended to customers, and interbank loans and cash, among other things. Liabilities include anything owed to others, such as deposits, borrowings, obligations to foreign offices, and other liabilities. The difference between the amount of assets and of liabilities is the value of the bank's equity.

In the US, the Board of Governors of the Federal Reserve System reports aggregate balance sheets for commercial banks in the United States and for foreign-related institutions (typically, institutions that are owned by non-US based entities) chartered in the United States.[27]

A few summary statistics are abstracted below:

ASSETS	Domestic	Intl. in US	Total
Bank credit	9,793.4	986.0	10,779.4
• Securities	2,759.9	189.8	2,949.7
• Loans	7,033.5	796.2	7,829.7
Interbank loans	64.0	19.9	83.9
Cash	1,474.8	1,098.0	2,572.9
Other	1,208.0	162.2	1,370.2
Total Assets	12,540.3	2,266.1	14,806.4

---

27 See the Board of Governors of the Federal Reserve System, H.8 Release, Assets and Liabilities of Commercial Banks in the United States - H.8, posted online at www.federalreserve.gov/releases/h8/current. Seasonally adjusted data are shown here, but raw data are available as well.

LIABILITIES			
Deposits	9,298.6	1,103.2	10,401.8
Borrowings	1,051.2	697.8	1,749.0
Related foreign offices	79.7	289.6	369.4
Other	502.4	148.1	650.5
Total Liabilities	**10,932.0**	**2,238.8**	**13,170.8**
Residual	**1,608.3**	**27.3**	**1,635.6**

Numbers do not add up due to rounding and other adjustments.

FIGURE 3.1 Summary Statistics—US Aggregate Balance Sheet H8 SA (USD billions), end-2014

Collectively, these statistics paint an impressive picture. Banks in the United States alone hold USD 14.8 trillion in assets, including USD 2.9 trillion in securities (mostly fixed income) and USD 7.8 trillion in loans. These are offset by liabilities of USD 10.4 trillion in deposits and USD 1.7 trillion in borrowings. The income, expenses, appreciation, and devaluation of these assets are all affected profoundly by fluctuations in interest rates and credit spreads. Figures provided by the Bank for International Settlements (BIS) paint a similar global picture. The reporting categories are different, but the figures approximately triple when scaled globally.[28]

3.2 Cash Fixed Income Instruments

This section examines fixed income instruments that trade on a spot or cash basis. The analogy in the FX market is a spot FX contract. Spot contracts have their own risks, and also form the basis for forward contracts and swaps discussed later in the chapter.

3.2.1 Loans and Deposits on the Interbank Market

Loans and deposits are traded between banks at fixed interest rates for an agreed period, or with interest rates that reset periodically. Maturities range from overnight to five years. However, there are not many trades that have a maturity of more than one year. Interest is paid on the maturity date with the repayment of the principal, unless the maturity is over one year, in which

---

28 http://www.bis.org/publ/qtrpdf/r_qa1412.pdf#page=7

case an interest payment is made on each anniversary of the transaction.[29] The interbank money market is where banks make loans and trade deposits with each other. It is also used by banks to take positions in anticipation of a favorable movement in interest rates. However, banks' need to match their funding requirements to maintain their liquidity positions drives much of the volume in the market. (Liquidity positions are explained in Chapter 3 in the *Asset and Liability Management* book of the GARP FRR Series.)

The largest interbank loan market for US dollars outside the United States is the LIBOR market, where London banks make USD loans to each other to help meet mutual liquidity and yield needs. Because it is not directly affected by US regulation or policies, the LIBOR rate is considered one of the best measures of USD interest rates. Since banks are vulnerable to default risk, however, LIBOR will typically trade at a small premium over comparable risk-free bonds issued by the US government.

The same is true, in turn, for the five other currencies covered by LIBOR: Swiss franc (CHF), Euro (EUR), British pound sterling (GBP), Japanese yen (JPY). The rate is calculated for 15 different maturities for each of these currencies at 11:00 a.m. each business day. The current submission and calculation agent is ICE Benchmark Administration Limited (IBA). LIBOR is a quote-driven, not an order/trade-driven, market.

A newspaper article in 2008 highlighted a practice among key players in the market of doctoring LIBOR submissions. This led, in 2012, to an official review of the rate setting process, led by Martin Wheatley, who became the Head of the UK Financial Conduct Authority. This review process, and many other parallel international investigations, has led to significant fines being levied in multiple jurisdictions against many of the best-known banks in the business. At the same time, the responsibility for receiving submissions, calculating LIBOR rates, and publicizing them daily has been transferred from the British Bankers Association (BBA) to the US Intercontinental Exchange, owner of NYSE Euronext.[30]

On October 10, 2008, the yield on three-month US government instruments was 0.24%, and the three-month LIBOR rate was 4.81%, reflecting a 4.57% credit spread–the highest this spread has ever been. This credit spread is also referred to as the TED (Treasury-Euro Dollar) spread and is seen as a general predictor of credit risk in the banking sector and the economy at large.

---

29   In some cases, when convention or business conditions necessitate, the interest payments are not made on an annual basis, but on a semiannual basis.
30   http://en.wikipedia.org/wiki/Libor_scandal

The TED spread has a long-term average of around 30 bp, peaking in times of crisis. On December 31, 2014 the spread was 24 bp.

3.2.2 Loans to Customers

On the asset side of the balance sheet, many banks generate most of their income from loans to customers. Unlike the standardized short-term interbank loans, customer loans can be highly customized instruments designed to meet the needs of customers while earning the highest possible interest rate for the banks. The loans can be short term or long term, fixed rate or floating rate, revolving lines of credit or fixed commitments.

The key difference between customer loans and interbank loans lies in the credit risk. Customers are less credit-worthy than banks on average, so yields are higher on average. Of course, banks can and do fail, but due to the continual exchange of information between banks active in the interbank market, there is a high degree of transparency that normally facilitates trading. When this transparency disappears—as happened multiple times during the credit crisis of 2007-2009—the risk premium paid on these interbank trades can increase substantially, and sometimes markets and trading disappear altogether. Several factors can cause customers to default, such as a downturn in their industry or adverse factors specific to a particular company.

The market risk of loans depends on how the loans are managed by the bank. In general, customer loans are not traded as frequently as bonds, even though they have similar payment and risk profiles. (The credit risk of bonds and loans is covered in later chapters.)

Loan Management
Most commercial loans are held indefinitely in the bank's portfolio, for three reasons:

1. Customer relations/flexibility to renegotiate
2. Attractive risk-return profile
3. Non-marketability of the loan

In the first case, a loan is held by a bank in order to maintain a good relationship with an important customer. By keeping a commercial loan in its portfolio, the bank signals to its customer that it has confidence in the customer and values the relationship. If the customer ever needs to renegotiate the terms of the loan, this is easiest to do if the bank retains the loan and does not sell it.

In the second case, banks may find that some loans have an attractive risk-return profile relative to alternative capital uses and may decide to keep a loan portfolio in the bank for that reason. While the trend for many banks has been to focus on origination and to sell the loans they produce, others keep selective loan portfolios on their books for portfolio reasons. See Chapter 6 for more discussion of a bank's portfolio motives.

In the third case, the loan is not sold because it is not marketable. The loan may be nonstandard, or the borrower may have had some documentation problems that were originally overlooked by the bank. Also, the borrower may have fallen on hard times, or had a poor payment history. In these cases, even if the bank makes the loan in anticipation of selling it later, the marketability of the loan is compromised and the bank may have no other option than to keep the loan in its portfolio.

Marketable Loans
The risk of holding loans depends in part on their marketability. For many loans, such as residential mortgage loans in the United States, the bank holds the loans for a short while until it can accumulate a portfolio that can be sold to a government-sponsored entity (GSE) such as the Federal National Mortgage Association, known as Fannie Mae (FNMA), or the Federal Home Loan Mortgage Corporation, known as Freddie Mac (FHLMC), or directly to private investors. In general, qualified loans receive government guarantees and are sold to GSEs, while nonqualified loans are sold to private investors. The process of accumulating loans for eventual sale is known as warehousing, since the bank "stores" the loans until they can be packaged and sold. Banks can also borrow using the transitional portfolio as collateral; these loans are known as warehouse loans.

For loans in the pipeline, i.e., loans that are in process but not yet originated, the bank incurs interest rate risk only to the extent it has pre-committed to a fixed funding rate. Even if the bank has collected a fee or taken other consideration for the commitment, the bank is left to manage that risk or decide if the risk is worth taking. Once the loan is originated, a fixed rate loan will carry interest rate risk and credit risk for the bank until it is sold. Once it is sold, the bank sheds these risks.

Securitization
Securitization is a form of marketable loan sale, where the underlying fixed income instruments are aggregated and structured for sale to investors.

Securitization has benefits and disadvantages, which are discussed in Chapter 3 in the Credit Risk Book in the GARP FRR Series.

3.2.3 Bonds

A bond is a transferable long-term debt instrument issued by a borrower or issuer on receipt of the principal amount from an investor or bond holder. The bond issuer is obligated to pay the holder a specified amount of interest, usually at regular intervals, during the life of the bond and repay the principal, usually at maturity.

Review of Bond Basics
Bonds are typically issued by governments, government agencies, or corporations. Each bond represents a financial claim on the issuing organization. A "vanilla" bond will normally pay fixed interest, known as a "coupon," on set dates during the life of the bond, with the principal repaid on maturity. The term "vanilla" is used to indicate a bond that has standard market features. However, bonds may also incorporate many other financial incentives to encourage investors. The price of the bond will be affected by the general level of interest rates and the financial standing of the issuer. Rating agencies, such as Moody's Investors Service and Standard & Poor's produce a wide range of risk-sensitive grades ranking the credit risk of bonds. These range from AAA (the issuer's ability to pay interest and principal is very strong) to D (in default). Bonds generate general interest rate risk and specific risk. Non-vanilla bonds may expose the holder to other types of risk, such as liquidity risk. Zero-coupon bonds are a special type of bond that does not pay interest until maturity, when the borrower repays the amount borrowed with the interest accrued.

3.2.4 Bond Classifications

Bonds can be classified by maturity, issuer, seniority, credit quality, payment formula, and embedded options.

Maturity
Most issuers prefer to issue long-term bonds so they do not have to worry about returning frequently to the market to raise capital to refinance their debts. The cost of these instruments, however, can be significantly higher than that of short-term bonds, so some companies prefer to issue short-term debt such as commercial paper to raise capital. Typically, short-term

bonds have maturities not exceeding five years, medium-term bonds have maturities not exceeding 10 years, and long-term bonds have maturities exceeding 10 years. There are also bonds that are perpetual—where the interest is paid in perpetuity and the principal is never repaid.

Issuer
If the issuer is a government, bondholders will look to the strength of the government issuing the bond as an indicator of credit quality. Sovereign debt can be risky: sovereign default occurs with relative frequency and several governments have repeatedly defaulted on their debts. Government agencies do not always have the full backing of their governments. Bonds issued by various government entities may also provide tax benefits to those who invest in these bonds, and this provides an additional incentive to invest in these bonds compared to non-government bonds. Corporate bonds are subject to many types of market, industry, and specific risks affecting the likelihood of default and the amount that investors can recover after a default.

Seniority
In corporate bonds, seniority refers to the priority of a bond or of bondholder interests in bankruptcy. Seniority is achieved by the bond contract. In case of bankruptcy, the first bondholders to be paid are those holding senior bonds. Unless overruled by a judicial authority, senior bonds are paid in full before junior or subordinated bondholders receive payment. A senior bond is considered more secure than a junior bond, since in the event of liquidation, payments due on senior bonds would likely be paid before payments due on junior bond. Therefore, senior bond credit spreads should be less than otherwise similar junior bonds' credit spreads; junior bonds usually have a lower credit rating than senior bonds.

Credit Quality
Many bonds are rated by the three major bond-rating agencies: Moody's Investors Service, Standard & Poor's (S&P), and Fitch Ratings. Agencies are usually paid a fee to study a firm's financials and interview management for the purpose of assigning a credit rating. There are eight major credit ratings, four are investment grade, and four are non-investment or junk grade. The S&P ratings (for example) are AAA, AA, A, BBB, BB, B, C and D, in declining credit quality. Generally, bonds with higher ratings will enjoy lower credit spreads.

Payment Formula
Issued bonds can carry either fixed coupons, floating coupons linked to various interest rate indices, or no coupons. Bonds without coupons are called zero-coupon bonds (ZCBs) and are the extreme form of "bullet" bonds, whose entire principal is redeemed at maturity. Interest rates on bonds are typically stated on an annualized rate, but the actual payment of interest on the bonds can be more frequent. Commercial and financial conventions may require semiannual interest payments on bonds in different parts of the world, such as in the United States. In other parts of the world, interest payments are typically made annually, but occasionally bonds might pay interest on a more frequent, even a monthly, basis.

Embedded Options
Many bonds have complex options embedded within them. Convertible bonds can be converted at the option of the investor into shares of stock. Callable bonds can be recalled by the issuer according to a pre-determined formula, which is done when interest rates fall and the issuer wishes to refinance. Convertible bonds, therefore, have an element of equity risk, while callable bonds have an element of prepayment risk, similar to that of mortgages.

3.3 Pricing Cash Fixed Income Instruments

In this section, we will look at the methods used to price fixed income instruments. The purpose of this exercise is to determine the factors that drive the valuation of these instruments, and thus the risk of these instruments, which are, in many cases, the inputs to the pricing formulas.

3.3.1 Yield Curves

All financial instruments with future cash flows are valued by calculating the present value of the future cash flows promised by the instrument. The present value of any future cash flow is calculated by discounting its future value using the appropriate current interest rate. For valuation purposes, a market interest rate is required for any date on which there is a cash flow. To calculate the required market interest rate, banks create a yield curve using a yield curve model. The description below is simplified to illustrate the construction of a yield curve. The yield curves used by traders are more complex and are derived from a number of instruments to ensure the curve is accurate and consistent. While there are commercially available yield curve models, banks typically derive their own yield curve models based on a wide variety of material factors specific to the bond issuers and the bond issues.

The inputs for our simplified model are the market interest rates for several periods. The periods will be 1, 2, 3, 6, and 12 months and 2, 3, 5, and 10 years. There are bonds with maturities exceeding 10 years, and yield curves can often cover 30 or more years, but for the following examples, a 10-year yield curve explains the relationship adequately. Figure 3.2 shows a sample shape of the curve at a given point in time.

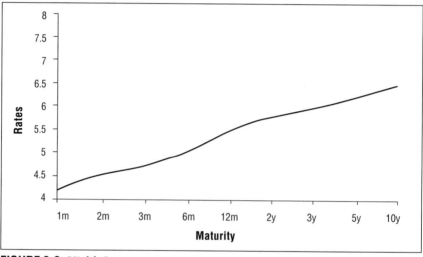

FIGURE 3.2 Yield Curve

Rates for the standard maturity dates can be observed from the curve, but any rates for other dates must be interpolated from the input rates.

The value of interest rate-related products, as well as all products with cash flows at a future date, will be sensitive to changes in the yield curve. A product's value may be sensitive to changes in one or more of the yield curve rates depending on the maturity and financial properties of the instrument.

The difference between the yield curves will primarily be the difference in the underlying instruments used to create the discrete points. Each major currency has its own set of yield curves—bonds issued in EUR can be issued by different entities, such as governments, corporations, institutions, etc. These bonds have different risk profiles and reflect different conditions that impact their yield, which often necessitates the creation of multiple yield curves for a currency. Even within a single currency, there will typically be many different yield curves corresponding to the different types of risk-free or risky instruments associated with the currency. The main types of interest rate-related yield curves are:

- *Cash:* These are used to revalue loan and deposit positions. The points on the curve are defined by the standard maturity dates traded in the interbank market, and are typically short-term instruments issued by governments or institutions with high credit quality.
- *Derivative:* These curves are used to value all types of derivatives including options. The points on the curve are determined by a mixture of instruments beginning with cash rates of the short maturities followed by forward or futures contracts. Finally, if other rates are not available, long-term rates are determined by swap rates for the standard traded periods. The mixture of instruments is closely related to the underlying hedge instruments used by banks to hedge derivative risk.
- *Bond*: These are valued on a price basis by taking the closing price for the day. However, some bonds are not actively traded, so they may not trade each day. Banks may use a bond curve to derive a notional closing price from the closing price of actively traded bonds. The curve is usually defined by the standard maturities traded in the government bond market. Bonds may then be valued as a spread over the corresponding government benchmark bond when a market price cannot be obtained. This reflects differences in the liquidity of the bond and the credit standing of the issuer.
- *Basis:* Not all interest rates are traded actively in the interbank market. Some primarily exist for historical reasons or to service customer demands. The rate set by the central bank for discounting bills (known as the Base Rate in the UK) is a good example. Basis curves are created to price instruments in these non-interbank-based rates. A curve is usually expressed as a spread over or under a standard curve. Each point on the curve will have a unique interest rate differential to its corresponding maturity on the standard curve.

EXAMPLE

US government bonds might be considered comparable to bonds issued by US municipalities, known as municipal debt, or, in short form, "'munis.'" While there are some institutional differences—some munis are tax advantaged compared to government bonds, and government bonds have a significantly lower risk of failing than municipal bonds, which do fail relatively frequently—there are features common to both types of bonds. The taxation power of the government often backs these bonds, which ordinarily reduces the likelihood of default.

However, the yield curves are very different. The following chart (taken from data provided by Bloomberg.com) shows the differences in the levels of interest rates. Furthermore, the muni curve is steeper than the government curve, reflecting a risk premium for longer-term municipal debt instruments. The difference between these curves can be called the municipal curve basis to treasuries.

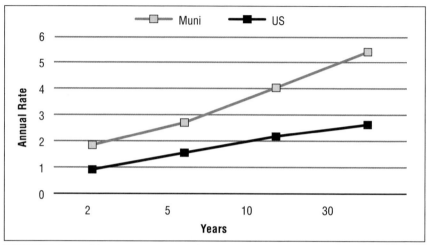

FIGURE 3.3 Yield Curves—December 25, 2008

One of the reasons for the spread is the different tax treatment of these securities for US investors. Uncertainty about tax rules after an election can be a factor in determining the slope of the basis between these two yield curves.

3.3.2 Theories of the Term Structure of Interest Rates

The term structure is usually upward sloping, reflecting higher annual yields on long-term debt than on short-term debt. The most widely accepted reason for this is that if short-term rates were equal to long-term rates, borrowers would prefer to issue long-term debt to lock in their funding, but lenders would prefer to buy short-term debt in order to keep their risks lower. To reach equilibrium in this market, long-term rates must rise enough to get some borrowers to borrow short term, and some lenders to lend long term. This theory is known as the Liquidity Preference Theory of the term structure. There are other qualitative theories of the term structure, such as the Preferred Habitat Theory and the Expectations Hypothesis, although these alternative theories each have critical weaknesses.[31] There are also quantitative theories of the term structure, but they are beyond the scope of this program.[32]

The Liquidity Preference Theory also implies that banks that lend loans long term and borrow deposits short term will tend to make money over time. However, being profitable on average does not guarantee banks will always be profitable. In fact, the Savings & Loan (S&L) crisis in the United States in the 1980s demonstrated forcefully how S&Ls could fail due to fluctuations in interest rates. The cost of the crisis was estimated to be USD 160 billion.

3.3.3 Drivers of Interest Rates

Interest rates are often divided into two components, a risk-free component that reflects the cost of borrowing for a lender that cannot default, and a credit spread, which measures the additional yield a creditor must pay due to its risk of default. The risk-free interest rate can be considered the "cost" of credit, and the credit spread can be considered the "cost" of risk.

This cost of credit is driven by many macroeconomic variables, all of which are related to the demand for credit. For example, greater willingness of consumers to defer consumption will imply lower interest rates in an economy. Higher inflation will increase demand for today's dollars, causing interest rates to rise. Returns on alternative investments also drive interest rates, since high returns on alternative investments—such as Certificates of Deposit or short-term loans—increase the demand for cash.

Interest rates can be affected by the relative risk of fixed income investments, as higher risk instruments command a higher average rate of return. The preference for liquidity will cause investors to want to hold more cash, to protect against the uncertainty of long-dated investments and against cash shortfalls. Finally, since different instruments are taxed differently, taxes influence the level of interest rates.

The Federal Reserve Board also provides historical interest rate data. The following chart shows the one-year, continuously compounded zero coupon bond rate for the USD from 1961 to May 2015.

---

31 The Preferred Habitat Theory postulates separate equilibrium rates in each time bucket without considering arbitrage relationships that regulate the relative rates of return. The Expectations Hypothesis does not account for risk aversion.
32 Some examples are models by Vasicek, Cox/Ingersoll/Ross, Brennan/Schwartz, Black/Derman/Toy, and others.

FIGURE 3.4 Daily History of One-Year USD Rates

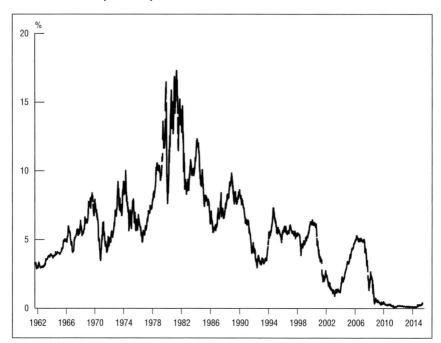

The history shows that USD interest rates can be quite volatile over long periods of time, from high inflation periods like the late 1970's to lower inflation periods similar to today's economic conditions. The historical volatility measured in percentage terms since 1961 was 23% per year.

3.3.4 Drivers of Credit Spreads

Credit spreads vary considerably, though the data are less readily available. This can cause the value of credit-sensitive instruments to fluctuate more than risk-free instruments.

The credit spread can be derived from three components:

$$Credit\ spread = PD \times LGD + RP.$$

PD is the probability of default of the issuer, and LGD is the loss given default of the issuer. Therefore, PD x LGD is the expected loss rate expressed as a percentage of the value of a loan or bond. RP is a risk premium that compensates the lender for taking credit risk. The risk premium depends on the lender's criteria and also fluctuates with the market. When credit "dries up," risk premiums increase, raising borrowing rates even when a company's fundamentals have not changed.

EXAMPLE

A bond trades at a 3% yield premium to treasuries. The probability of default is 2%, and investors are expected to lose 60% of their investment if the bond fails. Since the expected credit loss is 2% x 60% = 1.2%, the remaining 1.8% credit spread can be attributed to a risk premium earned by investors for holding the bond. Anything that changes a firm's probability of default, its recovery rate if there is a default, or the credit risk premium will cause fluctuations in the values of the bond. In general, it will be impossible to determine the source of credit-spread risk, because these three variables are not directly observable. For this reason, credit-spread risk is often considered as if it were a single variable.

3.4 Price Risk In Cash Fixed Income Instruments

The price risk in fixed income instruments can be linked directly to the volatility in interest rates. There are three popular risk measures used, all of which are based on the assumption of a parallel shift in the yield curve, i.e., short-, medium-, and long-term interest rates change by the same amount. This is an approximation of reality, since yield curves do not usually shift in this manner.

3.4.1 Present Value of a Basis Point (PVBP/PV01)

This measure computes the change in value of a bond under the assumption that the yields of all the payments increase by one basis point. For example, using a financial calculator, we can calculate that a five-year bond that pays a 4% annual coupon, paid semiannually, will be priced at USD 97.805 when the annual yield is 4.50%. If the discount rate were to rise by one basis point to 4.51%, the valuation would be USD 97.762, for a change of USD 0.04328. The PVBP is therefore USD 0.04328.

3.4.2 Modified Duration and Macaulay Duration

Modified duration measures the percentage change in bond price for a 100 basis point change in yield. Using the PVBP calculation above, a 100 bp change would be expected to lower the bond's price by approximately USD

4.328. As a percentage of bond value, this is 4.425%. This number is inexact due to the nonlinear relationship between a bond's yield and its price.

Macaulay duration, the original duration measure, can be calculated in two ways. First, it can be calculated as the weighted average life of the bond payments, where each payment life gets weighted according to the present value of the payment. Second, Macaulay duration can be shown to be equal to the modified duration (MD) multiplied by one plus the bond's yield, where the yield is divided by the number of coupon periods per year. Continuing with the example:

Macaulay duration = 4.425% × (1 + (0.045 / 1)) = 4.62 years.

This five-year bond has a weighted average payment life of 4.62 years. This means, for risk purposes, that a bond will respond to yield changes approximately in proportion to its weighted average life, with the exact calculation being determined by the modified duration. The general equation is the following:

Bond volatility (%) = Rate volatility (%) × Yield × Modified duration

Going from an individual bond to a portfolio, the modified duration of a portfolio can be calculated by taking the value-weighted average modified duration of the component bonds.

EXAMPLE

Macaulay duration
A 10-year bond has a yield of 6.2%, is priced at USD 95 per USD 100 par, and has a weighted average payment life of 8.6 years (Macaulay duration). The modified duration is 8.6/1.062 =8.098, implying that the bond value will drop 8.098% of its value—fall to USD 87.31—if yields increase 100 bp.

Bond volatility
Say the short-term rate volatility is 23% of yield. The bond volatility is therefore 23% of 6.2%, which is 143 bp, and 1.43 times 8.098 is 11.58%. This is the bond's short-term annualized volatility. Given the yield volatility, this is how much one can expect the bond price to increase or decrease with a given level of confidence.

To hedge a portfolio against a small parallel shift in the term structure (when the yield on all bonds, irrespective of maturity, changes by the same amount, e.g. 10), a hedge should be constructed that has the same value and the same duration as the current portfolio, but, of course, the opposite sign. For example, a long bond portfolio with duration of 8 and a value of USD 100 million should be hedged with a short bond portfolio with duration of 8 and a value of USD 100 million.

3.4.3 Convexity

Assuming a parallel shift in the yield curve, the change in yield of a bond affects the price of the bond in a nonlinear fashion. One way to measure the nonlinear relationship is to compute the degree to which the duration changes as the yield changes. This measure is known as a bond's convexity.

For plain vanilla bonds, as yields rise, duration will fall. For example, if a bond's modified duration is 8 and its convexity is 0.5, and if yields go up by 1%, we can expect the bond's price to fall by 8% and its duration to fall by 0.5.

Going from an individual bond to a portfolio, the convexity of a portfolio can be calculated by taking the value-weighted average convexity of the component bonds. To hedge a portfolio against a larger parallel shift in yield curves, the bank should match the values, the durations, and the convexities of the portfolios.

3.4.4 Nonparallel Shifts in the Yield Curve

While duration and convexity were designed to measure risks of parallel shifts in the yield curve, in practice, curves do not shift in a parallel fashion. For instance, short-term yields exhibit greater variability than long-term yields. The figure below shows six monthly snapshots of the yield curve during the second half of 1980, demonstrating clearly that the yield curve does not shift in a parallel fashion.[33]

---

[33] Some financial websites provide a "yield curve animation" which shows how the yield curve has changed historically. One example currently is http://stockcharts.com/freecharts/yieldcurve.php, which requires Java, but there are others available.

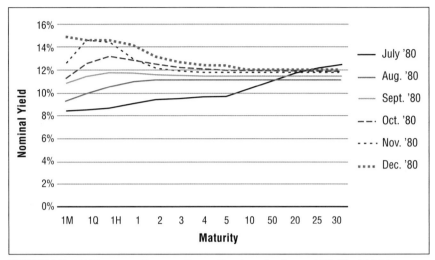

FIGURE 3.5 US Treasury Interest Rates During the Second Half of 1980

This was an unusual situation: interest rates were high and variable. However, even under normal circumstances, the short-term rate fluctuates a great deal more than the long-term rate. For this reason, most banks have multifactor models of the term structure to capture the risk of yields that do not change uniformly.

For example, a bank may separately model movements in short-term and long-term rates to determine risks of bond portfolios as they respond to different risk factors. Short-term rates are sensitive to central bank borrowing rates, whereas long-term rates are driven more by inflation and risk. A bank typically models different portions of the yield curve as separate, but correlated, risk factors. In general, the multiple factor methods are analytically more complex, but they improve bond risk measurement and management significantly compared to duration-based methods.

3.4.5 Floating Rate Risk

Floating rate bonds have coupon payments tied to floating interest rates. At first, it would appear these bonds are riskier than fixed rate bonds, since the payments vary. Actually, the risk of these bonds is lower. As interest rates rise, payments rise, counterbalancing the natural negative present-value effect on the bonds. When rates fall, payments fall and the discount rate falls—these changes have an offsetting effect.

Floating interest rate bonds can be issued for multiple reasons. A borrower expecting rates to decline in the future would normally prefer to issue floating rate bonds. Interest rate declines can be caused by several factors, such as the overall reduction of market interest rates, or the borrower's improved business conditions, which would reduce the likelihood that the borrower defaults and, consequently, the risk premium associated with the borrower. A borrower may also issue a floating rate bond because the interest rate demanded by the lenders would be relatively more advantageous if the borrower offers to pay a floating rate instead of a fixed rate. There are also lenders that have interest rate sensitive liabilities and seek a natural hedge against the impact of changing interest rates by investing in assets that pay floating interest rates.

A floating rate bond typically has a very small sensitivity to interest rates. For example, if the five-year coupon bond mentioned above were linked to floating interest rates, it might have a modified duration between 0 and 0.5. This short duration means small sensitivity to interest rate changes because the interest rate on the variable rate bond is reset every six months (0.5 years).

Usually, floating rate bonds have a small degree of interest rate risk for one of two reasons. First, part of the floating index may, in fact, be fixed, such as LIBOR plus 50 bp. The 50 bp part of the coupon is fixed, and gives the bond a fixed-rate feature. Secondly, many floating rate bonds calculate interest in arrears, so the next payment is known (and therefore fixed) even though future payments will vary.

The rules for computing modified duration of a portfolio including floating rate bonds are the same as for fixed rate bonds; the portfolio's modified duration is the value-weighted average of the components' modified durations.

EXAMPLE

Bond	Value	Modified Duration
5-year floater	USD 100 MM	0.25
10-year fixed	USD 150 MM	7.00
Portfolio	USD 250 MM	4.30

To compute the modified duration of the portfolio:
[40% (= 100/250) × 0.25] + [60% (= 150/250) × 7.00] = 4.30.

FIGURE 3.6 Example of Modified Duration Computation

A highly sophisticated form of floating rate bonds is a reverse floater. For these types of bonds, the interest rate level moves in the opposite direction to the movement of interest rates. When interest rates increase, the interest rate on a reverse floater decreases, and when interest rates decrease, the interest rate on a reverse floater increases.

3.4.6 Bond Risk and Bank Balance Sheets

Consider the simplified aggregate US bank balance sheet presented in Section 3.1.

Assets (USD tr)	Amt	MD	Liabilities	Amt	MD
Securities	5	5.00	Deposits	8	2.00
Loans	8	7.00	Borrowings	3	1.00
			Equity	2	0.00
Total or avg.	13	6.23		13	1.46

FIGURE 3.7 Aggregate US Bank Balance Sheets

The modified duration figures are based on the observation that for most banks, the duration of their assets exceeds the duration of their liabilities. For example, while the average loan life may be around eight years, the average deposit does not stay with the bank more than two years.

The modified duration for the assets (6.23) and the liabilities (1.46) is computed by taking the value-weighted average of the component assets and liabilities.

Now we can determine the impact of yield risk on the banks' collective balance sheet. A 100 bp rise in yields means that assets will fall 6.23%, or USD 810 billion, while liabilities will fall only 1.46%, or USD 190 billion. The net impact is a USD 620 billion impact—decrease—on aggregate wealth.

3.4.7 Overview of Bank Interest Rate Risk Management

In some banks, an Asset-Liability Management (ALM) committee is responsible for monitoring and managing the bank's interest rate risk on the banking book, i.e., loans, securities, and deposits. The committee generally seeks to either increase the duration of its liabilities or decrease the duration of its assets. This process is called duration matching. For example, deposit duration can be increased if demand deposits are shifted to time deposits. Loan duration can be decreased by shortening loan maturities or contracting for variable-rate loans. Finally, the ALM committee may elect to use interest rate swaps to balance the durations of the assets and the liabilities. Swaps are described in detail in the next section.

In other banks, the ALM function has been taken over by the Market Risk Management Committee, which also has responsibility for market risk management in the trading book. The overall function is not much different, but the scope of the risks considered is. Whereas the ALM committee focuses on interest rate risks in the banking book, the market risk management committee generally addresses all material market risks in the banking and the trading books. These processes are discussed in greater detail in Chapter 1 of the Asset and Liability Management book in the GARP FRR Series.

3.5 Fixed Income Derivatives

In this section, we discuss derivative instruments whose underlying instruments may be the spot instruments presented above or other derivative instruments. The general logic of Chapter 2 applies: derivative instruments inherit the risk of their underlying assets and add a layer of risks all of their own. However, there are also specific differences between fixed income derivatives and other derivatives that the student needs to understand.

3.5.1 Forward Rate Agreements

Forward rate agreements (FRAs) are OTC derivative contracts that enable banks to take positions in forward interest rates. The contract gives the right to lend (borrow) funds at a fixed rate for a specified period starting in the future. There is no exchange of principal, and on maturity a cash settlement is made for the difference between the rate of the contract and the current LIBOR rate for the period. FRAs are the OTC version of interest rate futures contracts (such as the Eurodollar futures traded at the CME) and provide more flexibility than futures. FRAs generate interest rate risk.

3.5.2 Interest Rate Swaps

Interest rate swaps are OTC derivatives that enable banks and customers to obtain the risk/reward profile of long-term interest rates without having to use long-term funding. Credit risk and liquidity requirements are a major constraint on a bank providing long-term funds to customers. Conversely, many customers have long-term projects that need long-term funding at a fixed rate. Interest rate swaps provide a solution by enabling counterparties to swap interest flows without swapping principal amounts. Interest rate swaps are traded for maturities of up to 30 years although most trades have maturities of less than 10 years. The maximum maturity varies by country and depends on the underlying bond market in the host country. This is because banks use local bonds to hedge unmatched swap positions.

Plain vanilla swaps have a fixed interest rate that is "swapped" against a floating rate index such as one-month, three-month, or six-month LIBOR. This means that the parties agree to exchange the difference between these two interest rates. Given that the LIBOR rate will change regularly, the net exchange will differ over time.

The interbank market mainly trades vanilla swaps but there are many variations traded with end-users to match their requirements. One side of the swap will be designed to match customers' interest flows with the other side set to match their funding requirements. Banks use a mixture of hedging instruments to manage the interest rate risk created by a swap. Interest rate swaps without offsetting swaps or hedges generate interest rate risk.

EXAMPLE

XYZ Company (XYZ) obtains a USD 100 million loan from Bank A for two years, paying a floating interest rate set every six months at LIBOR. The company projects interest rates will rise over next two years period and wants to "lock in" a fixed rate. However, Bank A did not wish to extend a fixed rate loan to XYZ because it needed to increase the volume of floating rate bonds on its books; instead Bank A offered XYZ a competitive, floating interest rate.

To create a fixed interest rate loan, the company, therefore, goes to Bank B and enters into an interest rate swap where the company will pay to Bank B a fixed rate of 5% every six months calculated on the same principal amount as the loan.

This amount is 5% x USD 1 million ÷ 2, or USD 25,000 per six-month period. In return, the bank will pay a floating interest payment based on LIBOR to the company. The floating rate payment is also calculated referencing the USD 1 million principal amount. Because there is no exchange of the principal payment in an interest rate swap, the USD 1 million amount is usually called the swap notional principal or simply notional amount.

The company is now paying LIBOR every six months on the loan and receiving the same fixed interest flow from the swap. This leaves the company with net interest flows equal to the fixed rate of 5% being paid via the swap. While we may think of a swap as the exchange of a fixed rate loan for a floating rate loan, since the notional principal is the same there is no actual exchange of principal at maturity. Figure 3.8 shows the interest flows from these transactions for XYZ company.

Interest Rate Markets, Instruments and Risk

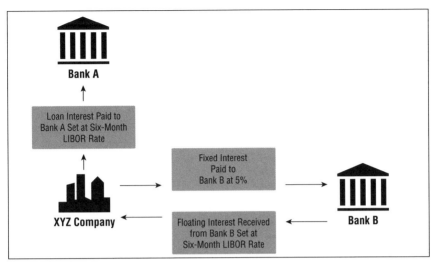

FIGURE 3.8 Interest Flows Diagram

The net effect of this arrangement is that XYZ pays fixed instead of floating interest rates on its debt. Bank A benefits from increasing interest rates, but not from floating interest rates. Bank B benefits from the swap transaction as long as the LIBOR rate is below the 5% stated interest rate on the swap. If the interest rates increase above that 5% fixed rate, Bank B will be paying the spread between the prevailing LIBOR rate and 5% to XYZ. From Bank B's perspective, declining interest rates are beneficial, but increasing rates are not. As a result of this swap transaction, XYZ insulated itself from the effects of changing interest rates, and the two banks assumed opposing exposures to interest rate changes. Bank B benefits from floating interest rates declining below 5% and Bank A benefits from increasing rates.

3.5.3 Currency Swaps

A currency swap has the same features as an interest rate swap except that the interest flows are expressed in different currencies. This product is used to swap, for example, USD interest flows for EUR interest flows. A key difference between interest rate and currency swaps is that with a currency swap loan proceeds and principal amounts are exchanged at the spot rate. Currency swaps generate interest rate risk in two currencies and foreign exchange risk. An example of a currency swap was given in Chapter 2.

3.5.4 Interest Rate Swap Valuation and Risks

At first, a swap appears to have a complex risk profile. However, a swap can be replicated with traded bonds, and therefore its valuation and risks are transparent. Using the example above, if XYZ pays fixed interest to Bank B and receives floating interest, the effect is the same as if B had issued a fixed rate bond to XYZ, and XYZ had issued a floating rate bond to Bank B. This back-to-back loan concept was the foundation of the first interest rate swaps and provides a key to understanding swap pricing and risk.

The value of a swap is simply the difference in value between a fixed rate bond and a floating rate bond. At inception, the value is zero since the bonds have the same value. Over time, the values will vary due to changes in interest rates. The value fluctuations of the swap will derive almost entirely from the value fluctuations of the fixed leg of the swap, and hardly at all from the floating leg. Therefore, interest rate risk on a swap is comparable to the interest rate risk of an equivalent fixed rate bond.

EXAMPLE

If a bank has a USD 200 million fixed rate loan portfolio and enters into an interest rate swap where it pays fixed and receives floating on USD 50 million notional, its interest rate risk is equivalent to a USD 150 million fixed rate portfolio. The benefit of using swaps instead of bonds to hedge is that the bank does not need to sell any bonds in order to reduce its interest rate risk.

Typically, swap transactions are conducted between a corporation, institution, or other entity and a bank or financial institution. Swap transactions lead to counterparty risk—the potential loss caused by default of the swap counterparty. At the inception of a swap, the contract is usually valueless, because the arrangement reflects the then prevailing market interest rates. Over time, interest rates change, and the value of the swap changes as well. As the swap nears maturity and fewer and fewer swap payments remain, the possible range of the swap's value tightens. However, the interest rate uncertainty increases with time: the further from inception, the greater the interest rate uncertainty. Thus, the counterparty credit risk is the greatest somewhere during the middle of the contract's time frame. It is during this period when it is most likely that one of the parties to the swap may default.

To reduce this risk of default, many swap dealers carry very high credit ratings. To further mitigate the negative effects of a default, collateral can be posted to provide additional payment support. Typically, the value of the collateral posted reflects the prevailing value of the swap agreement, and is revalued often to ensure continually sufficient collateral support.

3.6 Options and Exotic Fixed Income Instruments

Options and exotics have the same general properties in the fixed income markets as they do in the FX markets. There are some differences in both the products and their uses. This section discusses the most important differences.

3.6.1 Caps and Floors

The most widely used interest rate options are caps and floors. A customer who pays floating interest rates might want to buy protection against increases in rates, and so purchase a strip of interest rate options with the same payment dates and payment formula as the debt payments. A receiver of floating interest might want to purchase a strip of put options, i.e., a floor on interest rates to ensure earning a minimum yield.

EXAMPLE

A customer who is borrowing in GBP might want to protect against increases in the GBP LIBOR, and therefore purchases a strip of call options (cap) with maturities corresponding to the payment dates that pay off when the GBP LIBOR exceeds some threshold level. With the cap in place, high loan payments will be offset by proceeds from exercising the call options so that the net interest expense never exceeds the threshold level.

3.6.2 Exotics

There are hundreds of variations of exotic interest rate options, but most of them follow the exotic option patterns presented in the FX chapter. Option valuation formulas are similar, and the risk drivers are similar as well. One important exception is the index-amortizing swap.

Options can also be exotic because of their complex structure, such as embedded options. These instruments include mortgages, CMOs, structured debt, CDOs, and CDO-squareds as examples. Each of these instruments is discussed briefly.

Index-Amortizing Swap

Suppose the owner of a portfolio of mortgage-backed securities (customer) wants to change the profile from fixed rate to floating rate. Because of prepayment risk, i.e., some of the mortgages may be repaid prior to expiration, the notional value of the portfolio declines as mortgages are prepaid. For this reason, the customer would like to do an interest rate swap with a declining notional value.

For the customer, the two alternatives are: enter into an interest rate swap with the notional amount tied to the outstanding mortgage balance, or agree with the bank that a particular index will be used to amortize or reduce the notional balance over time. The notional balance will decrease more rapidly when interest rates decrease and more slowly when interest rates increase. The first alternative fits the customer's risk profile better, but is likely to be expensive, since the bank takes the full risk of the reduction in principal over time. The second alternative is an index-amortizing swap. It allows the bank to manage its risk more easily, but it does not fit the customer's profile as well, since the customer takes basis risk between the amortization of an index and the actual amortization of his own portfolio.

Mortgages (Whole Loans)

When a homeowner borrows and secures a loan with his property, the loan is called a mortgage. Unlike most credits, which pay interest plus a final face value payment, fixed rate mortgages have monthly payments and typically amortize fully over the life of the mortgage.

Fixed rate mortgages normally have a prepayment option that can be compared to the callability option of corporate bonds.[34] Corporate bonds are normally called when interest rates fall; mortgages are normally prepaid for any variety of other reasons, in addition to refinancing as interest rates fall. Life cycle events—divorce, death, career changes, retirement—can all cause mortgage prepayment. Because of this, mortgages have interest rate risk and default risk, like other bonds, but they also have prepayment risk, which is a behavioral risk element.

Collateralized Mortgage Obligations (CMOs)

CMOs are pools of mortgages that are divided according to the timing of cash flows. Typically, all tranches (investor groups) earn interest. The first principal payments go to the first, or highest, tranche, and later principal payments go to lower tranches. Therefore, the first tranche has less credit

---

34 There are commercial mortgages that expressly forbid full or partial prepayment.

uncertainty and prepayment uncertainty than the other tranches. For this reason, senior tranches of CMOs were considered acceptable short-term low-risk instruments suitable for bank investment.

After all the tranches are paid, the remaining payments go to the residual tranche. Banks that structured CMOs often kept the residual tranches, keeping high-risk, high-yield, hard-to-model instruments on their trading books. In their time, CMO residuals were truly the exotic instruments of the fixed income market.

3.6.3 Structured Debt, CDO, and CDO-squared

Following the success of the CMO market, banks got into the business of creating collateralized debt obligations, or CDOs. CDOs also have an underlying collateral pool, typically loans or bonds. The CDO waterfall is the set of rules that define which tranches get paid and how they get paid. Given the significant default risk on some underlying bonds, the CDOs were generally much riskier than CMOs.

To value a CDO, one must be able to value and assess the risk of all its components, simulate the waterfall, and determine the range of cash flows that the CDO is expected to generate. In addition to this daunting complexity, one must estimate the correlation among defaults in the CDO collateral. Underestimation of this correlation was blamed by many for the extreme losses in the CDO instruments in the 2008 credit crisis.

Some banks structured CDOs using CDOs as the underlying collateral, creating instruments that came to be known as CDO-squared. The extreme complexity of these instruments makes them almost impossible to value.

3.7 Fixed Income Risk Map

To summarize this chapter from a risk point of view, it is helpful to see how the risks in simple fixed income instruments become embedded in term risk, credit risk, forward positions, forward rate agreements, outright options, embedded bond options, and exotics.

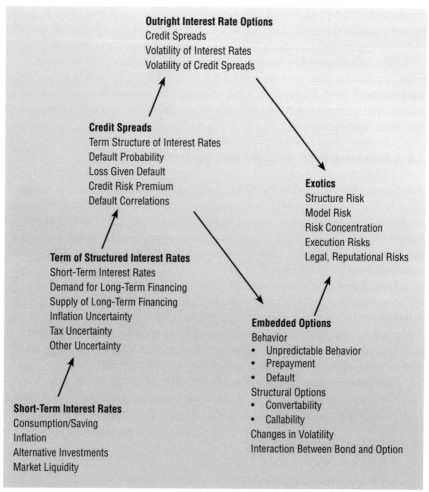

FIGURE 3.9 Fixed Income Risk Map

The benefit of this risk map is that it clearly shows all the risk drivers of all fixed income instruments. When undertaking a risk assessment, this provides a guide for how to calculate the impact of a bank's market assumptions on the risk of market instruments.

3.8 Summary

This chapter has expanded a number of introductory concepts in the FBR by studying interest rate markets and fixed income instruments in more detail.

The Importance of Fixed Income Instruments
- Collectively, banks in the US held assets of USD 3 trillion in securities and USD 8 trillion in loans, and liabilities of USD 10 trillion in deposits and USD 1.8 trillion in borrowings at the end of 2014. Global holdings are about double.
- Fixed income instruments comprise the vast majority of banks' assets and liabilities.

Cash Fixed Income Instruments
- Loans and bonds have similar characteristics, but differ in that loans are usually held by banks, while bonds are traded.
- Deposits are loans made by customers to the bank.
- Usually, loans are held in a bank's portfolio, but can sometimes be sold like bonds.
- There are several types of marketable loans; an important category is retail mortgages, which are originated by banks, warehoused, and sold as mortgage pools.
- A bank can make loans marketable by securitizing them, as is often the case with credit card receivables.
- Bonds are classified by issuer, maturity, credit quality, seniority, payment terms, and embedded options.

Pricing Fixed Income Instruments
- Yield curves determine discount rates for all varieties and currencies of fixed income instruments: cash, derivative, bond, and basis curves.
- Term structures are normally upward sloping, implying higher discount rates for longer-dated cash flows.
- The dominant qualitative term structure theory is the Liquidity Preference Theory. The theory explains that lenders prefer short-term lending while borrowers prefer longer-term borrowing, and to bring the market into equilibrium, the yield on long-term instruments must rise relative to expected yields.
- Interest rates can be volatile: USD one-year rates since 1961 had 23% annual percentage volatility.
- Interest rates are driven by the cost of money (inflation) and the cost of credit (interest rate).

- The cost of money is inflation and is influenced by consumption and economic factors.
- The cost of credit is driven by default likelihood, losses given default, and risk premiums required by the market for particular types of credit instruments.

Risk in Cash Fixed Income Instruments
- Bankers use PVBP/PV01, Macaulay duration, and modified duration as measures of interest rate risk.
- Duration is also a measure of the weighted average life of a fixed-rate bond.
- Bond volatility can be linked directly to interest rate volatility using modified duration.
- All these measures assume the yield curve shifts in a parallel fashion.
- Duration-matching is achieved when a long portfolio has the same value and duration as a short portfolio—it is immunized against a small parallel shift in the term structure.
- Convexity measures the stability of the duration; a convexity-matching strategy can protect against larger parallel shifts.
- The yield curve shifts in a nonlinear fashion, suggesting multi-factor hedging models will perform better than duration-based models.

Fixed Income Derivatives
- FRAs act like forward contracts on interest rates.
- Interest rate swaps enable bank customers to exchange floating interest expense exposure for fixed interest expense exposure and vice versa.
- Interest rate swaps can be performed in a foreign currency.
- A swap is equivalent to a position in a fixed rate bond that is offset with a floating rate bond. As a result its risk approximates that of a fixed rate bond.

Options and Exotic Fixed Income Instruments
- Caps and floors are basic interest rate options that behave qualitatively like FX options.
- Exotics are similar: a few specific exceptions are index-amortizing swaps, mortgages, CMOs, structured debt, CDOs and CDO squared.
- In these cases, the exotic options are embedded in the fixed income products.

Risk Map
- Consult the risk map in Section 3.7 to see the risk dependencies in fixed income products.

CHAPTER 4

Equity and Commodity Markets, Instruments and Risks

This chapter completes the discussion of traded instruments most widely used by banks. Chapter 2 covered foreign exchange instruments, Chapter 3 covered fixed income instruments, and Chapter 4 discusses equity and commodity markets. Though these markets are smaller from the point of view of overall bank trading and less important for most banks, they each have unique risks associated with them, such as less liquidity, higher transaction costs, and greater vulnerability to market manipulation. Trading risks are discussed more fully in Chapter 5.

The extent of a bank's trading in equities is influenced by regulation. In the US, many banks are prohibited from trading in equities unless the trade is made by the bank's trust department on behalf of its trust department clients, is for investment purposes as defined by regulators, or is within the range of activities that the regulators allow banks to participate. Some of the largest US-based banks, such as Citibank and Bank of America, have investment banking affiliates trade and underwrite equities actively.

On completion of this chapter the reader will have an improved understanding of:

- Equity instruments
- Commodity instruments
- Credit instruments
- Risks in equity, commodity, and credit instruments

4.1 Equity

The stock market is one of the largest markets in the world. The size of the world stock market was estimated to be about USD 60 trillion in October 2007, but just over half of that (USD 36.6 trillion) one year later. In October 2007, the seven largest exchanges accounted for about two-thirds of global equity capitalization, i.e., equity value, measured in USD trillions:

NYSE Euronext (US and Europe)	USD 20.70
Tokyo Stock Exchange	4.63
NASDAQ	4.39
London Stock Exchange	4.21
Shanghai Stock Exchange	3.02
Hong Kong Stock Exchange	2.97
Toronto Stock Exchange	2.29

FIGURE 4.1 Top equity exchanges[35] by capitalization in October 2007 (USD trillion)

Two years later, in October 2009, the seven largest exchanges and their market capitalization were:

NYSE Euronext (US and Europe)	14.1
Tokyo Stock Exchange	3.3
NASDAQ OMX	2.9
London Stock Exchange	2.6
Shanghai Stock Exchange	2.4
Hong Kong Exchange	2.2
TSX Group (Toronto)	1.5

FIGURE 4.2 Top equity exchanges[36] by capitalization in October 2009 (USD trillion)

---

35 World Federation of Exchanges—Statistics Monthly, October 2007
36 World Federation of Exchanges—Statistics Monthly, October 2009

NYSE Euronext (US and Europe)	19.4
NASDAQ OMX	7.0
Tokyo Stock Exchange	4.4
London Stock Exchange	4.0
Shanghai Stock Exchange	3.9
Euronext	3.3
Hong Kong Exchange	3.2

FIGURE 4.3 Top equity exchanges[37] by capitalization in December 2014 (USD trillion)

The exchanges collectively turned over equities at an average rate of about USD 7.5 trillion per month. Although the equity and bond market sizes are comparable, bank activity in the equity market is much smaller in comparison to their activities in the currency and bond markets. There are several reasons for this:

- Banks have no natural equity exposures that need to be hedged, managed, or traded.
- Customers do not use banks much for cash equity trading, but some customers trade equity derivatives with banks.
- Because many bonds have similar features—coupon rate, maturity, risk rating, yield—they can act as substitutes for other bonds. Thus, due to lack of available bonds that have the right coupon rate, maturity, risk rating, yield features, and other characteristics that the bank seeks, a bank is unlikely to have problems managing bond positions.
- Daily trading activity in equities is a small fraction of FX activity.
- Equities are not good substitutes for each other. In fact, some individual company shares are quite illiquid or have idiosyncratic risks that limit their use in portfolios.

4.1.1 Equity Cash Instruments

Common Shares
"Common shares" (also known as ordinary shares or common stock) refers to shares in the residual ownership of a corporation. Common shareholders

---
37 World Federation of Exchanges—
    http://www.world-exchanges.org/statistics/annual-query-tool

are entitled to share corporate profits; in the case of bankruptcy, however, they may claim only the residual value of the corporation, after liability claimants' and preferred shareholders' claims have been resolved. Private firms do not offer their shares to the public, but public firms offer their shares on recognized stock exchanges around the world or in other forms. The holder of common shares may expect to receive a regular dividend, if offered, which is paid from the profits made by the company. The holder will also gain from an appreciation in share value. For the purposes of this volume, we will limit our attention to publicly traded shares, as this constitutes the bulk of bank equity trading activity.

Preferred Shares
"Preferred shares" is a class of equity securities that have both debt- and equity-like features. Like debt, preferred shares have stated periodic payments, and payments to preferred shareholders have priority over payments to common shareholders. Unlike debt—preferred shares are subordinated to debt—the payments to preferred shares can often be withheld or postponed in difficult times. Also, preferred shares can be perpetual or have maturities far exceeding debt maturities.[38]

Equity Indices and Exchange Traded Funds (ETFs)
Equity indices are numerical calculations that reflect the performance of hypothetical equity portfolios. Equity indices do not trade in cash form, but are meant to track the overall performance of an equity market. Indices like the Standard & Poor's 500 or the FTSE indices (jointly owned by the Financial Times and London Stock Exchange) are capitalization weighted, so large firms have more influence on the index. Others, like the Dow Jones and the Nikkei indices, are price weighted, where all stocks in the index carry the same weight. Capitalization-weighted indices are generally considered better to track the performance of an overall market. Price-weighted indices give greater weight to shares trading at higher prices (but not necessarily to larger companies).

Indices are used to settle forward contracts (see below) and are also approximated in portfolio form. These portfolios are traded in a single equity instrument known as an exchange-traded fund (ETF). ETF index investors can expect their shares to perform broadly in the same way that the index it tracks performs. For example, there are ETFs that reflect the performance of the S&P 500, a broad based index of 500 large companies traded in the

---

38 Preferred shares receive a tax advantage in the US because only 15% of the dividend income is taxable if the preferred share is held by another corporation.

US markets. As such, ETFs are exposed to fluctuations in general market prices, but are less sensitive to the fluctuations of the value of any individual security.

4.1.2 Drivers of Equity Values

Common Shares
There are many different models of share valuation, each of which provides some insight into equity risk drivers. The simplest models are the price-to-earnings (P/E) multiple model and the discounted dividend or discounted cash flow model (commonly abbreviated as DDM or DCF, respectively). More advanced models are based on option pricing theory.

The P/E model suggests a benchmark for equity valuation that seems redundant at first:

$$Price = P/E\ ratio \times Earnings$$

The P/E ratio is taken from other comparable firms in the same or similar industries. The logic of this method is that firms in the same business should have (on average) the same valuation, scaled by their earnings level. Industry P/E levels reflect what investors will pay for earnings in a particular industry, which is a function of the cost of money, earnings volatility, a required risk premium related to aggregate risk aversion, and special industry factors. Earnings will depend on sales, cost management, and the general commercial success of a company, which depends on a wide range of factors. From a risk point of view, this suggests equity values will fluctuate with industry P/E levels and a company's individual earnings.

Extensions of the P/E model are the cash flow-based, relative valuation models such as the EBIT (Earnings Before Interest and Tax) or EBITDA (Earnings Before Interest, Taxes, Depreciation and Amortization) models, where the value of the company's shares is determined as a multiple of cash earnings under varying definitions.[39]

The discounted dividend model (DDM) suggests that the price of a share of stock should be the present value of its expected future dividends,

---

39 EBIT stands for Earnings before Interest and Taxes, and EBITDA stands for Earnings Before Interest, Taxes, Depreciation, and Amortization. Typically, EBIT reflects the corporation's core operating profit and profit contribution from non-operating activities, but excludes the effects of debt financing (interest payments) and tax liabilities. EBITDA usually measures cash earnings, without the effects of taxes, some accounting conventions, depreciation, and amortization, and the effects of debt financing (interest payments) and tax liabilities.

discounted at an appropriate risk-adjusted rate, where dividends serve as a proxy for earnings.

The risk-adjusted rate may be determined using benchmarks, or using a model such as the Capital Asset Pricing Model (CAPM), based on the security's sensitivity to the systemic risk of its market as measured by beta. In the CAPM, the required risk-adjusted rate of return on a stock is given by:

Required return = risk-free return + (beta × market risk premium)

In addition to the factors already identified, the DDM suggests that share prices will be sensitive to (a) the beta of the dividends, which is related to the correlation between dividends and the overall performance of the market, and (b) the market risk premium, as contrasted with the industry risk premium in the P/E multiple model.

The discounted cash flow model (DCF) suggests that the price of a share of stock should be the present value of the cash flow accruing to the shareholders, discounted at an appropriate risk-adjusted rate. The cash flow accruing to the shareholders is a residual cash flow that takes into consideration cash flow needed for debt repayment and certain investment purposes. The risk-adjusted rate may be determined using the corporation's cost of capital, which reflects the return demanded by shareholders, bondholders, lenders, and other providers of capital. In addition to the factors already identified for the DDM model, the DCF model suggests that share prices are also sensitive to (a) the overall cost of securing debt and equity financing, (b) the level of investments the corporation has committed to undertake, and (c) the level and structure of debt repayments.

Beta and Risk
Many equity traders use beta as their primary risk measure. This is based on the concept that, although equity values are driven by market factors and firm-specific factors, because of diversification, market factors are most important. In this context, beta is being used as a measure of elasticity:

Percentage change in stock = beta × Percentage change in market index

Using this measure, portfolio beta (the weighted average of the betas of the equities in the portfolio), can estimate the responsiveness of a particular equity portfolio to the overall market. There are no specific rules as to how to estimate beta and the change in market index; investors can use daily, weekly, monthly return data stretching back for many years. Moreover, there are methodological disagreements about the exact nature of a market index.

EXAMPLE

A trader has a long position in a stock with a beta of 0.8, and the market has gone up 3%. Therefore, the trader estimates that the stock has gone up 2.4%. To hedge this stock position against changes in the market, the trader should take a short position with the same value and beta.

Banks are less inclined to use beta as a measure of risk since it does not naturally integrate with risk measures in other markets. Also, there are no consistent approaches to estimate beta, which further compounds its shortcomings. For these reasons, banks prefer value-at-risk measures, which are explained fully in the next chapter.

Option-Based Equity Models
Option-based models of equity recognize two important and distinct options: one focuses on the present value of a firm's growth opportunities (PVGO) which may be realized if conditions favor the firm's growth, but have no cost to the firm if they fail to materialize. Another focuses on the idea that when a company is financed with debt, the equity owners hold an option on the assets of the firm, and therefore their shares behave like options.[40] Knowing what we know about options, this suggests that increased asset volatility will benefit shareholders of a firm.

Finally, knowing that many equity instruments are traded on margin, i.e., bought using borrowed funds, it is important to consider that fluctuations in equity values can prompt cash demands from margin lenders. This can be a significant risk in trading equities. Compiling a list of risk factors from these models we have:

Individual Equity Risk Drivers
- Company-specific projected earnings and earnings risk
- Macro-economic, systemic, or political risks affecting earnings
- Market pricing of industry risk
- Risk-free interest rates
- Market equity risk premium

---

40 Robert C. Merton, "On the pricing of corporate debt: The risk structure of interest rates," *Journal of Finance* 29 (1974) p 449-470.

- Asset volatility
- Market liquidity
- Margin cash demands

Preferred Shares
Since preferred shares carry a stated dividend that is paid ahead of common share dividends, they behave more like debt than like equity, provided the company is healthy enough to expect to be able to make those payments. When a company falls on hard times and the preferred payments are threatened, the preferred shares behave more like equity. Preferred shares that, under certain circumstances, can be converted into equity are called convertible preferred shares.

Because of the risk that preferred shares might trade like equity, they inherit all of the equity risk factors, but usually with proportionately less risk than equity.

Equity Indices and ETFs
In theory, equity indices and ETFs should inherit all the risk of the individual equities in the index or fund. In practice, the risk to any specific share in the fund tends to be negligible when considering the risk of the fund as a whole. Large equity portfolios of any kind are more exposed to the factors that affect all securities. We may therefore simplify the list of equity risk drivers above to reflect those that have the greatest impact on diversified equity portfolios:

Equity Portfolio Risk Drivers
- Aggregate earnings expectations
- Macro-economic or political risks affecting aggregate earnings
- Market pricing of risk
- Risk-free interest rates
- Market equity risk premium
- Aggregate asset volatility
- Market liquidity

4.2 Equity Derivatives

4.2.1 Individual Equity Forwards and Futures

Futures on individual equities, also known as single stock futures, were first traded in Europe on the London International Financial Futures and

Options (Liffe) and Eurex (DTB) exchanges. Since 2002, these instruments have been traded in the United States at Nasdaq/Liffe Markets (NQLX), a joint venture between Nasdaq and Liffe; OneChicago, a joint venture between the Chicago futures and options exchanges; and the American Stock Exchange (Amex).

An equity forward contract is an obligation to buy or sell (usually 100) shares of a particular stock at a fixed price on a future date. The structure of the contract is exactly the same as a forward FX contract. Therefore, using similar arbitrage arguments to those applied in the FX chapter, equity forwards and futures can be priced according to the following formula:

*Equity forward or futures price = market equity price
× [1 + (risk-free rate − expected dividend rate)]^t*

The expected dividend rate is expressed here as an annualized percentage rate applicable to the forward contract period. The equity forward price is reduced by the dividend because the owner of the long forward equity position does not receive dividends, in the same way that someone who buys currency forward does not receive interest on the currency prior to the forward date. This formula suggests risk drivers for equity forward prices. Equity forward positions are vulnerable to changes in spot equity prices, risk-free interest rates, and expected dividend payments. Most of the time, spot equity prices will be the most important driver of equity futures prices, but near dividend payment periods, the expected dividend can become an important risk factor as well.

EXAMPLE

If Microsoft stock trades at USD 19 per share, the annualized dividend yield is 2.7%, and the 6-month LIBOR is 2%, then the 6-month futures contract will trade at USD19 × (1+ 0.02 − 0.027)0.5 = USD 18.93. At any point in time, the dividend may be accurately adjusted to reflect known or planned dividends. If the stock increases 10%, so does the futures price. A 1% increase in LIBOR or a 1% decrease in the expected dividend rate would cause the price to rise by USD 0.095.[41]

Because futures typically require a 20% margin, equity futures behave like equity that is leveraged five times. For this reason, margin risk in equity futures is typically much greater than margin risk in spot equity investments.

---

41 Figures do not add up due to rounding.

Equity Forward and Futures Risk Drivers
- All risks affecting spot equity values for individual securities
- Changes in expected dividends paid prior to the forward date
- Risk-free rate of interest
- Margin risk
- Counterparty risk (forwards)

4.2.2 Equity Index Futures

Equity index futures trade on all major stock indices, including, for example, the DAX, FTSE 100, Nikkei 225, S&P 500 and the ASX 200. With a few small differences, the pricing and risk models discussed for individual equities apply to equity index as well.

The few differences have to do with (a) the reduction in firm-specific risk, (b) reducing dividend risk as a major factor in equity index futures, and (c) the increase in index composition risk. Index composition changes over time according to the criteria of the different indices. In general, as stocks increase in value and their market capitalization increases, their chance of entering the index increases. Conversely, as they shrink or decrease in value, their chance of leaving the index increases. Over long periods, the sector composition of an index may change. Over short periods of time, however, the change in index composition can be deemed a minor factor in the determination of overall equity futures index risks.

4.2.3 Equity Swaps

While there are many varieties of equity swaps, one of the most common is the total return swap (TRS). In a TRS, the receiver gets a payment equal to the total return—capital gains plus dividends—of a stock over a fixed period of time, usually a calendar quarter. In exchange, the receiver pays LIBOR plus a spread. The purpose of this trade is to create leveraged equity exposure for a receiver, but it accomplishes three other things for the receiver as well.

First, since the notional is reset every quarter, the total return receiver does not need to modify the size of the trading position, something that might be done in a formal portfolio rebalancing strategy. Second, the total return receiver does not need to incur the transaction costs of establishing and rebalancing an equity position. Third, compared to an equity forward position, the total return receiver gets paid the dividend while the equity forward position does not. One disadvantage of the TRS is that the receiver does not have any voting rights.

From the bank's point of view, a short TRS position is a way to hedge equity exposure without selling shares of stock. In general, banks tend to prefer not to sell their clients' stocks, and this provides a way to get the economic benefit of hedging without actually selling the stock. Ironically, the bank that makes a market in the TRS may sell the original bank client's equity to hedge its exposure.

4.2.4 Equity Options

Equity call options and put options are structured like FX options, except that the underlying asset is a share of stock or a stock index rather than a foreign currency. Equity options trade on many exchanges around the world, for example, the International Securities Exchange (ISE), the Chicago Board Options Exchange (CBOE), Eurex, Borsa Italiana, Meff, and Euronext Liffe. In addition, options on equity index futures trade on major futures option exchanges.

Most currency options, when exercised, lead to a physical transaction in the currencies. For example, upon exercise, a GBP call owner exchanges local currency for GBP. The owner of the call does not hold GBP, but seeks to exchange a different currency into GBP. Because the behavior of individual equity values around the close of trading can be erratic, options on individual equities normally require a physical transaction to settle the options. Some options are settled in cash rather than the underlying equities, such as the OEX S&P 100 options traded on the CBOE. Other options initiate a futures transaction when executed, such as the S&P 500 futures options traded on the Chicago Mercantile Exchange (CME). In all cases, the economics are approximately the same.

Like currency options, equity option values are driven by the underlying instrument value, the perceived volatility of the underlying, interest rates, strike price, and time to maturity. The difference is that equity options are sensitive to the expected dividend yield, since the buyer of a call option does not receive dividends prior to option maturity, and the buyer of the put option does not have to pay dividends prior to option maturity. Therefore, options inherit all the risk of the underlying equities, plus perceived volatility changes, future dividend yields, and risk-free interest rates.

Unlike most currency options, because most equity options have an American exercise feature (are American options), early exercise of call options is much more prelevant. The American exercise feature allows the option to be exercised at any time to the expiration of the contract. In contrast, the European exercise feature mandates that the option can only be exercised at the expiration of the contract. In the event of a high dividend for an in-the-money call option, exercise for an American option prior to expiration is virtually certain.

Equity Option Risk Drivers
- All risks affecting underlying spot or forward share or index values
- Changes in perceived volatility of the underlying
- Changes in expected dividend paid prior to the forward date
- Risk-free rate of interest
- Margin risk on short option positions
- Counterparty risk on long OTC option positions

4.2.5 Equity Exotics

On the individual security level, exotic equity options are quite rare. The reason for this is the high transaction costs of hedging in an individual equity instrument, and the occasional illiquidity of individual equity markets. However, some exotics do trade at the portfolio or index level.

One popular equity exotic is the basket option, which is a call or put option on a basket of equity instruments. The major complexity of this option from the bank's point of view is correlation risk, a key driver of value. Correlation is both unknown and unstable, leading to model risk and hedging risk for banks.

4.3 Commodities

4.3.1 Overview

Commodities can be divided into precious metals (gold, silver, and platinum), industrial metals (copper, nickel, aluminum, lead, tin, zinc, and palladium), energy (oil, gasoline, natural gas, heating oil, fuel oil, coal, jet fuel, electricity, and ethanol), and agricultural commodities (corn, oats, soybean and soybean products, rice, wheat, cattle, hogs, pork bellies, lumber, milk, cocoa, coffee, sugar, cotton, and orange juice).[42]

Most banks do not trade physical commodities, but some trade OTC derivatives that enable the bank's customers to hedge their actual exposures to various commodity price risks. There are also banks that provide financing for corporations engaged in the commodities markets. Some banks may also

---

[42] Source: *The Wall Street Journal* financial pages

trade futures and OTC contracts for speculative purposes. The notional value outstanding of banks' OTC commodity derivatives contracts in 2007 was USD 9 trillion. Global physical and derivative trading of commodities on exchanges in 2007 was estimated at 1,684 million contracts. Over 40% of commodities trading on exchanges was conducted on US exchanges, while about 25% was conducted in China. Because of their emergence as significant commodity consumers and producers, trading on exchanges in China and India has gained in importance in recent years.

By contract volumes in millions, the top exchanges in 2007 were the New York Mercantile Exchange (353), The Dalian Commodity Exchange in China (186), the Chicago Board of Trade (173), ICE Futures in London (138), the Zhengzhou Commodity Exchange in China (93), the London Metals Exchange (93) and the Shanghai Futures Exchange (86).[43]

Though commodities represent an important global market, banks do not typically have significant exposure to commodities for the same reasons that they do not have much exposure to equities.

Noteworthy points on commodity exchanges include:

- Banks have no natural direct exposure to commodities.
- Customers rarely trade physical commodities with banks.
- Banks trade in OTC contracts primarily to serve clients and facilitate client hedging and lending.
- Commodity markets are relatively illiquid compared to FX and debt markets

4.3.2 Commodity Cash Instruments

Physical Commodity Trading
Physical commodity trading is the buying and selling of actual commodities for delivery. Products are bought and sold for physical delivery at a specified location on an agreed date, or in some cases delivered on a range of dates. There is a spot market for many commodities, and each product has additional features that relate directly to its physical properties.

---

43 Commodities Trading 2008, IFSL Research, June 2008, www.ifsl.org.uk, now www.thecityuk.com

EXAMPLE

In Cushing, Oklahoma, several different major crude oil pipelines connect. Coupled with large storage facilities, this small town has emerged as one of the main markets for physical crude oil in the United States. Another major physical market is Zeebrugge in Belgium where natural gas is available for trade. In the Scandinavian countries, a multinational exchange for electricity trading, NordPool, enables power suppliers and consumers to trade electricity for delivery.

Buying and Storing Physical Commodities
The cost of trading commodities is not limited to the commodity price. Buyers typically get an adjustment on price due to quality fluctuations between what is promised and what is delivered. For example, a coal shipment may have higher sulfur content than expected. Rather than reject the shipment, the value of the coal is discounted according to a pre-agreed formula. Buyers also pay the cost of transport, insurance, and inspection. Finally, if the commodity is not used immediately, it must be stored.

Some commodities can be stored easily. For example, aluminum can be stored in warehouses. Other commodities, such as crude oil, require specialized storage facilities that comply with safety and environmental regulations. Grain storage is maintained so as to minimize the cost of spoilage. Storage of live animals requires feeding and caring for the animals. Orange juice must be kept frozen, and gold is usually kept in certificate form. Electricity can only be stored in very limited quantities at a high cost.[44] In addition to technical considerations that vary by commodity, the cost of storage is also determined by supply and demand for storage services, and may not be easy to predict.

Selling and Short-Selling Physical Commodities
Commodities are often sold on organized spot markets, as mentioned above, or in physical direct contracts between producers and consumers of the commodities. Selling is an expensive process because it involves transporting the commodity, insuring the commodity, and risking spoilage, evaporation, death, and other losses in transport.

In all the markets discussed so far (FX, interest rates, and equities), it is possible to sell or short-sell the instruments at relatively low costs. In most commodity markets, shorting is prohibitively expensive or does not exist. This is because a lending market in commodities makes little sense if

---

44   Electricity can be stored in batteries, but the loss rate is high. Similarly, some power plants pump water uphill at night to create potential energy to meet peak demand the following day.

people plan to consume the commodities. Furthermore, since each short sale requires a cover, the high physical transaction costs would have to be borne twice in order to short-sell and to cover a short sale.

The one important market that allows short selling is the gold market. Gold trades in certificate form. Central banks auction off the right to "borrow" the stored gold, on paper, in exchange for a fee. This fee is called the lease rate and is expressed as an annualized percentage of the gold value. The certificate model works for gold because it is a commodity that is stored and not consumed.

4.3.3 Physical Commodity Risk Drivers

Commodity prices are driven by demand and supply. Demand is determined by consumer preferences, prices of substitute goods, consumer wealth, general economic activity, and other macroeconomic drivers. Supply is influenced by production uncertainty, technological innovation, production costs including interest rates, the value of the commodity in alternative uses, and macroeconomic and regulatory forces. In many commodities, such as natural gas, local supply and demand are greater price determinants than for a global commodity such as crude oil. Prices are affected by factors such as inflation, and also factors such as market arrangements that may favor buyers or sellers.

4.4 Commodity Derivative Instruments

Historically, gold was the most important commodity for banks, who traded and held gold in large quantities. However, the importance of gold declined and by 2007, many large international banks actively traded and speculated in other commodities, including oil.[45] The following description focuses on oil and gold derivatives. Each market has its own idiosyncratic features that determine pricing, and we will not cover all of them, but some of these general principles apply.

4.4.1 Commodity Forwards

Commodity forward pricing differs from forward pricing in other markets. Forward prices in foreign exchange, bonds, and equities are governed by arbitrage relationships.

---

45   Commodities Trading 2008, op. cit.

In the foreign exchange, bond, or equity markets, if the forward price becomes too high, an arbitrageur can buy the spot with borrowed funds and sell forward at the elevated forward price in order to lock in a sure profit at maturity. If the forward price becomes too low, the arbitrageur borrows the underlying, sells it short, invests the proceeds, and agrees to buy the underlying back at a depressed price in order to lock in a sure profit.

Commodity forward arbitrage generally fails because of the lack of a market for short selling, and because of the market-determined (as opposed to fixed) costs of storage.

EXAMPLE USING OIL

If the cost of oil is USD 40 a barrel, and the six-month forward contract trades at USD 30, a bank looking to arbitrage this relationship might want to short-sell physical crude oil and take a long position in the futures contract. This would be impossible due to the inability to short oil. Alternatively, if the forward contract traded at USD 45, a bank might try to buy oil at USD 40 a barrel, pay the interest on the money used to buy the oil, store it for six months, and sell it at a previously contracted rate of USD 45. However, the costs of storage, transport, and exchange are so high they would render that trade unprofitable. In fact, the forward price could trade anywhere between USD 30 and USD 45 without any arbitrage pressure from traders or banks to reach any given price level.

EXAMPLE USING GOLD

Since gold trades in certificate form, the only cost of holding gold is the cost of money, i.e., the risk-free rate of interest; the cost of shorting gold is the lease rate. Hence, we have two equations for the gold forward price:

Gold forward ≤ *Gold spot* × *(1 + risk-free rate)t*
Gold forward ≥ *Gold spot* × *(1 + risk-free rate − lease rate)t*

Gold may theoretically trade anywhere in this range, though it usually trades at the bottom of the range. If gold forward prices traded anywhere outside that range, arbitrage would be profitable.

Oil forward prices are driven by two factors: the expected future oil price, and the value of locking in fixed oil prices. Effectively, oil forwards have no upper or lower arbitrage bounds. The lower bound does not exist because there is no active market for borrowing oil. The upper bound does not exist because if forward oil prices rise, the cost of storage will rise in response. The reason for this is that oil storage is in fixed supply, and the demand for storage increases as forward prices rise. Therefore,

Oil forward price = Expected future oil price ± Oil market risk premium

The expected future oil price is driven by the same factors that affect current oil prices. The oil market risk premium is driven by the demand and supply of market participants wanting to hedge or speculate in the market. Note that the commodity forward pricing formula differs significantly from the forward pricing formula for other markets.

Backwardation and Contango

When forward prices are lower for longer maturities, the commodity market is said to be in backwardation, a term originated by John Maynard Keynes. The following chart shows 13 oil forward curves corresponding to the beginning of each of the months in 2007. In that year, oil traded in both contango and backwardation.

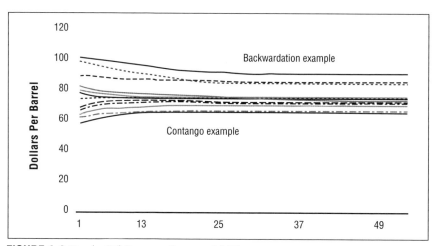

FIGURE 4.4 Crude Oil Futures Curves, 2007

Backwardated markets can be interpreted in at least three ways:

1. Market participants expect commodity prices to fall.
2. The market is signaling to producers that spot commodity availability should increase.
3. The commodity forward risk premium is negative.

As of November 2008 most commodity markets were in contango, where forward prices exceed current spot prices. Contango derives from the Latin word contangere, "to hold." Some markets (like gold) are always in contango, and the slope of the curve is equal to the carrying costs (i.e., holding costs).

The interpretations of contango are the opposite of the interpretations for backwardation, with the additional proviso that precious metals are forced into contango due to arbitrage activity. Without the forward lending market in precious metals, it is unlikely the forward prices would exhibit contango consistently.

Backwardation and contango represent risks for commodity trading departments of banks. Market prices can move from backwardation to contango, driven by changes in short-term commodity prices, long-term commodity prices, or both.

Customer Uses of Commodity Forwards
Bank customers trade with banks for strategic and transactional purposes. Strategically, bank customers that produce commodities often experience significant cash flow risk due to fluctuations in commodity prices. For example, the income of corn farmers depends entirely on the amount of corn they produce and the price they can sell it on the market. Corn prices can be very volatile. Also, corn production depends on rainfall, temperature, and sunshine. Because of these factors, a farmer's income may be very volatile, and due to questions about his ability to repay he may have trouble borrowing to finance his production.

EXAMPLE

The farmer hedges by going short on corn futures contracts, protecting the harvest price level provided the hedged amount is produced. However, the farmer is then exposed to margin fluctuation from futures contracts. By entering a customized forward contract with the bank to link the volume of the hedge to the volume of production, the farmer may be able to pass some of the production risk to the bank, and may be able to negotiate a credit line that would reduce the risk of his margin calls.

Bank customers may trade commodity forwards with banks in order to express trading views, reverse undesired short-term exposures created from fixed price commodity sales, or to reach short-term budgetary targets.

4.4.2 Commodity Options

Banks trade a full battery of commodity option types, roughly approximating the types of options traded in other markets. The risks of the options include all the risks of the underlying plus additional risks related to volatility and market illiquidity. For example, call options on crude oil futures and put options on soybean futures behave as expected, given knowledge of the FX option markets (see Chapter 2 for a review). There are some features that are unique to some commodity options. Two examples are Asian options and flexible volume options.

Asian Options
Most consumers of natural gas do not have the ability to store it. As a result, they contract with suppliers to receive a flow of natural gas equal to a certain number of MMBTU[46] per day. The pricing of natural gas is usually based on a daily spot index, such as Henry Hub. If the consumer wants to protect against price increases, the concern is not the price on one day (expiration), as it is with an FX option; the concern is with the average price over the course of a month. For this reason, the underlying contract for the Asian option is the average of the daily prices throughout the month, rather than the spot price.[47] In other markets, these averaging options are considered exotic, but in commodity markets, they are considered "plain vanilla."

Flexible Volume Options
Many consumers of commodities do not know how much of the commodity they will need. For example, an office building will require more electricity when air conditioners have to run longer than expected, a function of the weather. While it seems logical to allow the customer this sort of option, for risk management purposes, banks must consider the risks associated with variable customer volumes. The customer cannot simply buy electricity forward, since forward contracts normally specify a fixed volume. Therefore, it is in the interest of the customer to enter a contract with the bank that takes volumetric flexibility into account.

---

[46] MMBTU is one million BTU, and BTU is the amount of heat required to increase the temperature of a (US) pint of water (which weighs exactly 16 ounces) by one degree Fahrenheit. One cubic foot of natural gas produces approximately 1,000 BTUs, thus 1 MMBTU is approximately 1,000 cu. ft. of gas.

[47] Asian options are also called average value options, where the pay-off from the option is not determined by the price observed at one particular point of time, but rather by the average of the prices observed over one or several specific time periods.

Flex options are considered exotic in other markets, but standard in commodities. They are valued based on assumptions about consumer behavior, and how behavior is affected by outside variables, in this case, temperatures. Due to the high costs of hedging and the relative illiquidity of the underlying commodity markets, most banks and customers do not trade exotic commodity options like those seen in other markets.

4.4.3 Commodity Derivative Risks

In addition to the specific risks particular to each commodity, the main commodity derivative risks are: basis (product, location, quality), term, seasonality, and correlation.

Basis
Because of the different demand-supply balance in each region and the cost of transporting the oil between regions, a tanker of West Texas Intermediate (WTI) crude oil in the US will have a different value to a US buyer than a tanker of Arab light crude oil in Malaysia. Different oil sulfur content and gravity levels will also make the oil unsuitable for some refineries.

When banks hedge an Arab light OTC forward position with WTI crude oil forwards, they have the benefit of using the most liquid OTC market to hedge, but at the cost of significant basis risk between WTI and Arab light. Similarly, the basis reflects the location or geographic differentials. For instance, the price of natural gas delivered in different ports in the Houston ship channel is different; these differences are determined by the cost of transportation between two points as well as localized supply and demand factors.

Calendar Spreads
Calendar spreads represent a special case of basis risk. For example, a trader might take a position in March natural gas futures and offset it with a position in April gas futures, on the theory that relative prices will come into alignment and that the trader is protected against absolute price movements.

Some calendar spreads move in reliable patterns, but others can be quite volatile. Perhaps the most famous example of a calendar spread gone wrong is illustrated by the history of Amaranth Advisors. Typically, natural gas prices decline during the spring months, starting in March and April, when natural gas inventories begin to rise. Amaranth made a bet on the direction of the spread between two natural gas futures prices: the 2007 March and April contracts, respectively. Amaranth expected that the spread between these two contracts would rise and built up a substantial position in these contracts. However, the spread narrowed considerably. In September 2006, as a result of the unexpected move of the spread, Amaranth lost 65% of its USD 9.2 billion asset base and closed its fund.[48]

The company had made an active bet on increasing natural gas prices during the previous year, when Hurricane Katrina curtailed production; the bet was successful for the year, and Amaranth had shown an impressive performance during 2005.

A reason why calendar spreads are an important source of risk for banks is the small number of traded contracts in some markets. While futures contracts for equity indexes, interest rates, and currencies may have a regular, monthly expiration calendar, there are multiple commodities where there is only quarterly expiration. This makes hedging an exposure accruing during a month different from the expiration of the futures contract difficult to hedge, because there is an inherent mismatch between the maturities of the contracts and the exposure.

Term
In other markets, forward prices move approximately in proportion to spot prices. This does not hold for commodities, except for precious metals. For most commodities, the shortest-term forward contracts are the most volatile, and the longest-term contracts are the least volatile. This is because supply and demand factors for nearby forward positions are changing daily, while information about long-dated expectations does not change as frequently.

Failure to understand this phenomenon cost Metallgesellschaft (MG) over USD 1 billion in 1993. Using front month oil futures (the contracts that are nearest to expiry) to hedge long-dated forward positions in gasoline and heating oil proved to be disastrous, particularly because the hedge ratio was taken to be one barrel for one barrel. The prices of long-dated contracts tend to move much less than the prices of short-dated contracts, even if they are somewhat correlated. The actual short-term hedge should have been much smaller than it was. MG's problems were exacerbated by extremely high liquidity risk and by the illiquidity of the near month oil futures market relative to MG's hedging demand.[49] MG became the largest trader in the front month oil market, and therefore found it extremely difficult to revise and reverse its trades.

---

48   "How giant bets on natural gas sank brash hedge fund trader,"
     The Wall Street Journal, Sept 2006
49   Franklin Edwards and Michael Canter, "The collapse of Metallgesellschaft: Unhedgeable risks, poor hedging strategy or just bad luck?" *Journal of Futures Markets* v 15 no 3: 1995.

Seasonality
Some commodities are prone to seasonal price fluctuations. Planted agricultural commodities in cold climates are harvested once or twice a year, leading to seasonal peaks and troughs. Prices of fuels used for heating (heating oil and natural gas) have seasonal variations in climates that can be hot or cold. Power prices exhibit high variations where the demand for air conditioning and daily usage is highly variable. Furthermore, as a result of these market characteristics, price volatility can be greater during some seasons and less during other seasons.

The following chart from January 2008 shows how the US natural gas market can both be in backwardation and have a strong seasonal component:

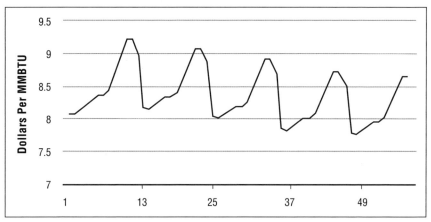

FIGURE 4.5 Natural Gas Future Curve, January 2008

Correlation
While there may be no day-to-day correlation between copper and aluminum, during times of extreme price movements we can expect to see prices moving in the same direction due to long-term substitutability of one metal for another. The same analogy can be applied to ethanol and corn; the former, made from the latter, can correlate with grains or with fuels depending on the price environment. Finally, as we saw in 2008, all commodity prices tended to correlate together as global demand for commodities increased. Taken together, changing correlation represents a significant risk for banks with commodity portfolios.

4.5 Credit

Credit-related instruments of all types are subject to credit risk. Credit risk can be measured from a number of different perspectives, including credit default risk and credit price risk. Credit default risk is the subject of the Credit Risk Management book in this series and is not the subject of this section.

Credit price risk, on the other hand, is concerned with the risk of loss due to a change in market perception for a credit risky asset and hence in the price of that asset. As an example, an investor who is long a credit bond will suffer a loss if the yield of that bond goes up.

The yield is composed of two factors, the risk-free yield and the credit spread. The bond is subject to interest rate risk if the risk-free yield goes up, and credit price risk if the credit spread goes up. It is possible that changes in the two components of yield could counteract one another, leaving the bond price largely unchanged. This does not reduce either of the two risks, however, which must be analyzed individually.

The following two sub-sections describe the most common instruments in both the cash markets and the derivatives markets for credit.

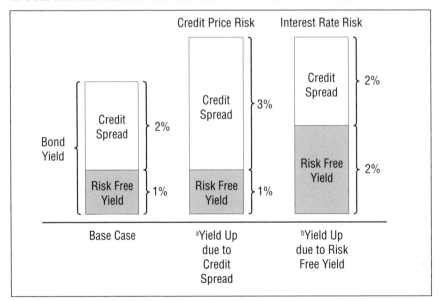

FIGURE 4.6 Yield Spread Ratio

Most bank loan assets are illiquid. This is not only because of the difficulty and cost involved if one bank should attempt to sell one consumer mortgage or one SME working capital facility to another bank, but also because many loan agreements do not include a transferability clause. Without a right to transfer the ownership of a loan to a new owner, a bank would have to ask the borrower's permission before attempting to sell it. The difficulty and inconsistent outcomes of such an enterprise mean that most banks are reluctant to actively trade their credit book.

4.5.1 Credit Instruments

Corporate Loans
Large corporates and some sovereigns are frequent borrowers in the international syndicated loan markets. Many syndicated loan documents include clauses allowing the lender to transfer or assign the loan participation to any subsequent holder or owner. This opens the possibility that the loans can be sold. Given sufficient volumes of supply and demand, a two-way market can be established. When trading liquidity and market reporting mechanisms become stable and dependable, it then becomes possible to mark the loan participation to market on a daily basis. The credit margin payable by the debtor in the loan will be described in the original loan document, but may trade either higher or lower than that in the daily market. Any variation in the traded credit margin gives rise to credit price risk.

In some cases corporate loan interest is charged on a fixed rate basis. The interest charged will be similar to the coupon on a bond. If not clearly illustrated in the loan document, investors will first have to work out how much of the fixed rate is due to the risk free interest rate and how much to the credit spread. From then on the sensitivity to a 1 bp credit spread change (CS01) becomes trivial to compute.

Bonds
A bond will typically have negotiability or transferability clauses written into its terms. This allows any owner, or holder in due course, to sell, give, or assign owner's rights to anyone else without recourse to or special permission from the issuer or debtor.

Bonds are typically sold with fixed rate coupons, although a subset of that market allows variable or floating rates of interest (via floating rate notes or FRNs).

The bond price sensitivity to a 1 bp change in credit spread (CS01, also sometimes called credit spread value of 1 bp) is a key metric to understanding credit price risk.

4.5.2 Credit Derivatives

Single-name Credit Default Swap (CDS)
A credit default swap (CDS) is an over-the-counter (OTC) derivative which references an approximation of the credit spread on an underlying credit asset (loan or bond). The buyer of a CDS buys credit default protection, while the seller sells credit default protection on the underlying credit. A CDS buyer is short the underlying credit risk, while a CDS seller is long the same credit risk. A CDS buyer will typically use the position as a hedge for a long position in the real underlying credit, thereby partly or fully insuring against a credit default.

The CDS fee, or spread, is paid, usually quarterly, by the buyer to the seller, and is measured in basis points per annum. The seller will not make regular payments in return. Payments by the seller are triggered by an actual default as defined in the CDS contract and may be either 100% of the face value of the underlying, or 100% minus the Recovery Rate (RR), depending on whether physical or cash settlement was stipulated in the contract. If a CDS contract is triggered by a default it expires and any future CDS coupons become void.

A single-name CDS, as its title suggests, references just one credit and is specifically referencing the seniority of the claim, such as senior secured, senior unsecured, junior/subordinated secured, or junior/subordinated unsecured. A senior secured CDS and a junior unsecured CDS on the same reference credit has two different prices.

Following the global financial crisis of 2007-2009, the International Swap and Derivatives Association (ISDA), publisher of CDS standard contract terms adopted many changes. Whereas previously the CDS price was payable periodically at its full risk-based value, the CDS fee is now standardized at either 100 bp or 500 bp per annum, with any discrepancy to the true CDS spread discounted to present value and settled up front from buyer to seller or seller to buyer, as the case may be.

Also, in the event of a default, ISDA calls an auction to be held immediately after the event. Traders will have an opportunity to "net off" and compress CDS outstanding to the smallest possible amount and then bid for the settlement price of the remaining stub. The official auction result becomes the settlement terms for the payout under each remaining non-netted CDS contract. This is an accelerated process that helps market participants realize losses early, while allowing arbitrageurs to speculate in the possible difference between the auction result and the final bankruptcy payout, which may turn out to be higher or lower than the auction result predicted.

Finally, it is now commonplace that CDS sellers post collateral to the buyer in a range from 0% to 100% depending on the credit standing of the protection seller and the PD of the underlying credit. This is done to mitigate losses in the event that the seller defaults at the same moment as the underlying credit.

Single-name CDSs can, in principle, be written on any credit, though CDS liquidity is only assured when written against the largest loans and bonds by outstanding debt amount.

Index CDS

Credit default swaps tracking a bond index are analogous to equity index-linked swaps tracking a stock market index, although functionally different. There is a multitude of internationally traded credit indices, most calculated by Markit Ltd, in particular the iTraxx and the CDX index series. Each series is divided into geographical regions (North America, Europe, Asia) and further into investment grade (IG), high yield (HY), or one of several other sub-categories. Each of these sub-groups reference 100 or 125 names. For example the CDX.NA.HY.23 references 100 speculative grade North American names in the 23rd series, starting September 22, 2014. Each index gets rebalanced in six-monthly rolling series with new index constituents entering and others leaving.

Buyers of index CDS pay a periodic fee, much like single-name CDS buyers. However, in the event of a default in an index constituent, the index CDS fee payments continue, while those of the single-name CDS would be wound up. In the single-name CDS, the underlying principal goes to zero in the event of a default, while in an index the remaining underlying principal goes down by 1% or 0.8% per default and the index CDS continues at that level.

An index CDS has a fee/coupon just as a single-name CDS, hence, for example, a protection buyer may be asked to pay 90 bp/annum in quarterly installments. This would be translated into the 100 bp standard fee with the extra 10 bp/annum discounted to present value and paid back to the buyer.

If an investor simultaneously buys US Treasuries and sells the same notional amount of CDX index swaps (i.e., sells credit protection), the result is a diversified synthetic loan portfolio comprising 125 equally weighted, high quality, North American corporate borrowers. It will not be a real loan portfolio, but the credit default and the credit price risks will be identical.

4.6 Risk Maps

Risk maps can be constructed for equities and commodities in the same way we have constructed them for FX and interest rates. Compiling the risk factors in this chapter, the important drivers of spot, forward, option and exotic risks can be reviewed.

Spot Risks	• Company-specific projected earnings and earnings risk • Macro-economic or political risks affecting earnings • Market pricing of industry risk • Risk-free interest rates • Market equity risk premium • Asset volatility • Market liquidity • Margin cash demands
Preferred Risks	• Reduced equity risks • Corporate debt risks including credit spreads and interest rates
Portfolio Risks	• Aggregate earnings expectations • Macro-economic or political risks affecting aggregate earnings • Market pricing of risk • Risk-free interest rates • Market equity risk premium • Aggregate asset volatility • Market liquidity
Forward Risks	• All risks affecting underlying • Interest rate risk • Dividend risk
Option Risks	• All risks affecting underlying spot or forward share or index values • Changes in perceived volatility of the underlying • Changes in expected dividend paid prior to the forward date • Risk-free rate of interest • Margining risk on short option positions • Counterparty risk on long OTC option positions
Exotics Risks	• All risks affecting equity options • Model risk • Additional execution risk • Legal & reputational risk • Operational risk

FIGURE 4.7 Risk Map—Equity

Spot Risks	• Consumer preferences • Prices of substitute goods • Consumer wealth • General economic activity • Other macroeconomic drivers • Production uncertainty • Technological innovation • Production costs including interest rates • Value of the commodity in alternative uses • Regulatory forces
Forward Risks	• All factors affecting spot prices • The cost and characteristics of storage • Costs and availability of short-selling • Demand for fixed price protection • Commodity risk premium • Basis risk • Calendar spread risk • Seasonality
Option Risks	• All factors affecting forward prices • Perceived volatility • Seasonal volatility • Unstable correlations • Behavioral variables

FIGURE 4.8 Risk Map—Commodities

4.7 Summary

This chapter addressed risks associated with equities and commodities beyond those covered in the FBR book.

Equity
- Equity is generally a relatively small part of bank trading activity, even though it is a large component of global markets.
- Common shares represent residual ownership of an enterprise.
- Preferred shares are a hybrid between equity and debt, acting more like debt for healthy firms and more like equity for unhealthy firms.

- Exchange traded funds (ETFs) are useful to banks and investors to obtain equity index exposure without having to trade all the index components.
- Common shares are driven by firm-specific factors, such as earnings, industry factors, and macroeconomic factors, such as discount rates.
- ETFs are driven by macroeconomic factors affecting equity markets.

Equity Derivatives
- Forward positions provide a leveraged way to obtain equity exposure.
- Equity forwards are priced like FX forwards except that dividends are deducted from the forward price, since the long forward position does not receive dividends.
- Equity swaps may provide more efficient risk-taking and hedging opportunities for banks than outright equity positions.
- Equity options have the same qualitative characteristics as FX options.
- Equity exotics on individual equities are rare, but one popular equity exotic is the basket option.

Commodities
- Some banks have significant commodity trading activities while others have none.
- Bank trading activity in commodities is usually limited to financial rather than physical contracts.
- Commodities are fundamentally different from financial assets: they are costly to trade and store, and often impossible to sell short.
- Commodity prices are driven by all economic factors affecting supply and demand.
- Commodity forwards are not priced by arbitrage, but arbitrage bounds are relevant in some commodities, particularly upper bounds defined by cash-and-carry arbitrage.
- Commodities may trade in backwardation or contango; the shapes of the forward curves are determined by expectations of future spot prices and the commodity forward risk premium.
- Bank customers use commodity trading to hedge their price exposures, reduce their risks and, in some cases, increase their ability to borrow from the bank.
- Commodity options tend to be "plain vanilla" although plain vanilla options in some commodity markets are Asian options, that is, contracts with volumetric flexibility.

- Major commodity derivative risks include basis, calendar, seasonality, and correlation.
- Consult the risk maps in Section 4.6 for a summary of risk dependencies.

Credit Instruments
- Credit instruments come in two formats: funded (loans and bonds) and unfunded (derivatives).
- Among credit derivatives, single-name CDS and index CDS contracts are used more frequently than any other form of credit derivative.
- CS01 is a key metric to understand credit price risk.
- It is possible to create a synthetic credit bond by buying a government bond and selling a CDS in the same currency.

CHAPTER 5

The Risk Measurement Process

In Chapters 2–4, the sources of FX, interest rate, equity, and commodity risks were discussed at length. However, the risks were never quantified. The purpose of Chapter 5 is to study the methods used by banks to quantify risk.

This chapter discusses the most common of these methods, value-at-risk (VaR), and the limitations of VaR-based methods. It also addresses substantive choices in quantitative VaR and risk modeling, and the processes by which banks determine their overall VaR levels. Advanced quantitative modeling procedures will not be covered.[50]

On completion of this section the reader will have an improved understanding of:

- The meaning of VaR (Value-at-Risk)
- How to determine the VaR of a single factor
- The differences in implementation between parametric and non-parametric VaR models
- Important correlation assumptions and their implications for VaR

---

50 Readers interested in an advanced quantitative treatment of VaR may consult Philippe Jorion, *Value at Risk: The New Benchmark for Managing Financial Risk*, 3rd ed., McGraw-Hill Professional 2006, or Moorad Choudhry, *Introduction to Value-at-Risk*, 5th ed. (New York: Securities Institute 2013).

- Adapting VaR for option positions
- Risk aggregation methods including variance-covariance and full revaluation
- The process by which banks aggregate and measure risk
- Viable alternatives to VaR

5.1 Value-at-Risk (VAR)

VaR is both a concept and a calculation. The concept of VaR is forward-looking in nature, but the calculation is usually backward looking.

5.1.1 Definitions

Definition of VaR
VaR is the maximum likely loss on an instrument or portfolio over a given time period with a given degree of probabilistic confidence.

EXAMPLE

If a bank has a USD 10 million one-day, 95% VaR, this means that the chance of a loss exceeding USD 10 million in one day is 5%.

Because it is a forward-looking measure of risk, the true VaR cannot be known, so banks use numerous means to estimate it. Most of the methods in practice use historical data, but some methods use forward-looking data, such as option-implied volatilities or independent risk forecasts, to determine the VaR. Regardless of the method used, no risk manager should ever conclude that the estimated VaR is truly representative of the future, since past risks are only an indicator of future risks. Nevertheless, it would be inappropriate for a bank not to compute VaR, as the bank should understand as much as possible about the risk of its current positions based on price movements in the past.

5.1.2 Parametric VaR and the Normal Distribution

VaR can be computed for a single contract, trading position, or portfolio, and can also be computed at the level of the entire bank. Broadly speaking, there are two types of VaR calculations: parametric and nonparametric methods. Parametric methods generally assume that future profits and losses

(P&L) are normally distributed, while non-parametric methods make no distributional assumptions. One benefit of a parametric method is that for a normal distribution, the loss probabilities are known:[51]

Confidence Level	Probability of Loss Greater Than VaR	Number of Standard Deviations
90%	10%	−1.282
95%	5%	−1.645
99%	1%	−2.33

FIGURE 5.1 Normal Distribution Probability Levels

EXAMPLE

To calculate a VaR at a 95% confidence level, the bank may estimate the standard deviation of future P&L to be USD 3 million, and then determine the VaR by multiplying by 1.645 to obtain VaR = USD 4.935 million.

The standard deviation is a measure of dispersion that has the same interpretation for every normal distribution. Using historical data, the standard deviation can be computed using Microsoft Excel, a statistical calculator, or any statistical software package.[52] Figure 5.2 below shows the probability ranges that apply to every normal distribution. The number of standard deviations is shown on the x-axis, and the approximate probabilities associated with each range are shown in the respective ranges.[53] A normal distribution will assume a bell curve.

"Zero" corresponds to the mean of the normal distribution, "1" to one standard deviation above the mean, "−1" to one standard deviation below the mean, and so on.

---

51 These can be computed in Excel using normsinv(0.10) or can be found in tables of the standard normal distribution.
52 Mathematically, the standard deviation is the square root of the average squared deviation (difference) of a random variable from its mean.
53 More exact probabilities can be found using Excel, e.g. normsdist(3)-normsdist(2)=0.0214.

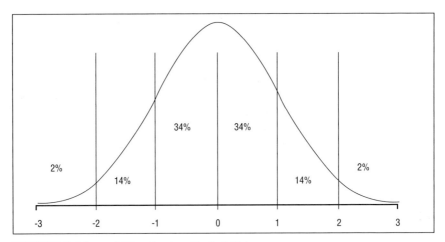

FIGURE 5.2 Normal Distribution Probabilities

EXAMPLE

If the standard deviation of P&L is USD 3 million, and the mean is USD 1 million, then the probability of experiencing P&L between USD 1 million and USD −2 million, i.e., between 0 and −1 standard deviations, is 34%.

Nonparametric VaR methods, such as historical simulation, do not make any assumption about the shape of the probability distribution and therefore do not rely on the standard deviation as a measure of risk. Historical simulation is explained in section 5.1.4.

5.1.3 VaR Conversions and Conventions

In some cases, banks will measure the standard deviation of portfolio returns instead of portfolio P&L. The annualized standard deviation of portfolio returns is the volatility of the portfolio. Volatility can refer to different time periods, such as daily volatility or monthly volatility, but without a modifier it is assumed to refer to annualized return volatility.

To convert the standard deviation of daily returns into the standard deviation of annual returns, we make the assumption that the probability distribution of returns from any day to any other day satisfies the following assumptions:

- Identical standard deviation
- Independent returns from one day and any other day

Note that it is not necessary to assume normally distributed returns. We begin by computing the daily return variance, which is the square of the standard deviation. Since the returns are assumed to be independent, the variance of the sum of daily returns is the sum of the variances. If there are 252 trading days in the year, for example, the annual variance is 252 times the daily variance. To obtain the annual standard deviation, we take the square root of 252 times the daily standard deviation.

$$\text{Annual volatility} = \text{Daily volatility} \times \sqrt{252}$$

Note that the choice of 252 trading days will differ according to the year, and how a bank decides to measure holidays. The choice of the number of days per year to use at a given bank is a matter of bank policy.

Continuing the logic of this calculation, any periodic volatility can be converted to another by multiplying or dividing by the square root of the number of smaller time periods in the larger time period.

Finally, to convert a percentage standard deviation or volatility into P&L standard deviation or volatility, multiply the percentage by the size of the portfolio in currency terms.

EXAMPLE

A bank estimates its annualized portfolio volatility is 15%. This estimate was based on the statistical properties of the portfolio's returns. The portfolio is worth USD 100 million. Its one-month 95% confidence VaR is therefore computed using the following steps:

Monthly volatility = 15% ÷ √12 = 4.33%.
Monthly 95% confidence percent VaR = 1.645 x 4.33% = 7.1231%.
Monthly 95% confidence P&L VaR = 7.1231% x USD 100 million = USD 7.1231 million.

5.1.4 Estimating the VaR From Historical Data

To simplify the discussion of VaR, we restrict our attention to a single variable, the total return value of the S&P 500 stock index, which can be found in electronic form on http://finance.yahoo.com. These publicly available data are used so the student may replicate the data and results below if desired. We included the Nasdaq index as well for the discussion on correlation in the next section.

Our goal is to estimate future risk of the S&P index but, regrettably, we have only past data to inform our estimate. The most common VaR approach is to compute the VaR using the historical volatility of the index, giving equal weight to all the historical observations.

The historical index series was taken for one full year, from January 2, 2014 to December 31, 2014.

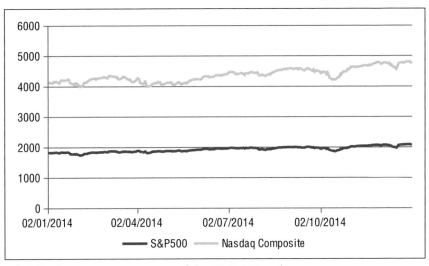

FIGURE 5.3 One Year's History of the S&P 500 and NASDAQ Indices 2014

The index axis is on the left and the S&P index values appear lower than the NASDAQ values on the chart. From this index we are able to compute daily returns, the percentage change in the value of the index between two days, and the statistics corresponding to daily returns.

	Daily	Annually
Mean	0.05%	11.43%
Standard deviation	0.72%	11.37%
Skewness	-0.40	
Kurtosis	1.34	
5th Percentile	-1.22%	
VaR @ 95% CI	1.18%	18.70%

FIGURE 5.4 S&P 500 Return Statistics, 2014

The mean (average) return, standard deviation, skewness, and kurtosis are computed in Excel or any standard statistical package. Skewness is a measure of asymmetry of returns; negative skewness implies relatively high likelihood of high negative returns compared to high positive returns. Kurtosis is a measure of "fat tails," i.e., the relative probability of extreme returns compared to usual returns. Normal distributions have zero skewness and zero kurtosis.[54]

The annual mean return is found by multiplying the daily mean by 252 days, the assumed number of trading days in a year. The annual standard deviation is the daily standard deviation multiplied by the square root of 252.

5.2 Critiques of VAR

The parametric method of computing VaR discussed in the last section has several advantages. Most importantly, it can be computed easily and quickly, which is necessary for banks with millions of positions that need to be aggregated and assessed for risk on a daily basis. However, analytic convenience comes at a price. In this section, we address the weaknesses of the assumptions made in the last section and mention some alternatives.

5.2.1 Constant Parameters

When the standard deviation of returns is computed in the parametric method, the implicit assumption is made that the mean and standard deviation of returns is constant. However, markets and financial instruments

---

54 We are using kurtosis here in the sense of "relative kurtosis." The absolute kurtosis of the standard normal distribution is 3.

generally go through periods with varying expected returns and volatilities, so the assumption can be best seen as an approximation to true returns in practice. For example, most market participants believed that true market volatility increased in the last quarter of 2008, while in 2014 they believed market volatility was decreasing. Also, many forecasters expressed the view that, due to fundamental changes in the capital markets, future expected returns would be lower.

5.2.2 Normality of Returns

While many VaR calculations assume factor returns are normally distributed, i.e., distributed according to a symmetric bell-shaped curve, the assumption is only approximate. For example, in this example, the S&P 500 index returns are not normally distributed:

- The skewness is generally negative (−0.40 in our sample), indicating higher relative probability of negative returns than positive returns.
- The kurtosis is generally positive (1.34 in our sample), indicating higher relative probabilities of extreme events than non-extreme events.
- The 5th percentile value was a return of −1.22%, indicating that 5% of the daily returns are less than −1.22%. In a normal distribution, this number would have been −1.18%. Therefore, the downside risk was slightly larger in the S&P index in 2014 than a comparable normally distributed index.

We can graph the actual frequency distribution of the data against the theoretical normal frequency with the same mean and standard deviation to see how the empirical distribution differs from the theoretical distribution. These data are organized so that "2.0" on the x-axis means "between 1.50 and 2.00 standard deviations."

The Risk Measurement Process **119**

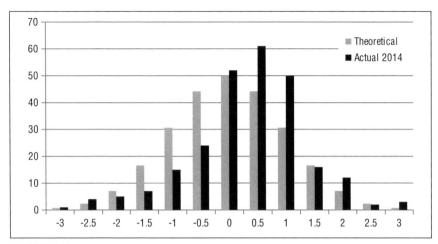

FIGURE 5.5 S&P 500 Return Frequency 2014

This graph confirms that actual returns appear to be more negatively skewed with greater kurtosis than the normal distribution would imply. Taken together, these statistics suggest that a bank that uses the normal distribution to assess risk may underestimate the risk of a long position in the S&P. The positive kurtosis indicates higher probability of extreme returns, while the negative skewness implies higher relative probability of extreme negative returns than extreme positive returns. Figure 5.6 shows the data used in constructing Figure 5.5.

SD	Theoretical	Actual
-3.0	0.75	1
-2.5	2.34	4
-2.0	7.04	5
-1.5	16.59	7
-1.0	30.61	15
-0.5	44.19	24
0.0	49.95	52
0.5	44.19	61
1.0	30.61	50
1.5	16.59	16
2.0	7.04	12
2.5	2.34	2
3.0	0.75	3
Total	253.00	252

FIGURE 5.6 S&P500 Frequency Distribution Data[55]

---
55 Note that the theoretical expected number of days will always be fractional, since the probabilities are not round numbers.

The table shows that a −3 standard deviation loss was more likely to occur in the historical data than would have been predicted by a normal distribution with the same standard deviation—an outcome of 1 instead of 0.75 in a sample of 252 observations.

If returns had been distributed normally, there would have been only one day (0.75 occasions would be 1 day) when the returns were more than 3 standard deviations from the mean return. In reality, there was exactly 1 day when the returns were less than 3 standard deviations from the mean.

However, the table also shows that a 3 standard deviation gain was more than three times as likely to occur in the historical data than would have been predicted by a normal distribution with the same standard deviation—3 outcomes instead of 0.75—captured by the positive kurtosis of returns. Differently put, if returns had been distributed normally, there would have been only one day (0.75 occasion would be 1 day) when the positive returns were more than 3 standard deviations from the mean return; in reality there have been exactly 3 days in 2014 when positive returns were more than 3 standard deviations from the mean.

5.2.3 Equal Weighting of Historical Data

When calculating historical volatility, the choice of historical timeframe is always difficult. Should an analyst use one year of returns or five years of returns? If a shorter time period is used, the focus is on time periods closest to the present—a good idea if future risks will look like present risks. However, a longer historical time period may be needed to capture all the risks that might be present in future markets.

The following chart shows how the resulting S&P 500 historical volatility varied on September 26, 2008 as a function of the number of days of history used to calculate it. Note that the time scale runs backwards, showing a decline in historical volatility (in this case) as the length of the sampling period increases.

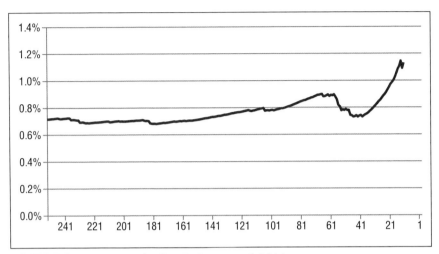

FIGURE 5.7 S&P 500 Volatility Estimate, end-2014

In this case, the shorter historical period of 10 days yields a daily volatility estimate of 1.14%, whereas the 252-day sample yields a daily volatility of 0.72%, as computed earlier.

A second problem with equal weighting is that the volatility calculation is very sensitive to the passage of time. For example, if a bank uses a 200-trading-day period to capture the VaR, then when an extreme outcome first occurs, it causes the VaR estimate to increase rapidly. This is perhaps a good thing, since risk may indeed have increased and may be expected to remain high. However, after 200 days pass and the extreme outcome falls out of the data set, the VaR drops quickly, without a good market-based reason. Because of this, banks have sought alternatives that put more weight on recent observations that contain higher informational content about more current market events and less weight on older observations.

The most well-known model of this type is the Exponentially Weighted Moving Average (EWMA) model introduced by JP Morgan under its RiskMetrics program. In the RiskMetrics weighting methodology, returns are given less weight in the volatility calculation the further they are in the past.

The model uses a daily decay factor, lambda (λ), which is taken to be equal to 0.94, to calculate the weights of different data points in computing the volatility. This means that the weight of a data point two days in the past has 94% of the weight of a data point one day in the past. Similarly, the weight of a data point three days in the past is 94% of the weight of a data point two days in the past, and so on.[56] After 80 days, historical data have virtually no weight when $\lambda=0.94$.

T = 0	T = -1	T = -2	T = -3
Weight = 1	Weight = 0.94	Weight = 0.94^2	Weight = 0.94^3
Actual weights are multiplied by 0.06 so that they sum to one.			

FIGURE 5.8 Relative Weights in the RiskMetrics Methodology

The benefit of this method is that when an extreme return enters the dataset, it causes VaR to increase. Under the exponential weighting scheme, the extreme return never vanishes, but its weight lessens so that its impact on VaR becomes smaller and smaller, and therefore does not cause the volatility estimate to drop suddenly as the extreme return becomes more distant in the past.

The six-month historical volatility estimates (starting six months prior to the last data point) can be compared to the volatility produced by the RiskMetrics algorithm. The daily updated volatility estimates were as shown in Figure 5.9.

The historical volatility estimate is fairly stable, but is that desirable? Given the volatility in the US markets in September 2008, it seems the RiskMetrics approach is better at picking up the increased volatility.

---

56   The value of 0.94 was chosen to optimize out-of-sample daily return volatility forecasting ability. For monthly volatility forecasting, λ is estimated to be 0.97.

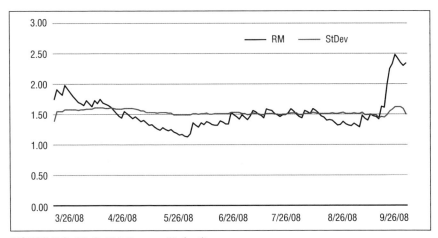

FIGURE 5.9 S&P 500 Return Volatility

5.2.4 Forward-Looking Volatilities

Some critics of VaR suggest that banks would be better served by looking at current market data rather than historical data where available. In some markets, like the S&P 500 for example, there are options traded that can be used to estimate the volatility of the underlying factor. This is done by determining what volatility level is consistent with observed option prices, called the implied volatility. This measure of volatility is considered superior in some ways to both historical volatility and historical simulation, since it is forward rather than backward looking. Also, since implied volatility is determined from a market price rather than a statistical calculation, it is judged to be a superior input. This is because traders have bought and sold options at that price and stand to gain or lose based on their view of volatility.

While this concept is theoretically appealing, there is no guarantee that implied volatility is the best predictor of future actual volatility. The reason for this is that the implied volatility also reflects relative demand and supply of options in the marketplace, and is influenced by those factors as much as by the volatility forecast. For example, implied volatilities in the S&P options market seem to exceed, on average, the actual volatility estimates.

Even if there is a bias, however, there may be useful information in implied volatilities. Therefore, some banks forecast their most important risks using a combination of implied and historical volatility.

5.2.5 Other Volatility Forecasting Methods

Some banks will overlay volatility estimates from expert forecasts, or from models that simulate market fundamentals to determine factor volatility. These sources may provide valuable input into future volatility estimates but, as the material is subjective, they should be tested to verify that the forecasting power of these sources exceeds the forecasting power of alternative historical and implied volatility models.

5.3 Nonparametric Methods and Historical Simulation

One of the strongest criticisms of VaR questions the assumption of using any predetermined probability distribution of returns, including the normal distribution. The argument is that markets will not conform to any theoretical distribution. To address this argument, researchers have developed methods that do not rely on theoretical probability distributions. As theoretical statistical distributions are generally characterized by their parameters, such as their mean and standard deviation, the methods that do not use prescribed distributions are called nonparametric. The most important of these methods used for VaR purposes is known as historical simulation.

Applying historical simulation to the S&P 500 results listed above, the VaR for a one-day period is determined from the actual historical observation that corresponds to the 5th percentile return, which for the S&P was $-1.22\%\%$ in one day. To determine the VaR for a two-day period, simulate returns for the first day and for the second day using historical returns, and choose the combined return representing the 5th percentile two-day return.

The Risk Measurement Process **125**

EXAMPLE

To determine the 10-day VaR using historical simulation, the following algorithm is used:
- For Day 1, choose one of the 252 S&P500 returns from the sample randomly
- Repeat for Days 2-10
- Compute the compound return and the frequency distribution for the compound return
- Calculate the 5th percentile of the frequency distribution

An alternative algorithm is the following:
- Construct the frequency distribution of returns for every 10-day period occurring in the sample
- Calculate the 5th percentile of this frequency distribution

Each of these methods has its problems. Both assume the historical return distribution applies to the future. The first assumes statistical independence of returns from one day to the next. The second has overlapping time periods, which are necessarily correlated and cannot be used to construct a distribution.

Historical simulation does solve the problem of assuming normally distributed returns, but invites the criticism that the historical periods sampled may not best represent the current market risk situation. For example, when oil prices are over USD 100 per barrel and highly volatile, historical time periods when oil was USD 20 per barrel and not very volatile would most likely be irrelevant.

Historical simulation can also be exponentially weighted to give less importance to older returns, by lowering the probability of selected older returns, similar to the method used for exponentially weighted historical VaR.

5.4 VaR for Multiple Factors

Once a bank has developed models for all the individual factors that affect its risks, it must understand how those factors interrelate in order to get a picture of the risk of its positions. The most common method for characterizing these interrelationships is the correlation. In this section we show how the correlation is used to compute risks of multiple factor positions, and the criticisms of using correlation as a measure of interrelationships. Like parametric VaR, correlation makes computation simple and quick, but it makes several assumptions that do not always apply in practice.

5.4.1 Correlation and Covariance Definition

Correlation is a single measure of association between two variables, and establishes the strength of a statistical relationship. It also forms the basis for statistical regression.

The correlation and covariance between factor returns can be calculated easily using built-in functions of Excel (CORREL, COVAR) or other programs.

The correlation can also be computed directly using factor returns and the formula:

$$\text{Correlation } (\rho) \text{ between } X \text{ and } Y =$$
$$\text{Covariance } (Cov) \text{ between } X \text{ and } Y$$
divided by product of their standard deviations (σ), or
$$\rho_{x,y} = Cov(x,y)/\sigma_x \sigma_y$$
Covariance = Average product of the deviations of X and Y from their respective means, or
$$Cov(x,y) = E[(R_x - ER_x)(R_y - ER_y)]$$

Definition and Properties of Correlation
- A measure of how closely one factor can be predicted as a linear function of the return of another factor
- Assumes constant mean return and standard deviation for both factors over the given time period
- Ranges from -1 (perfectly negative linear relationship; the factors move in opposite directions but with equal magnitude of movement) to 1 (perfectly positive linear relationship; the factors move in the same direction with equal magnitude of movement)
- Zero correlation indicates no co-movement relationship between the factors

Sample Calculation
Adding the Nasdaq returns to the S&P return results above, the following statistics were computed in Excel.

	S&P500 Daily	Nasdaq Comp Daily	S&P500 Annually	Nasdaq Comp Annually
Mean	0.05%	0.05%	11.43%	13.57%
Standard deviation	0.72%	0.89%	11.37%	14.14%
Skewness	-0.40	-0.46		
Kurtosis	1.34	0.88		
5th percentile	-1.22%	-1.47%		
VaR @ 95% CI	-1.18%	-1.47%	-18.70%	-23.27%
Correlation	93.06%			

FIGURE 5.10 NASDAQ Return Statistics

The computed correlation of returns is 93.06%, indicating a strong positive linear relationship between the two returns.

5.4.2 The VaR of a Two-Asset Portfolio

In this section, we study how to compute the VaR of a two-asset portfolio, using the S&P500 and the NASDAQ indices as the two assets.

The squared VaR of a two-asset portfolio is given by the following equation, where N1 and N2 are the sizes of the positions measured in dollars:

$$Portfolio\ VaR^2 = N_1^2 VaR_1^2 + N_2^2 VaR_2^2 + 2 \times N_1 \times N_2 \times \rho_{1,2} \times VaR_1 \times VaR_2$$

The VaR is found by taking the square root of this expression. If there are more than two factors in the position, then the portfolio's squared VaR includes all the components' squared VaRs and all possible paired correlation terms.

EXAMPLE

Suppose a bank has a long position of USD 100 million in NASDAQ securities hedged with a USD 100 million short position in the S&P 500:

N1 = 100 (NASDAQ); N2 = –100 (S&P)

Portfolio VaR^2
 = $100^2(0.0147^2) + (-100)^2(0.0118^2) + 2(100)(-100)(0.9306)(0.0147)(0.0118)$
 = 2.1609 + 1.3924 − 3.2284
 = 0.3249
Portfolio VaR = $\sqrt{0.3249}$ = 0.57

The one-day portfolio VaR is USD 0.57 million, and the annual VaR (252 trading days) is USD 9.05 million (0.57 *$\sqrt{252}$).

Therefore, even when there is a high, positive correlation, hedging one equity index with another still has significant risk (discussed in Section 5.5.1).

5.4.3 Bucketing with Correlation

Many institutions and banks will consider for aggregation purposes that a NASDAQ position is similar to an S&P 500 position and will therefore group them together in one bucket. Given the high correlation between the returns, this is a reasonable assumption. Simplistically, we could have added USD 100 to −USD 100 in the last example to get a bucket equity US exposure of zero. Bucketing, as described in more detail later, assigns exposures of similar kinds and types into one specific and generic range.

The NASDAQ positions can be converted to S&P positions for risk purposes using the following formula, assuming S&P (in this case Asset 2) is the bucket.

Position equivalent mapping Asset 1 to Asset 2 = $(VaR_1 \times \rho_{1,2})/(VaR_2)$

In the NASDAQ case, this is (100 x 0.0147 x 0.9306) / (100 x 0.0118) = 1.159. Therefore, the NASDAQ position could be represented as 1.159 S&P positions. The resulting bucket would be USD 115.9 S&P long and USD 100 NASDAQ short, for a net S&P long position of USD 15.9 million.

The one-day VaR of the bucket S&P position is found by multiplying the net S&P position by the one-day VaR shown in the table, which is USD 0.19 million (= USD 15.9 × 0.0118), much smaller than the VaR of USD 0.57 million computed in the last section.

This illustrates the principal risk associated with bucketing, which is the tendency to underestimate position risk for offsetting positions.

5.4.4 Criticisms of Correlation as a Measure of Interrelationships

Critics of correlation point to major problems with correlation calculations: the inability to capture increases in factor co-movements in extreme market scenarios, and the inability to recognize nonlinear pricing relationships. These are summarized below.

Instability	Correlation estimates can change widely over time. This can happen as a result of changes in the true correlation. However, it is more likely that changes in the correlation are caused by incorrect assumptions. For example, if we assume the mean and standard deviation are constant over the sample period, but they are not, the resulting miscalculation is captured in the correlation estimate. The changing correlation may show the amplified effect of changing means and volatilities.
Movements	For many risk factors, there may be little correlation between them for small price movements. However, when one factor changes dramatically, a second factor can become highly correlated. Unfortunately, the VaR calculation focuses on large price changes, so if the average correlation is used, risks will not be properly estimated for extreme factor movements. For example, in the first half of 2008, an equity investor using average correlation to model returns in the financial sector would have underestimated the risk of the sector by not realizing that that correlation could increase in times of panic.
Effects	For some risk factors, the degree of correlation may change due to other outside drivers. For example, foreign exchange rates may be highly correlated when major currencies move in value, but much less correlated when there is not a major currency movement. An average correlation measure misses the true correlation in both cases.

FIGURE 5.11 Criticisms of Correlation as a Measure of Interrelationships

All of these issues can be addressed with better correlation modeling by banks. One example of a class of models that allows nonlinear correlations are copula models, which are widely used in credit models to correlate default risks between multiple borrowers and can be used to estimate market risk as well. A copula creates a multivariate distribution from several univariate distributions in such a way that various general types of dependence can be represented, and the copula distribution artificially combines the features of the individual univariate distributions and the interrelationship across the individual univariate distributions.

5.4.5 Historical Simulation and Correlation

In the historical simulation methodology, correlation problems are avoided by choosing combinations of factor movements that actually occurred on a given day. This ensures that the historical frequency with which, for example, interest rates and equity prices moved in the same direction is preserved in future risk simulations. There is no need to calculate a specific parametric correlation. For this reason, many analysts prefer historical simulation. The preference is justified as long as historical time periods chosen represent the present time period as well as possible.

5.5 Position Mapping and Aggregation

In this section, we show how banks simplify risk aggregation by bucketing positions of similar risks together. The discussion begins with plain vanilla positions and then proceeds to option and exotic positions.

5.5.1 Bucketing and Mapping Plain Vanilla Positions

Interest Rates
While we may refer to a general concept of factor risk, it is often the case that the factor itself has many dimensions. For example, the phrase "interest rates" refers to many different bank rates, in different countries, at different maturities, and reflects different levels of credit risk. While it would seem to be ideal to include every possible rate as a factor, this is inappropriate for two reasons. First, it sometimes makes the calculation problem extremely large and intractable. Second, if we assume jointly normal returns, the risk model may not capture natural relationships in the data (e.g., the prime rate is always higher than LIBOR). Thus, a large set of data must be reduced in order to make the process computationally efficient and workable.

The process of reducing a large number of factors into a small number of factors is accomplished in two ways. The first process is called mapping, and the second is called bucketing. The mapping process shows how to convert selected risk factors into combinations of other risk factors. The bucketing process shows how to group similar positions by type or time period.

Suppose a bank has a small number of products linked to Interest rate 2, and wants to map Rate 2 to Rate 1 in its risk calculation.

Month	Rate 1	Rate 2
Jan	5.77%	6.25%
Feb	5.87%	6.42%
Mar	6.02%	6.62%
Apr	6.03%	6.54%
May	6.02%	6.56%
Jun	6.38%	6.88%
Jul	6.43%	6.94%
Aug	6.52%	7.00%
Sep	6.27%	6.65%

FIGURE 5.12 Sample Historical Data

By performing a regression of Rate 2 on Rate 1, we obtain the following relationship:

$$Rate\ 2 = 0.0100 + (0.9195 \times Rate\ 1)$$
$$R^2 = 95\%$$

Using this equation, the pricing of any instrument based on Rate 2 can be mapped to 0.9195 units of Position 1. The high R2 (squared correlation) tells us that the statistical relationship is highly reliable.

Basis Risk
In the mapping exercise conducted above, Rate 2 risk is being modeled as a function of Rate 1 risk alone. Although the relationship is fairly strong historically, with a R^2 of 97%, there is a risk that Rate 2 will fail to follow Rate 1 so closely. This risk is termed basis risk. Most VaR models do not capture basis risk, but try as much as possible to capture risks that can be mapped to traded risk factors and therefore quantified.

Risk Bucketing
Risk bucketing is accomplished by grouping maturity ranges of interest-rate-sensitive products together. These ranges are typically not evenly spaced, but rather tightly spaced for short-term maturities and more widely spaced for longer-term maturities. For example, a typical interest rate bucketing scheme might have the following ranges:

0–3 months
3–6 months
6–12 months
12–24 months
24–60 months
60+ months

A 10-year bond in this example would have its coupon payments and principal payment assigned to each of the 6 categories. A conversion factor would be applied to all the payments to give them the correct representation in each bucket.

The goal of the bucketing process is threefold:

- First, for cash flows assigned to a particular bucket, to estimate the correct sensitivity of those cash flows to the index factor chosen to represent the bucket.
- Second, to have enough buckets to capture a significant majority of the interest rate risks across the spectrum.
- Finally, to have as few buckets as feasible so we can reduce the size of our computational problem.

Overall, a bank may have thousands of different interest rate exposures, but through mapping and bucketing it seeks to reduce the number of factors to a manageable size while still giving a realistic risk picture.

Foreign Exchange
Foreign exchange positions can be mapped to cash positions and forward positions. Cash positions are treated as a risk factor unto themselves, though currencies that are less important to a particular bank may be mapped to other currencies. Forward foreign currency rates are determined exactly by interest rate arbitrage. Hence, the risk of forward currency positions is known when both the spot rate risk and the risk to the risk-less yield curves of the two countries are also known.

Equity
Equity positions can also be mapped into cash positions and forward positions, though the latter are relatively rare. Cash equities are usually mapped to their regional indices. For example, Microsoft may be estimated to have a beta of 0.87, implying that a 1% movement in the S&P 500 will move Microsoft's stock by 0.87% in the same direction. For purposes of risk

mapping, a USD 100 million investment in Microsoft is equivalent to a USD 115 million investment in the S&P 500, as 0.87 × 115 = 100.

Commodities
Commodities are most similar to interest rates, with the possible exception that there is usually much less visibility and liquidity in the commodity markets, and as a result risk models are more difficult to build. A commodity-trading group may have five different oil exposures out to five years, two different gasoline exposures to six months, and one 10-year ethanol position. In monthly terms, this would be 432 positions:

$$(5 \times 12 \times 5) + (2 \times 6) + (10 \times 12) = 432.$$

The ethanol position in particular would be difficult to model, because there is no liquid forward curve with prices out 10 years. For this reason, ethanol may be modeled as a combination of other fuels, such as unleaded gasoline and natural gas. For risk purposes, then, the ethanol position would be mapped into an equivalent risk position in unleaded gasoline and natural gas.

5.5.2 Conversion of Option Positions

The challenge with options is that they are valued as a nonlinear function of their underlying risk factors. For example, a far in-the-money call moves almost like its underlying, but a far out-of-the-money call barely moves at all. Hence, the risk model needs to capture the "moneyness" (amount in the money) of options to reflect the true risk of option positions.

We can approximate this risk knowing the delta of the option, which is the change in option value per unit change of the underlying instrument. This provides good sensitivity estimates for small underlying changes. However, this method can give an illogical risk measure for large underlying price changes. For example, suppose the underlying instrument is priced at USD 100, the option has a delta of 0.5 and a value of USD 10. If the underlying instrument drops USD 1, we have no trouble discounting the option USD 0.50. But if the underlying instrument drops USD 30, the option cannot fall by USD 15, since it cannot fall below zero. Therefore, if we rely on deltas, we will overestimate the risk of long option positions and underestimate the risk of short option positions when price movements are large. This applies to both calls and puts.

Delta-Normal
In the delta-normal method, we convert all options to their delta equivalent and thereby convert them to a factor position. There may be more than one delta if the option has more than one driver. This would be the case in a basket option or a spread option, for example.

EXAMPLE

A bank holds a put option on the S&P 500 with a delta of –0.4. Therefore, for risk purposes, the position is mapped to a short S&P position equivalent to –0.4 units.

EXAMPLE

Suppose a bank holds a crack spread option, which pays off if the difference between crude oil prices and heating oil prices (expressed in barrels) exceeds the strike price of the option. If the option has a crude oil delta of 0.6 and a heating oil delta of –0.6, the option risk can be approximated by a position that is long 0.6 barrels of crude oil and short 0.6 barrels of heating oil.

Delta-Gamma
In the delta-gamma method, all options are converted into a delta position on the underlying factor and a gamma position on the square of the change in the underlying factor. The delta-gamma VaR is computed as follows:

$$VaR = (|Delta| \times Factor\ VaR) - (0.5 \times Gamma \times (Factor\ VaR)^2)$$

|Delta| is the absolute value of delta. The second term in the equation, 0.5 Gamma × (Factor VaR)2, causes a reduction in the risk estimate for long options (as the gamma is positive), and an increase in the risk estimate for short options. In some cases, delta (Δ or δ) and gamma (Γ or γ) will be written as their Greek-letter equivalents.

It should be noted that the delta-gamma method effectively fits a curved line, or more specifically a parabola, to the option-pricing curve, which is more accurate than fitting a straight line using the delta-normal method, but does not fully capture option risk, particularly for extreme price movements.

EXAMPLE

The following chart shows the value of a short call position for various levels of the index using the S&P 500 index option, the index at 1,200, dividend yield at 1.5%, and annualized volatility of 37.78%. It also shows how well the option position is approximated by the straightline (delta normal) index position and the quadratic (delta gamma) position. For extreme loss scenarios, i.e., rising S&P values, the delta-normal underestimates risk in this case, while the delta-gamma method overestimates the risk.

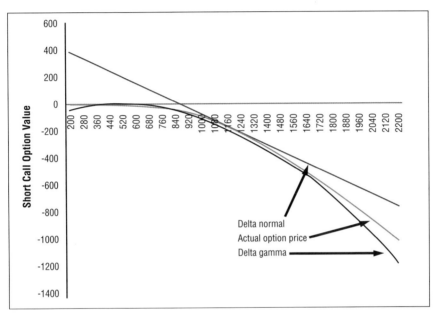

FIGURE 5.13 Linear and Quadratic Option Approximations

Complex Options and Structured Deals
Most banks enter transactions that are more complex than plain vanilla options. If the options were custom-tailored for a particular client, there is a good chance there is no easy pricing model for the product. In this case, the bank's quantitative staff are responsible for building a benchmark model or a simulation model to price the option, and providing the necessary delta and gamma calculations.

Once the option can be reduced to the deltas and gammas with respect to its traded factors, its risks can be approximated with the delta-normal or the delta-gamma approach as appropriate.

5.6 The Daily VaR Process

Banks normally compute VaR on a daily basis, following the closing of bank and trader positions for the day. Best practice requires banks to calculate the VaR on all their positions, whether they are subject to mark-to-market accounting or not. While processes differ slightly from bank to bank, they share the same general components, as shown in Figure 5.14.

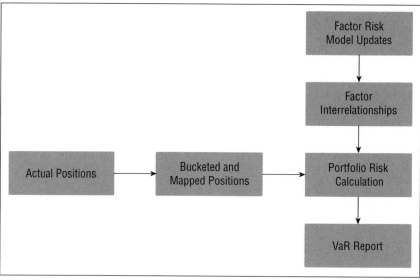

FIGURE 5.14 Overview of the VaR Determination Process

Factors include market risk factors such as interest rates, foreign exchange rates, and equity and commodity prices. Factor risk models are the statistical models built by banks to describe the risk of these factors individually. These models are typically updated on a daily basis. The bank will have established policies for measuring and updating the risk measurement of a single factor, and will review these policies over time. Some use a parametric technique, such as historical volatility, while others use a nonparametric technique, such as historical simulation. In both approaches, the risk measure changes slightly every day with the addition of the new day's market information.

Factor interrelationships refer to the update in the correlation estimate or other measure of association between two variables. Banks that use historical simulation avoid the problems associated with correlation as a means to quantify a relationship between two variables, but they introduce other problems, such as consistency and suitability.

The position simplification process is extremely important, since it allows complex or unique transactions to be bucketed and mapped into an alternative simplified form. In the simplified form, the complex trades can be combined with the plain vanilla (cash and forward) positions of the bank. The goal of this process is to be able to include all the bank's positions in its risk measure, even if the simplifications cause the computation to lose some level of precision.

Portfolio risk calculation has to do with how the profit or loss (P&L) is computed for each position based on each risk factor scenario, and how these P&Ls are aggregated into loss distributions. Two widely used methods are the variance-covariance method and the full revaluation method.

The variance-covariance approach takes the variance and covariance of all the factors, and combines this with the positions in order to compute an overall risk estimate. The full revaluation approach simulates the factors jointly, and then re-prices all the instruments in the bank's portfolio to reflect those factor changes. Variance-covariance is quicker, but full revaluation is more accurate. Some risk models combine the two approaches by using the variance-covariance approach for small price changes and the full revaluation approach for larger price changes; this approach has computational speed benefits.

5.7 Quality Control in VAR

Most banks check the predictive accuracy of their VaR models by backtesting. The backtesting process requires the following procedure:
- Keep track of the VaR estimate on a daily basis (as positions change)
- Plot the positive VaR and its negative complement over time (note the mirror image of the VaR boundaries on the following Figure 5.15)
- Plot the subsequent day's P&L along with the range of VaR's
- Determine the fraction of P&Ls falling below the VaR
- Compare this number to the target probability of falling below the VaR

EXAMPLE

Using the S&P data and the RiskMetrics volatility calculation, we backtest to see if the estimated VaR at the 95% confidence level produced losses outside the VaR range about 95% of the time. Using the last half of the data sample, the following chart was produced, using a VaR range of 1.645 times the RiskMetrics volatility estimate.

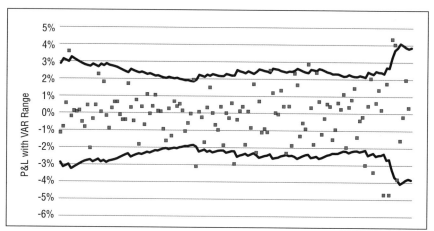

FIGURE 5.15 VaR Back Test—RiskMetrics—S&P 500

The chart indicates that there were six loss exceptions out of 130 predictions where the actual P&L was below the VaR limit, or 4.62%, slightly lower than the 5% expected level, but well within the expected range.[57] By means of comparison, the standard volatility calculation using six months of historical data had similar results, with seven exceptions out of 130 predictions.

VaR backtests are usually conducted on a periodic basis by banks to verify the continuing accuracy of their VaR estimates. These tests can be done at the level of individual trades, the level of a given trading unit, or even on the bank as a whole.

5.8 Alternatives to VaR in Light of the Financial Crisis

Although VaR has now passed two decades of global adoption and use, it has acknowledged shortcomings, both as a concept and as a set of methodologies.

When dealing with very large datasets and time-series data—a very common occurrence in financial institutions—it quickly becomes convenient, indeed required, to find ways to treat these datasets in a compact, reduced form. In addition, many activities in finance are forward looking, with the

---

57 The maximum error in measuring the outlier frequency with 95% confidence is given by $1.96 \times p(1-p)/\sqrt{n}$, where p is the percentage of outliers and $n>30$ is the number of observations. In this case, it is 0.76%.

result that probability theory finds a natural home, not only in product pricing, but also in risk management.

There are large numbers of probability distributions to choose from, but only a few contain elements that can be adapted to financial markets. The standard normal distribution has long been the favorite due to its simplified features and its well-understood mathematics.

To aid comparability between risks in different financial assets, it is usual to convert price series to return series before applying further calculations. This is a simple task, subtracting yesterday's closing price from today's closing price and dividing the result by yesterday's closing price. This produces the relative percentage gain or loss since yesterday. It is therefore the daily losses or gains that are used in the further statistical analysis.

The standard normal distribution has one peak and two tails. The tails drop away quite quickly from the mean in both directions, meaning they display insignificant probability values from the 3rd to 4th standard deviation outwards. In financial market terms this means that there is an insignificant probability for making large gains and, more importantly in this context, large losses.

When doing test runs of financial market return series, however, it can be seen that these are consistently not normally distributed, but produce probability curves that are both more peaked and dense in the middle, and converge less rapidly towards the x-axis in the tails. This produces the "fat tail" effect, which technically is referred to as "leptokurtosis."

Unfortunately, VaR models cannot compensate for this effect, even if it were constant. To make matters worse, leptokurtosis is not constant, but rather varies over time, sometimes being less and sometimes more.

In a sense, VaR risk models are like a set of defective seatbelts in a car. Every time the car is in normal use, its occupants would use the seatbelts and things would be fine. However, the moment the car had an accident, the seatbelts would all malfunction simultaneously and injure or kill the occupants.

It has long been known that VaR models display the same characteristics as the seatbelts in this analogy. In times of reasonably orderly markets they function perfectly well and give risk managers a sense of security that loss predictions are not exceeded. However, the moment a market malfunctions and leads to dramatic price changes, VaR loss predictions are quickly distorted, causing unexpected financial loss.

The issue is not that VaR calculations are inappropriate, but rather that forecasting actual losses beyond the VaR confidence interval is difficult and unreliable. What is needed is a tool to deal with "tail risk."

5.8.1 Expected Shortfall

To deal with tail risk, it is important to know what happens if the VaR confidence interval is broken. Once a daily market risk loss exceeds the daily VaR number there is very little certainty about how large the loss could be.

On one hand, the maximum loss is the full principal value of the position/portfolio in question, but that is not helpful. It is also not true for leveraged positions, where the loss could in some cases exceed the principal amount.

On the other hand, an analyst could look at the portfolio and identify concentrations of market risk exposure and then multiply this exposure with any number of scenarios that would cause just those market risk exposures to change. Then, assign a probability to each market risk factor change, multiply by the market risk exposure and aggregate the results. This exercise in scenario analysis and its result—the sum-product of exposure × price change × probability—has served as an essential yardstick for just how bad things can get when they go wrong.

Although better than any traditional alternative, this method was never very scientific or reliable. Scenario analysis is slow work and in any case portfolio concentrations can change rapidly, rendering most scenarios useless, or at best impractical. To make matters worse, probability assignments could be misestimated and market price swings could significantly deviate from earlier projections, undermining the whole effort to collate the information in the first place.

Expected shortfall (ES), on the other hand, is an attempt to solve this problem. Although sometimes billed as a replacement for VaR, it should instead be seen as a complement to it. ES attempts to compute not the maximum market risk loss beyond the 95%/99% quartile, nor the most likely, but the average. It asks, "On average, how much will we lose if, in spite of our best efforts to keep losses within the confidence interval boundary, they turn out to exceed the VaR number?"

ES is an average of losses past the risk threshold, so for 99% VaR, ES will represent the average of outcomes in the worst 1% of cases. This way ES looks at the distribution of losses beyond the previously determined threshold (which could conveniently be the VaR limit) and returns the average of experienced losses.

For example, a bank has 99% daily VaR of USD –4. If the worst 1% of losses experienced by a bank are USD –5 USD –6, and USD –7, then the expected shortfall is USD –6 (–(5+6+7)/3). In reality, the calculation is slightly more complicated, but this serves as an illustration of the principles involved.

ES is also referred to as Conditional VaR (CVaR) or Expected Tail Loss (ETL).

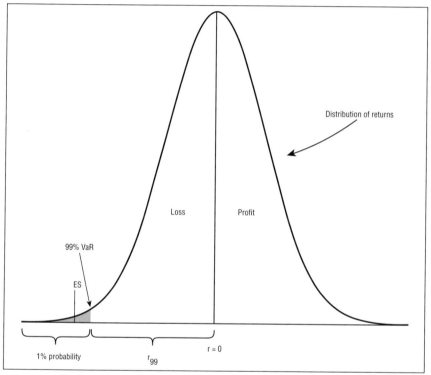

FIGURE 5.16 Expected Shortfall (ES)

In summary, VaR does not produce the maximum possible loss, but neither does Expected Shortfall. However, where VaR fails to adequately manage tail-events, ES at least gives some direction.

5.9 Basel III Treatment of Market Risk

For as long as banks have existed, market risk has been a feature of banking activities. However, it was not recognized by regulators in the first Basel Accord (Basel I) of 1988. Rather, Basel I emphasized the importance of converting positions in market-risky instruments into credit, or loan, equivalent values. As a result, Basel I completely ignored the possibility of financial loss due to changes in market rates and focused instead on credit losses, even in derivatives portfolios, due to counterparty/obligor default. Any associated capital requirement was intended to keep a bank in business with a reasonable expectation of success, even in the unlikely event of a catastrophic counterparty loss.

This unilateral focus on credit risk may seem naïve in hindsight, but it was not seen as unreasonable at the time. Very few banks were active to any significant extent in market risky transactions (such as derivatives). Even those who had invested significantly in developing derivatives markets found more often than not that their overall market risk exposures were insignificant compared to their banking book credit risks (in the case of corporate and universal banks), or of their bond underwriting and inventory credit exposure (in the case of investment banks).

The Growth of Over-The-Counter Derivatives

The situation changed rapidly after 1988. Several banks, mostly North American—and in particular JP Morgan—found that their customer limits were filling up with mark-to-market exposure from derivatives at an alarming rate. Then, as now, the largest group of counterparties were other banks, with whom the large derivatives houses would frequently engage in multiple transactions in largely similar derivatives. Sometimes these positions were long, sometimes short. However, with the bankruptcy legislation of the day there was no facility for counterbalancing a long exposure with a simultaneous short exposure between banks, as only the positive exposure of the two would be recognized for exposure purposes. Negative credit exposure was an alien concept to most credit risk managers then.

Seeing the trend, JP Morgan sent its head of derivatives to work for a full year at the International Swap and Derivatives Association (ISDA) in order to craft new standard documentation which could incorporate the possibility of bankruptcy netting. The result was the 1992 Standard Documentation. Bankruptcy legislation was slowly changed in a number of countries to allow for bankruptcy netting in financial instruments in the case of a bank default. This change put over-the-counter (OTC) derivatives on an equal footing with their exchange traded siblings, where clearing rules and daily margin adjustments had long since included this feature by default.

Effects of New ISDA Master Document

This turned out to cause a major shift in the development of OTC derivatives. As long as a bank could keep a reasonable balance in long and short positions with their counterparties, they were virtually assured a neutral credit exposure on their books. Derivatives activity boomed everywhere.

Banks now found that the increased activity in their derivatives businesses produced portfolio sizes in notional principal amount (NPA) terms that far outstripped their on-balance-sheet asset values. Although not intimidated by this, due to the beneficial effects of the ISDA netting clause, banks nevertheless became concerned that even minor imprecision in valuation and hedging of these positions might lead to losses that would have to be discharged against current year income. The result was a new race between banks to develop a market risk management methodology that could compute a specific loss that, with some certainty, would not be exceeded. Although many of these models survive in use, it was Value-at-Risk (VaR), promoted by JP Morgan, which caught the world's attention and continues to do so today. In what was a significant coup for the bank, JP Morgan published a technical document on the then nascent Internet for anyone to download. In addition, the bank supplied daily volatility and correlation statistics on a very broad range of markets, also for free.

The Basel I Market Risk Amendment
This clear-sighted development caused regulators to take notice. Within two years, in 1996, Basel I was updated with the Market Risk Amendment, which allowed banks to treat the market risk in their books for capital adequacy purposes. Two approaches were introduced: The Standardized Approach (SA) and the Internal Models Approach (IMA).

The SA was in essence a continuation of Basel I market risk treatment, but much more prescriptive and with significant additions related to time bands for each of four market risk categories: interest rates, foreign exchange, equity, and commodities. A separate treatment for options was added later.

The IMA was almost entirely a copy of the JP Morgan VaR description of two years earlier. There were significant freedoms available for early adopters, who could choose between three different methods for market risk calculation: the variance-covariance approach, the historical simulation approach, and the Monte Carlo simulation approach. Banks were required to seek approval for their own internal models, as well as stress test against time series of known market stresses. Banks were furthermore required to back test their models: compare previous predictions with actual P&L for consecutive future three-month rolling periods.

Basel II
The transition to Basel II in 2004 is covered elsewhere in this series (see Asset and Liability Management, Chapter 4). However, it is important to note that for all the significant changes that Basel II made to Basel I, the market risk capital charge and the methods used for its calculation were left unchanged. The market risk and capital charge calculations were already significantly more sophisticated than their credit risk equivalents and, for all the turmoil resulting from the changes to credit risk—the introduction of operational risk, Pillar 2, and Pillar 3—regulators decided to leave the market risk capital charge alone.

Basel III
The first steps towards Basel III had just been taken when the global financial crisis of 2007-2009 began. The effect of the crisis caused significant changes to the wording of the new Accord. The pre-announcement documents include the July 2008 First Consultative Document, the January 2009 Second Consultative Document, the July 2009 Final Document, as well as the February 2011 Update. The Basel III proposal itself was published in June 2010 and was originally to be introduced between 2013 and 2015. This was first extended in April 2013 to March 2018 and later to March 2019.

Although Basel III is mostly about capital, leverage, and liquidity, there are several changes of importance to market risk management, including Stress VaR, Incremental Risk Charge, Comprehensive Risk Measure, and CVA.

5.9.1 Stressed VaR

Stressed VaR is an evolution of classic VaR and is intended to meet some of the criticisms of the poor performance of VaR with respect to appropriate capture of tail risks. Stress VaR (SVaR) was defined by the Basel Committee on Banking Supervision (BCBS158, July 2009):

This measure is intended to replicate a value-at-risk calculation that would be generated on the bank's current portfolio if the relevant market factors were experiencing a period of stress; and should therefore be based on the 10-day, 99th percentile, one-tailed confidence interval value-at-risk measure of the current portfolio, with model inputs calibrated to historical data from a continuous 12-month period of significant financial stress relevant to the bank's portfolio.

The big difference to classic VaR is the period and the calibration. The period is 10 days instead of one. This will cause the SVaR number to be $\sqrt{10}$

(3.16) times higher than classic VaR. Classic VaR is calibrated to the most recent past, in other words current conditions. The requirement for stress calibration is similar to normal stress testing of portfolios, only here applied to VaR calculations.

Overall the SVaR number is going to be a great deal larger than normal VaR. However, banks have been given freedom to select which stress scenario is relevant for them and also to set the appropriate correlation coefficients between portfolio components. This is a clear regulatory risk, as it gives banks a strong incentive to game the system by choosing low volatility stress periods and low correlation assets. As a result, SVaR is being phased out for regulatory purposes and will be "moving to a single ES calculation that is calibrated to a period of significant financial stress."[58]

5.9.2 Incremental Risk Charge

Incremental Risk Charge (IRC) is an incremental charge for default and ratings migration risks for non-securitized products and is subject to at least a weekly computation. Non-securitized in this context means flow products, such as bonds and CDS, and may include listed equities.

5.9.3 Comprehensive Risk Measure

Comprehensive Risk Measure (CRM) is an incremental charge for correlation trading portfolios and is also subject to at least a weekly computation.

Although initially considered part of securitization positions, correlation trading portfolios are "carved out" of the standardized charge and subject to CRM and a "floor" (the CRM cannot be lower than 8% of the standard charge). It applies to correlation instruments and their hedges (including CDS), but without "re-securitization positions," e.g., CDO-squared or Leveraged Super Senior issues.

Default and migration risk (as in IRC) and all price risks (multiple defaults, credit spread volatility, volatility of implied correlations, basis risks, and recovery rate) must be simulated in the CRM model. Rebalancing may be taken into account via shorter liquidity horizons coupled with a "constant level of risk" concept.[59]

For CRM, the modeling of dynamic hedging and its cost are allowed.

---

58 BCBS Fundamental review of the trading book, October 2013, http://www.bis.org/publ/bcbs265.pdf
59 European Institute for Financial Regulation, http://www.eifr.eu/files/file4108236.pdf

Both IRC and CRM are based on the 99.9% loss quintile at one-year capital horizon. This contrasts with VaR and stressed VaR, which are much shorter term. This is a highly unrealistic percentage, which will only generate one acceptable data-point roughly every three years (1,000 days). It would take a 100-year data series to even get 33 reliable data points.

Additionally, the 8% floor is an issue for regulated banks, where under certain circumstances it can require less capital to hold an unhedged correlation position than would be required if the position were hedged. Additionally, banks are discouraged from trying to develop models that minimize the market risk exposure of correlation trades, as they would be subject to the 8% floor the moment the simulated market risk exposure would be less than 8%.

Substantial elements are still outstanding before work on a Comprehensive Risk Measure is complete. Many of these elements are described in the Basel Committee's "Fundamental review of the trading book: Outstanding issues," December 2014.

5.9.4 Credit Valuation Adjustment

The Basel Committee defines Credit Valuation Adjustment (CVA) as an adjustment to the mid-market valuation of a portfolio of trades with a counterparty. This adjustment reflects the market value of the credit risk due to any failure to perform on contractual agreements with a counterparty. This adjustment may reflect the market value of the credit risk of the counterparty or the market value of the credit risk of both the bank and the counterparty.

In this way CVA is effectively the market price of counterparty credit risk. Most banks add a CVA charge to OTC derivatives pricing, in particular to interest rate swaps. Rather than have each trading desk try to work out the relative credit rating difference between itself and its counterparty, banks have set up centralized CVA desks that are tasked with calculating the CVA charge each dealer has to quote. This way the dealer is absolved from dealing with counterparty risk and can concentrate on risk-free pricing in a specific product market.

In December 2014, the Basel Committee stated that it was "Considering further work on the treatment of CVA and CVA hedges, with a view to future consultation."

5.10 Summary

This chapter has introduced the value-at-risk methods for assessing risks in bank portfolios, along with the limitations of these methods.

Determining the Risk of a Single Factor
- To determine the VaR of a single risk factor (using historical volatility):
  - Determine historical time period and sampling frequency (usually daily).
  - Compute factor returns.
  - Compute standard deviation of factor returns.
  - Multiply by the price level to get dollar figures.
  - Multiply by the square root of the number of trading days in the VaR calculation.
  - Multiply by the number of standard deviations consistent with the desired confidence level (e.g., 95% corresponds to 1.645 standard deviations).
- The historical volatility method is criticized because:
  - The historical time period is arbitrary.
  - The methodology gives equal weight to all past returns.
  - An extreme factor movement moves historical volatility up when it enters the dataset and down again when it exits.
  - Many return series are not normal (i.e., the 1.645 standard deviation applies only to normal distributions).
- The exponential weighting method introduced by RiskMetrics is deemed to be better because:
  - More weight is given to more recent observations.
  - There is no explicit time interval chosen.
  - The decay rate can be chosen to give more or less weight to more distant historical observations.
  - Extreme observations gradually fade into insignificance.
- Advocates of historical simulation over historical volatility recommend it because:
  - It avoids the assumption of normally distributed returns.
  - Its future scenarios can be identified with actual past events.
  - Correlation between risk factors need not be computed.

Determining Risk Interrelationships
- ■ Two important measures of linear association are the covariance and correlation:
  - Covariance is an intermediate calculation.
  - Correlation is a scaled parameter between −1 and 1 indicating the strength of a relationship.
  - Both are based on historical data.
- ■ Correlation is criticized frequently for the following reasons:
  - Correlations appear to be unstable, usually because the calculation assumes that means, standard deviations, and correlations are constant.
  - Correlation fails to distinguish the relationship between short-term price movements (usually weak) and extreme movements (usually strong).
  - As a linear measure, correlation fails to capture the impact of nonlinear relationships, including those that might be driven by outside factors.
- ■ The alternative to using correlation is detailed modeling of inter-relationships, including the use of copulae for nonlinear relationships.

Position Mapping and Aggregation
- ■ The actual number of positions held by most banks is enormous, considering that similar variables, such as interest rates, can differ by bank conventions, country of origin, maturity date, issuer, credit grade, and month of cash flow.
- ■ The purpose of mapping is to model less important risk factors as combinations of the risk factors used in the VaR calculation.
- ■ The purpose of bucketing is to group positions by time to maturity, perhaps with some small adjustments.
- ■ The result of mapping and bucketing is to reduce the number of factors to a manageable level that does not compromise the quality of the risk measure too much.
- ■ Option positions can be mapped in two ways:
  - The delta-normal method provides that options are converted into underlying factor risks according to their deltas to those factors.
  - The delta-normal method is simple, but it overstates long option risks and understates short-option risks due to the nonlinearity of the option position.
  - The delta-gamma method corrects the nonlinearity problem by fitting a parabolic curve to the risk rather than a straight line.

- The risk of extreme option price movements is not captured perfectly with either method. For these options, a full revaluation simulation might be appropriate.
- After all the positions have been mapped to factors, aggregation can proceed in two ways:
  - The variance-covariance method computes the total position risk by taking the elements of the variance-covariance matrix, multiplying each by the position sizes, and adding them up. It is a fast method, but not as accurate as full revaluation.
  - The full revaluation method simulates the factors and then revalues all the positions at the simulated factor levels. The position P&L numbers are aggregated to find the fifth percentile value, which defines the VaR.

Components of the Daily VaR Process
- Banks undertake this VaR process daily by:
  - Updating individual risk factor models;
  - Updating factor interrelationships;
  - Bucketing and mapping actual positions to factors;
  - Computing portfolio risk by variance-covariance or full revaluation;
  - Producing the VaR report.

Quality Control in VaR
- Banks undertake quality control exercises periodically.
- The simplest tests verify that realized P&L stays within the predicted range with the appropriate frequency.
- A 95% VaR should yield P&L losses in excess of VaR roughly 5% of the time, or 1 in 20 trading days.

Problems with, and alternatives to, VaR
- VaR is a statistical measure of most likely maximum losses during normal market conditions.
- VaR does not say anything about the expected losses when markets are not normal.
- VaR models built on an assumption of lognormal returns in financial time series are often found to display "fat tail" or leptokurtic characteristics.
- This renders them largely without predictive power.
- Expected shortfall (ES) builds on the VaR concept by finding the most likely mean loss, should the earlier VaR number be exceeded.

Basel III Treatment of Market Risk
- Basel III requires banks to stress their VaR models with data from a known period of stress, i.e., the Credit Crisis of 2008. Stress VaR (SVaR) uses a 10-day time horizon, which is approximately 3 times larger than a one-day time horizon.
- The Incremental Risk Charge (IRC) is a market risk capital charge for unsecuritized positions.
- The Comprehensive Risk Measure (CRM) is a similar charge for securitized positions, subject to a controversial floor.
- Credit Valuation Adjustment (CVA) is intended to take credit quality of a counterparty into account, when pricing and valuing a derivatives position.

CHAPTER 6

Risks in Bank Trading Strategies

Chapters 2-4 explored risk in a bank's products and trading instruments. Chapter 5 examined VaR as one measure of the risk of a given portfolio. In practice, bank portfolios are dynamic, so VaR cannot be expected to represent the complete risk of a bank's trading function. In this chapter, we study the types of strategies banks often follow, and the risks of those strategies, some of which are within the control of the bank, and some of which are not.

On completion of this chapter, the reader will have an improved understanding of:

- Basic types of bank trading activities
- The life cycle and trading of bank products
- Bank use of leverage in trading
- Structural carry trades in a bank
- Trading through clearinghouses vs. OTC
- External market risks affecting bank trading performance
- Bank management of market risk

6.1 Overview of Bank Trading Activities

To understand the risk of bank trading activities, it is useful to begin with the major types of trading activities. In this section, we explore the major types of bank trading and hedging activities including the process by which a bank introduces new products and thereby new trading activities.

6.1.1 Development of Trading Activities

A bank's trading operations buy and sell financial instruments in the bank's name. The aim is to create short-term profit from a favorable move in market prices. This activity also means the bank risks losses should the value of the financial instruments change adversely.

Banks may adopt one of three broad trading strategies for each product that they trade. The strategy with the least market risk is when a bank runs a "matched book." A matched book strategy means the trading desk matches all customer positions immediately with an equal and opposite position by trading internally or with another bank. The only market risk taken is the chance that market prices will move in the time between executing the deal with the customer and executing the offsetting transaction, known as a "covering" or "hedging" transaction.

The second strategy is to manage positions in the product by executing covering or hedging deals at the discretion of the trading desk. In this strategy the trading desk would have a market risk or VaR limit in order to control the risk the bank would have at any one time. The positions could be taken because of customer transactions or by the traders creating positions by dealing in the market. This strategy allows the traders to time their position-taking activities to take advantage of favorable moves in market prices.

The third strategy is to be a "market maker" for a product. This means that the traders will quote a buy and sell price to customers and other banks and trade at the relevant price on whichever side of the market (buy or sell) the customer chooses. This strategy relies on the market being both liquid and having a number of other market makers the traders can cover their risk with.

A market maker that attracts buy and sell orders can make a profit from the spread quoted between the buy and sell price. Market makers can also benefit from the market information they get from the trades they are asked to execute. This helps them predict future movements in market prices. The risk in this strategy is that traders have to take positions that may quickly incur a loss. Traders must therefore be disciplined in the management of the risk, and the bank must set and monitor appropriate limits.

Banks have tended to change strategy as their business grows, and there will be more than one strategy in use across the products in a bank's trading book. Historically, many banks' trading activities grew from their desire to service their customers' commercial activities.

EXAMPLE

The FX market has become one of the most freely traded markets in the world, but its origins can be traced back to the introduction of floating exchange rates in the 1970s. For customers engaged in international business, this created new risks, which they managed through the services offered by their bank.

Retail exchange rates are those given by banks to their customers (primarily corporate customers) that include a margin over the wholesale rate that is available in the interbank market. Early in the market's development, the margin was large and banks' income grew quickly with the increased market activity even though their own positions were relatively small. As volumes increased and banks became more confident in their ability to manage foreign exchange positions, the activity changed from a customer-driven service to a wholesale trading operation.

Those banks with a large customer base and a large volume of foreign exchange transactions were able to use these "retail" positions to influence short-term movements in the wholesale foreign exchange market. This presented profit-making opportunities over and above the margin available from customer business.

To exploit this opportunity banks began to hold larger positions in their books. This process continued to develop and as competition increased, margins on customer business decreased. As a result, interbank trading now dominates the markets in the world's major currencies, such as USD/EUR, USD/JPY and USD/GBP, with customer volume accounting for a relatively small part of the market.

The development of the foreign exchange market is a good illustration of how trading in any instrument tends to develop within a bank. The first stage is where a bank will maintain a matched position in an instrument. This means the bank deals with a customer and immediately hedges its risk by entering into a transaction with another bank that perfectly matches the customer transaction. The profit for the bank would come from the difference in the price given to the customer and the interbank price. An example is given below.

Foreign Exchange Matched Position Trading
Bank A's customer wants to sell USD and buy JPY, as it wishes to pay its Japanese supplier JPY 100 million. Bank A does not hold yen so it asks for a quote to buy JPY in the market. The market rate is 100. The bank quotes a selling rate of 101 to its customer, sells JPY 100 million to its customer, and receives USD 1,010,000.

It immediately buys the yen in the market at 100 and pays USD 1,000,000. This leaves the bank with no market risk and a profit of USD 10,000.

The second stage in the development of a bank's trading activity occurs when the bank "holds" the position created by a customer transaction in anticipation of a favorable move (for the bank) in market prices over a short-term period. The trader's permitted holding period lengthened as the bank became more experienced in trading the instrument. Ultimately, this development process leads to the bank initiating a trading position in anticipation of a move in market prices. At this point, the trading activity no longer depends on customer activity.

6.1.2 Position Management and Hedging

Market risk affects both the banking book and the trading book. Positions held as part of the banking book, although not held for trading purposes, will create market risk because they are valued using current exchange, interest, and commodity rates. Management of interest rate risk in the banking book is usually carried out by the bank's Treasury function.

Management of market risk in the trading book is carried out continuously in bank dealing rooms by traders who are authorized to take market risk positions up to the limits set by the bank. The traders are authorized to execute deals in the bank's name and commit the bank to a financial liability. This activity must have rigorous controls independent of the traders to ensure the bank has full knowledge of the risks in its books.

Traders manage their risk by trading in instruments closely matching their current risk position. However, this is not usually the most profitable method of covering their risk so they often use hedging techniques. Traders can hedge their risks by taking an appropriate position in the underlying instrument. However, they could also hedge the portfolio risks by taking a position in a different instrument.

The instrument may have different characteristics but changes in its market value will mirror those of the original transaction. Therefore, changes in market prices will produce little or no change in the market value of the fully hedged portfolio. Often, a number of hedge positions will be required to match the underlying transaction completely.

EXAMPLE: COMMODITY HEDGE

A bank buys 25 metric tons of copper for delivery in four months. After a month the bank becomes concerned that the price of copper could fall. To hedge against this risk the bank sells a copper futures contract. This offsets the risk from the bank's future purchase of copper as it sets the price for selling the copper in three months. The bank has now hedged against a movement in the copper price by using a liquid futures contract.

Traders will regularly hedge with a more liquid instrument than the underlying transaction so that they are able to execute their hedging strategy quickly. In addition, dealing costs are generally lower in more liquid markets, which helps reduce costs. Traders can hedge all or part of their risk, allowing them to create the risk position they expect to be profitable without trading in the underlying instrument.

While customers often ask banks to provide underlying cash transactions such as loans, hedging is usually accomplished using derivative instruments. This is because, in general, derivatives have the following advantages over cash instruments:

- Lower credit risk
- Lower funding requirements
- Lower capital charges
- Greater liquidity
- Lower dealing costs

Hedging has many advantages but it does require careful management, as the instruments used are not identical to the original transaction. There will usually be some residual risk that is left uncovered and this must be measured and controlled. In some cases, the interaction of the hedge and the original risk position can create new risks for large trading positions.

6.1.3 New Product Development

Trading activities have become more complex as markets have become more liquid and sophisticated. In addition, some banks have felt the need to trade a portfolio of instruments more widely than the demand generated by its customer base. This has led to banks buying trading expertise to expand their trading portfolio. It is important in these circumstances that banks also invest in their control structures to ensure that they have the expertise to manage the risks created by the new trading activity. It can be tempting for a bank to move into a new market without waiting for the development of an adequate control structure.

A key element in the inspection of a bank's trading activities by its supervisors will be the independence of its approval procedure for the introduction of new trading products. It is important that there is a rigorous approval procedure that involves all relevant departments within the bank.

The approval procedure should address the following issues where applicable:

- Regulatory approval: Does the bank need approval for this product?
- Regulatory capital impact: How will the product affect the regulatory capital requirement of the bank?
- Tax issues: Will the product create new tax issues?
- Accounting procedures: Can the bank account for the product within its existing procedures?
- Legal and documentation procedures: Have all the legal requirements been satisfied and the documentation approved?
- IT system requirements: Will the current trading and settlement systems need enhancing?
- Operational support: Can the bank accurately book and manage the settlement of the transactions?
- Risk management reporting: Can the bank's risk systems capture and report the risk position created by the product?
- Pricing and valuation: Has the pricing and mark-to-market procedure been approved?
- Funding requirements: Will the product make a significant impact on the bank's funding requirements?
- Credit risk implications: Does the bank have sufficient credit lines to support the product?
- Compliance procedures: Will the product require the development of new compliance procedures?

The questions raised above highlight the kinds of issues that a bank's management must consider when introducing a new product. Following approval of a product it is important that the volume of trading is monitored. This is to ensure that if the product is a business success, it does not become a management problem.

Moving into new markets or products is often a sign that a bank's trading operation is successful and that it is looking to expand its portfolio to increase its revenue. However, it is also a testing time for a bank's management as it may be necessary to curtail profitable business to ensure that it maintains prudential control over the risks and the capital required to support the new trading activity.

6.2 Bank Trading Strategies

Most trading activity takes place on proprietary trading desks, but trading also exists wherever banks make markets or hedge customer risks. In theory, hedging activities have no trading risk, so long as perfect hedges with no counterparty risk are executed simultaneously with an offsetting trade. In practice, few transactions are or can be perfectly hedged and even apparently perfect hedges lose precision when market rates change. The bank has discretion in timing the hedge, choosing the hedging instrument, setting the percentage of the risk that will be hedged, and in some cases, choosing the counterparty it hedges with. All of these decisions, while they have the potential to add value for the bank, also add risk.

Similarly, proprietary trading can be a source of both significant profit and risk for the bank. "Prop" desks monetize a bank's views on capital markets by trading positions to reflect that view. "Monetize" means "convert into money," so monetizing a view is making a trade that is expected to profit if the view is correct. Such a trade can be either speculative or built on informed judgment. If the bank's views are more often correct than incorrect, the bank can expect to profit from this activity.

6.2.1 Basic Trading Strategies

Buy and Sell
If a bank has a view on currencies, rates, equities, commodities, or credit, it can take simple positions to monetize those views. If a bank has a view that the EUR will strengthen, it can purchase EUR with foreign currency on hand, hoping that the value of the position will rise. If the bank expects interest rates to fall, it buys risk-free bonds. If it expects credit spreads to

widen, it sells corporate bonds but hedges the interest rate risk. If it thinks emerging market equities will strengthen, it may purchase portfolios of emerging market stocks.

In all these cases, the instrument bought or sold is either a cash instrument or a forward on a cash instrument. When the trading desk believes that prices will rise, the bank buys the instrument entering into a long position. When the trading desk believes that prices will fall, bank sells or shorts the instrument, perhaps to be repurchased at a lower price.

Long and Short
There is a subtle difference between the terms long and short when compared to the terms buy and sell. In casual conversation, "long" and "buy" may be used interchangeably, as may "short" and "sell." The difference arises due to the fact that long and short positions do not necessarily imply the expense or receipt of cash in the transaction. For example, in the futures market, the investor who is long the S&P 100 index (OEX) will profit if the OEX rises in value, but that investor has not paid cash to own the underlying securities.[60] A long position can also refer generally to a forward agreement to buy something in the future. At the point of the transaction in the future, the long position becomes a purchase (buy).

Bankers speak in general about their exposures using the terms long and short. For example, a trader trading on behalf of the bank using the bank's own money (also called prop trader (from "proprietary")) may say the trading desk is long JPY, recognizing that the exposures come from combinations of cash, forward, and option positions. This statement implies that if the JPY strengthens, the prop trader's trading desk will profit. Similarly, if the bank is short the Nikkei 225, the implication is that the combination of its positions is expected to profit if the Nikkei index falls.

Long and short positions are usually expressed in position equivalents. In the example above, the JPY exposure would be expressed in terms of an equivalent cash JPY holding with similar risk. The short aggregated Nikkei position would be computed in terms of the number of index units the bank is effectively short, as if it had sold the stocks.

EXAMPLE

If the bank is long USD 1 billion in JPY, short USD 200 million in delta-equivalent JPY options, and long USD 50 million in JPY-denominated stocks, its net JPY position-equivalent is

---

60 The S&P 100 is an index that includes 100 leading US stocks with exchange-listed options, and is a subset of the widely recognized S&P 500 index.

USD 850 million. This is the amount of JPY exposure that would be shown in the aggregated risk reports.

Short Selling

Short selling carries a special meaning that is distinct from being short an exposure. In short selling, a bank wishes to establish a short position in a security but does not own the security. Therefore, the security is borrowed from a third party and sold in the marketplace with the expectation that the bank will repurchase the security at a lower price in the future. This is called "covering the short." If the security price falls, and the bank covers at a price lower than the selling price, it profits. If the security price rises, the bank covers at a higher price and loses. When the bank repurchases the security, it is returned to its original owner. Note that the exposure created by the bank is a short exposure, so the terms short and short selling are related in this sense.

EXAMPLE

A Microsoft short sale with three possible outcomes demonstrates massive loss potential relative to potential profit.

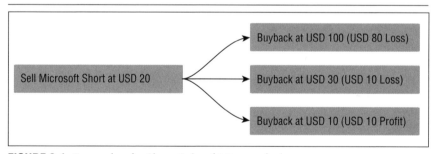

FIGURE 6.1 Example of a Short Sale of Microsoft shares

Mechanics of Short Selling

Short selling mechanics differ by market, but they share many common characteristics. In order to be specific, we consider the case of US equities, with the understanding that practices may differ by product and geography.

The institutional short seller, i.e., the bank, first locates the securities to be borrowed to ensure that it can affect the trade. If the bank does not do this, it is called naked short selling. Naked short selling means that the bank sells shares short that it cannot borrow. Naked short selling is very risky and presents the risk that the bank may not be able to borrow the security, causing a failure to deliver and subsequent losses to the bank. The securities are usually found by stockbrokers at custody banks and funds management firms, and can be borrowed without permission from the security's owner if the securities were bought on margin. Normally, the cash proceeds from the sale serve as collateral. The bank may or may not earn interest on the short sale proceeds.

If the stock pays a dividend, the bank is obligated to pay that dividend to the security owner. The securities lender retains the right to receive dividends, but gives up the right to vote its share. The lender generally has the right to demand the shares back from the bank, which forces the bank to either cover, or locate another securities lender to replace the shares.

Unique Risks to Short Selling
The primary risk to short selling is the potential for extreme losses. In fact, losses are theoretically unlimited. The risk to purchasing a security is limited to the cash paid for the security. However, in a short sale, the borrowed share's price may increase by a large multiple, causing the short seller to have to cover at a significant loss.

A second risk to short selling is the availability of shares to borrow. During times of change in control or important shareholder votes, it may be difficult to find lenders willing to give up their voting rights and lend the shares. And it is particularly during times of change in control, contested takeovers, or important shareholder votes when short sellers are demanding shares to borrow. With a clear price view, short sellers can generate substantial profits by shorting stocks in anticipation of an outcome that can adversely impact the share price. But to do so, they have to be able to borrow shares.

A third risk to short selling relates to market behavior. The NYSE and NASDAQ report short interest, which is the percentage of a firm's shares that have been sold short. They also report a short interest ratio, which is the short interest in shares divided by the average daily trading volume. If either of these indicators is large, it implies that there is a risk that many shorts will have to cover their positions within a particular timeframe, putting upward pressure on share prices.

Finally, short selling creates significant liquidity risks from cash margin calls when security prices are rising. In this case, banks must deposit additional cash to collateralize their short sale positions.

6.2.2 Leverage in Trading

There are at least four ways to achieve leverage in long positions in trading. First, securities may be purchased with borrowed funds using a bank loan or similar credit. Second, securities may be purchased on margin, i.e., by taking a loan from the broker. Third, securities may be purchased and repo'ed (see section below on Repurchase Agreements) to generate cash for further security purchases. Fourth, the bank may enter into a derivatives transaction, such as a total return swap, that requires little or no collateral but mimics the performance of a long or short position in the underlying instrument.

Leverage is received implicitly in short positions through short sales, where no amount of collateralization can cover the maximum loss. Leverage on the short side is also achieved by taking short derivative positions.

Margin Purchases (and Purchasing With Borrowed Funds)
In the United States, stock investors may borrow up to 50% of the value of their securities from their brokers. Regulation T of the Federal Reserve Bank, also known by its short name "Reg T," sets this limit. If the value of the margined securities falls, the investor must pay down the margin loan. That is, in a falling market environment, the investor has to produce additional cash to satisfy the Reg T requirements. Failing that, positions will be liquidated and the margin loan repaid.

Many market participants question the efficacy of Reg T since brokers have no way of knowing if investors are using borrowed funds to buy securities in the first place.

Repurchase Agreements (Repo's)
A repurchase agreement is affected when the owner of a security sells the security with an agreement to repurchase the security at a future date according to a pre-specified interest formula. The repo therefore acts like a collateralized loan, with the seller getting loan proceeds in exchange for paying interest. If the repo'ed security is a low-risk instrument, such as a short-term treasury bond, the lender will lend at full face value. If the repo'ed security is risky, the lender may take a "haircut" (a percentage reduction in assessed value for collateral purposes) and provide a fraction of the value in cash. In addition, the lender may require ongoing collateralization if the security falls in value.

EXAMPLE

A bank wants to take a leveraged position in Collateralized Debt Obligations (CDOs), and CDOs can be repo'ed with a 20% haircut. Starting with USD 100, the bank could buy USD 100 in CDO's, and repo the CDOs to receive USD 80. The USD 80 could be invested in securities, and the securities repo'ed again to receive USD 64.

Theoretically, the bank could continue that process and eventually receive USD 500 in purchasing power to buy CDOs. The maximum leverage factor equals 1/haircut = 1/0.2 = 5.

The danger in leverage is that while the cash investment may not increase, the risk estimate increases in proportion to the leverage. In the CDO example just given, the bank is exposed to the possibility of USD 500 in losses from spending USD 100 in cash. Even if the VaR on a USD 100 position were estimated to be USD 30, the VaR would also increase by the leverage multiple to 5 x USD 30, or USD 150—still greater than the USD 100 initial investment. Of course, this raises the risk that the VaR model could be incorrect, a risk that was not fully realized in CDOs until the global financial crisis of 2007-2009.

Derivatives as a Leverage Tool
For risk purposes, a long futures position resembles a leveraged asset purchase, where the leverage multiplier is determined by the margin requirement. For example, a 5% margin requirement implies leverage of 20 times. The long position has the same cash risks as a margined purchase, as the margin requirements must be continually satisfied in a dropping market.

Options are another form of leveraged position that provide higher degrees of exposure at less cash cost, but the difference is that losses to long option positions are limited to the premium paid.

6.2.3 Carry Trades

Many banks run large carry trade positions. In a typical carry trade, a bank will borrow funds in a low-interest currency and place the funds on deposit or lend in a high-interest currency. Carry trades produce income on paper, and are profitable so long as spot exchange rates do not change.

EXAMPLE: FOREIGN EXCHANGE CARRY

Under the theory of interest rate parity introduced in Chapter 2, the higher yielding currency should depreciate at a rate just enough to offset the interest differential. In practice, investors generally get a positive return from the carry trade, but are occasionally negatively surprised when the higher yielding currency devalues more quickly.

EXAMPLE: FIXED INCOME CARRY

In this instance, short-term borrowing is used to fund long-term debt. This can be done in the trading book by selling short-term debt instruments and buying long-term instruments. Commercial banking is in a way like a carry trade, since short-term deposits are used to fund long-term fixed rate loans. Whether in the banking book or the trading book, the fixed-income carry trade is also generally profitable, except when long-term rates rise relative to short-term rates.

EXAMPLE: COMMODITY CARRY

An oil futures trader may buy oil for delivery at one date in the future and sell at another point. In a backwardated market, where longer-term prices are lower than shorter-term prices, the carry trade is profitable as long as the curve stays in backwardation. Similarly, in a contango market, short-term commodity futures are bought while longer-dated positions are sold, a profitable strategy only if the curve stays in contango.

From a risk management point of view, carry trades can look deceptively profitable while containing hidden and occasional devastating outcomes. Historical evidence may show that a particular carry trade is profitable 95% of the time, but historical analysis may not provide the results of the worst possible breakdowns in carry relationships.

6.2.4 Trading Through Clearinghouses

Bank trading, as we have discovered, creates not only market risk, but counterparty risk and liquidity or margining risk, covered more fully in Section 2.4 and Section 3.4.6 of the Credit Risk Management book in the GARP FRR Series. The purpose of a clearinghouse is to reduce counterparty risk and liquidity risk.

A clearinghouse describes a number of different types of entities which may include clearing of cash payments, such as the Automated Clearing House (ACH) in the United States, or the central counterparty clearing mechanisms established in futures, options, and OTC markets.

The central counterparty clearing structure requires that the central counterparty be the counterparty to all trades. For example, in a direct trading system, A may contract to buy a security from B in the future. In a clearinghouse system, while A and B may agree to trade, they assign the trade to the clearinghouse, so that A is buying from the clearinghouse and B is selling to the clearinghouse. Essentially, the clearinghouse becomes the counterparty to every trade. This would seem to add an unnecessary component to the trading process but it accomplishes several objectives:

- *Centralized administration:* A and B can get a single aggregate position and risk report
- *Netting:* If A subsequently takes an offsetting position with a third party, the clearinghouse nets and cancels the transactions without affecting B's position
- *Collateral:* The clearinghouse requires A and B to post collateral to guarantee their performance, but the collateral is computed based on the net combined exposures, not the sum of the individual exposures
- *Credit quality:* A and B are concerned with the credit quality of the clearing-house, not each other, and the credit risk is generally minimal
- *Contract risk:* Since clearinghouses use standardized contracts, there is no risk that A or B missteps in offsetting a transaction

Clearinghouses are generally owned by banks or clearinghouse members, who take the residual risk of clearinghouse failure after other credit support layers have been exhausted. Some clearinghouses are backed by outside insurance companies to provide an additional layer of protection. For this reason, banks that trade through clearinghouses normally consider the counterparty credit risk of the clearinghouse to be minimal. The greatest direct benefit is the reduction in collateral requirements for traders who go both long and short.

EXAMPLE

Suppose a small bank has gone long with one large bank and short an identical trade with another large bank. Each large bank requires a 20% initial collateral deposit and does not itself provide collateral. As prices move in either direction, one large bank will ask for additional collateral, and the risk of loss to the other large bank will increase. By running the trades through a clearinghouse, the small bank will eliminate its collateral requirement, protect itself against increases in future collateral, and better protect itself against the risk of the failure of one of the large banks.

6.2.5 OTC Clearinghouses

Realizing the benefits of clearinghouses for standardized trades, a number of entities have sought to establish clearinghouses for nonstandard OTC trades. One notable clearinghouse for OTC trades is the London Clearinghouse, or LCH. On the LCH platform, standardized non-exchange traded contracts can be easily adapted. For these contracts, the clearinghouse values the transactions, collects collateral based on the mark-to-market, and performs all of the functions of a central counterparty clearing mechanism.

For unique trades, centralized clearing remains an unattained goal. While a clearinghouse can process trades and collect collateral, risk assessment and netting present difficulties that cannot be resolved within the standard clearinghouse model. Nevertheless, innovations in the markets will make it likely that some aspects of these trades could be cleared in a centralized fashion.

6.3 External Risks in Bank Trading

There are many risks in bank trading, which can be classified into several broad categories:

- Market liquidity and depth
- Market behavior
- Trading style
- Margin requirements
- Basis hedging
- Option hedging
- Failure of trading controls
- Mark-to-market

While some of these risks might be called banking risks (margin) or operational risks (failure of trading controls), they all have an element of market risk and are therefore discussed briefly here.

A Note on Defining "Liquidity"
The term liquidity can mean three different things in finance. First, market liquidity relates to the ease of trade in a market. For example, major FX markets are far more liquid than the markets for individual stocks. Second, liquidity can refer to having cash on hand to meet short-term obligations. For example, the bank treasurer usually manages liquidity risk. Third, liquidity

can refer to the ability to fund future cash payments. For example, the bank liquidity plan should account for vulnerability of future receivables.

In this section, we use liquidity to refer to the ease of trade in a market, and we use the term margining to refer to the cash requirements of trading.

6.3.1 Market Liquidity and Depth

Market liquidity can be measured in many ways, but the most common method is to measure typical bid-offer spreads in the market. The offer price is the higher price paid by a buyer in a market order, and the bid price is the lower price received by a seller in a market order. A market order is one that is placed for immediate execution at the price prevailing at the market when the order was received for execution by the broker. The bid-offer spread is the average cost a trader pays to initialize and reverse a position.

Market depth refers to the volume of potential trades that could take place near the market price. While there is no mathematical definition of depth, one indicator is the size of a limit order book, i.e., the listing of counterparties who would buy slightly below the current market and sell slightly above the current market.

The bid-offer can be expressed as a price difference or as a percentage. While large FX trades will have bid-offer costs of a few basis points, equity and commodity trades will typically be much higher, depending on the volume of trade and risk in the market.

The following factors generally explain the bid-offer spread in a market:

- Market volatility
- Market depth
- Competition among market makers

The bid-offer spread is not constant, but varies with these market forces. A good example is the CDO market in 2008. As markets became more volatile and market participants—both transactors and market makers—disappeared, the bid-offer spreads grew incomprehensibly wide, leading to a complete halt in trading of the instruments, or a "frozen market."

Buy-and-hold traders need to be concerned about liquidity risk. At position inception, a decision can be made if a trade is expected to be profitable at a particular price level. However, when the trader needs to exit the position, what will liquidity look like then? The best bank trading departments try to forecast a range of liquidity scenarios to properly estimate their expected costs of closing out a position.

Some strategies require constant changes to a position, such as the replication of an option. These strategies can become extremely costly due to paying the bid-offer spread every time a trade is made.

6.3.2 Market Behavior

Markets can behave in many different ways, in some cases not at all like the "random walk" theories postulated by economists. In these theories, the likelihood of up and down price movements relative to an average cannot be predicted. In some market scenarios, however, some market participants can predict prices better than others.

Market Manipulation
The Australian Securities Exchange defines market manipulation as follows:[61]

> *"Market manipulation describes a deliberate attempt to interfere with the free and fair operation of the market and create artificial, false, or misleading appearances with respect to the price of, or market for, a stock. This is typically done either by spreading false or misleading information in order to influence others to trade in a particular way, or by using buying and selling orders deliberately to affect prices or turnover, in order to create an opportunity for profit."*

One example of manipulation is a market corner, in which a group of traders has a large enough position to have undue influence on prices. In commodity markets, for example, it is possible for market corners to have long positions that exceed the deliverable supply of the commodity. A related manipulation is the squeeze, or short squeeze, wherein shorts needing to cover find they cannot purchase securities at expected prices.

Market manipulation is illegal, but nevertheless presents a trading risk for banks caught on the wrong side. Because manipulated markets are generally smaller and less liquid, manipulation occurs more frequently in equities and commodities than other capital markets. However, manipulation in major markets has been attempted, sometimes successfully. George Soros is famously known for manipulating the GBP and "breaking the Bank of England" on Black Wednesday in 1992. It was a daring trade, made possible by the lenient or non-existent market manipulation regulation at that time.

---

61 Further examples of market manipulation: http://en.wikipedia.org/wiki/Market_manipulation

Market Disappearance

In many markets, regulations dictate that exchanges halt trading after large price moves. These regulations are called "circuit breakers," since they halt trading in the markets during periods of extreme activity or fast change. Large price movements often suggest strategic position change, either cashing out gains or cutting losses. However, banks will find that exchange liquidity can vanish for short periods of time.

Liquidity can also disappear from trading counterparties off of the exchange. OTC liquidity can vanish altogether if market makers pull out of trading in their markets. A bank may enter an OTC position and find no way to unwind the position when it wants to terminate. This is particularly problematic for nonstandard or exotic trades.

Market Gapping

Markets gap—move suddenly upward or downward—in response to sudden changes in information or trading patterns. A bank that hoped to close out a position if the price fell 10% might find that it could not close out the position without taking a 12% loss. Stop-loss orders placed with exchanges or OTC counterparts also have execution risk. There is no guarantee the stop-loss order can be executed efficiently once it is activated. A stop-loss order is an order to a broker to sell a security once it reaches a certain, typically, lower price. Bid-offer spreads can also be expected to increase when markets gap.

EXAMPLE

Suppose BHP Billiton is trading at USD 45 on the NYSE. A bank purchases 10,000 shares of BHP and places a stop-loss order at USD 40 to achieve a maximum loss of USD 5 per share or USD 50,000. Markets move quickly, and BHP shares drop 20% to USD 36. When the first transaction below USD 40 occurred, the stop-loss was triggered, but the next executed price was USD 36, causing a USD 90,000 loss for the bank.

Crowded Trades

Bank traders get the same signals from the markets and often end up following similar trading strategies. Also, when new products or trading strategies are introduced and marketed aggressively to banks and funds, it is not surprising that many of them end up with similar positions. Positions held by many market participants following the same strategy are known as "crowded trades."

A bank in a crowded trade will be competing with others to get into and out of positions. Market liquidity is moving against them whenever they want to trade. In other types of situations, de-risking or risk-reducing strategies followed by investment funds can have simultaneous effects across many otherwise unrelated traded markets. In other words, a bank trader can experience losses due to correlated fund trading activity in other markets.

6.3.3 Trading Style

Most banks calculate their trading risk by looking at the VaR of the positions. Unfortunately, this only tells part of the story. In many cases, the changes in position drive more risk than the positions themselves. For this reason, it is often better to look at volatility of historical trading profit and loss, or P&L, as an indicator of trading risk than a forward-looking static VaR calculation on the current portfolio.

EXAMPLE

A bank estimates the VaR of its THB (Thai baht) position to be USD 3 MM, but over the course of a trading day, the emerging markets group changes the position by 30% on average, up or down. The actual VaR may therefore go from USD 3 MM to USD 2.1 MM or USD 3.9 MM without any change in the currency market.

The most popular trading styles are security selection and market timing. Those who follow security selection strategies try to pick individual long and short positions that appear to be mispriced relative to their benchmarks. Those who time the market are more likely to attempt to hold long positions when markets are rising, and hold short positions when markets are falling. Other styles include technical trading, black box models, momentum trading, mean-reversion strategies, merger "arbitrage," and many others. The details of these strategies are beyond the scope of this program, but it is important for the student to know that diverse funds can follow similar strategies leading to similar style risks and, in some cases, systemic risks.

To get an estimate of trading style risk, some banks use outside style indices to compare the performance of internal proprietary trading with the performance of outside funds managers. Style indices provide information on both performance and risk, helping banks decide if their proprietary trading activities benefit shareholders.

6.3.4 Margin Requirements

The financial impact of margin requirements is discussed in more detail in Section 3.4.6 in the Credit Risk Management book in the GARP FRR Series. Many trading strategies can be derailed by unanticipated margin demands. For example, a bank hedging an un-margined forward position with futures contracts may face significant cash flow fluctuations even though the trade was designed to reduce risks. A famous example of this occurred when Metallgesellschaft hedged its long-term customer contracts with short-term futures—the customer contracts were not margined but the futures were. A billion-dollar margin call triggered the company's failure. For this reason, banks need to assess margining risk as one of the more critical trading risks, in addition to market risk.

6.3.5 Basis Trading

Basis risk is one of the most significant residual risks usually found in a portfolio of similar deals. Basis risk is the risk of a change in the relationship between the price of a risk position and the price of the instrument used to hedge the risk position. Basis risk arises in situations where the underlying market prices are different for each type of instrument, but which are still very closely related. Where the divergence in the daily movement of the different rates is generally small, a bank will tend to hedge the general market movements and manage the basis risk separately.

EXAMPLE

A US company is paying the prime lending rate on a loan from Bank A. The prime rate is a floating rate charged on loans to customers with the highest credit rating. Bank A wants to lock in and fix the rate on the loan as it believes rates are going to fall. Bank A enters into an interest rate swap with Bank B to receive a fixed rate and pay six-month LIBOR. It proposes to offset the prime rate interest received from the loan against the six-month LIBOR interest paid on the swap. Bank A believes that the favorable level of the fixed rate received from the swap compensates for the difference in the floating rates. This creates a basis risk because the difference between the prime rate and the six-month LIBOR rate will fluctuate over the life of the swap. Any changes in the difference between the rates will have an impact on the revenue of Bank A. The figure below shows the relationship of the rates over a three-year period.

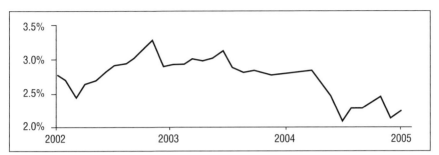

FIGURE 6.2 Difference Between Prime Rate and 6-Month LIBOR

6.3.6 Option Hedging Risks

There are a number of trading risks that are specific to option trading and hedging. The effect of bid-offer costs on option strategies is twofold, since the bid-offer must be paid on both the option position and the hedge position. If the hedge position varies, the bid-offer spread is paid continually.

Gapping markets present additional risks for option hedging. Arguably a trader who buys options to create an exposure removes the risk of being able to participate in a gapping market. The option premium represents the price paid for eliminating the execution risk of the delta-hedging strategy.

Finally, since option models are imperfect, particularly exotic option pricing models, valuations and hedge ratios may give traders the wrong signals for buying, selling, and hedging these instruments. The model risk, in other words, creates its own kind of market risk.

Some option risks can be reduced using static hedging techniques instead of dynamic techniques. In a static hedge, options are approximately replicated with other options that have less of a need to be rebalanced. Any residual risk may be dynamically hedged.

EXAMPLE

A bank writes a call option to a customer on Unilever with a strike price of GBP 1,600 and a maturity of one year. If that option does not trade on an exchange, the bank may hedge the option dynamically by taking stock positions based on the option delta. Alternatively, if a GBP 1,500 strike call trades at a six-month maturity, a hedge can be designed by purchasing the GBP 1,500 strike call, examining the basis risk, and managing the basis risk using the net option delta.

6.3.7 Failure of Trading Controls

While trading control failure is an operational risk, it has implications for market risk as well. This occurs when traders are "overlimit," or when the bank does not know that particular positions have been entered on its behalf.

Overlimits
The most common trading violation occurs when a trader exceeds his position or risk limit in a given market. This can occur because of trader error, hubris, or desperation to rescue a failing position. A trader who is "overlimit" (over-the-limit) creates a portfolio concentration and reduction in diversification benefit for the bank. As a result, it is a market risk issue as well as a compliance issue.

Most risk systems report risk at the end of a trading day and because of this, traders can often establish intraday positions well in excess of their limits. Since these positions are closed by the end of the day, they never show up as being overlimit.

Intraday trading causes a disparity between predicted P&L and actual P&L that introduces additional sources of risk. For example, a bank may think it is long 500 crude oil contracts as a result of its position limits, but not realize that a trader has increased the position to 1,000 crude oil contracts during the course of the day.

Rogue Traders
If a trader persists in violation of trading controls or manipulates reporting systems to hide his trading activity, the trader is a rogue trader. One famous example was Nick Leeson, whose unchecked risk taking in the Singapore branch of Barings Bank caused the bank's collapse in 1995. Mr. Leeson has commented on rogue trading:

> "I think rogue trading is probably a daily occurrence amongst the financial markets. Not enough focus goes on those risk management areas, those compliance areas, those settlement areas, that can ultimately save them money."[62]

From a market risk perspective, two problems with rogue traders are the under-reporting of their trading risks and the overconcentration of trading positions.

---

62   See www.nickleeson.com

6.3.8 Mark-to-Market Process

In large trading operations positions will change minute to minute as traders manage their risk positions. Therefore, it is important for the senior management of a bank to have a robust mark-to-market procedure in place to monitor traders' performances.

This is usually a daily process where a department, independent of the traders, will obtain and verify market prices for all the instruments held in the trading book. For any market where trades are made directly with counterparties, closing prices will be obtained from brokers who are active in the relevant markets. Brokers are independent of the banks and, by the nature of their business, know the current market price.

Some prices may be obtained from official fixing rates that are set daily. An important example of this is the daily fixing of LIBOR interest rates by the Intercontinental Exchange Benchmark Administration Ltd (IBA) in London. These rates are used to settle many derivatives contracts as well as for historical analysis. Official "fixings" occur in many centers around the world for different types of rates.

In addition to brokers and official fixings, closing rates for some instruments are obtained from official exchanges. For example, equity closing prices are officially set by the stock exchange where the share is quoted. These are used for mark-to-market equity positions. Futures contracts and options on futures are traded on futures exchanges around the world. Each exchange sets an official closing price each day that is used to revalue all positions. Futures contracts are traded for interest rates, foreign exchange, bonds, commodities, energy, and stock market indices. Futures exchanges are constantly developing new contracts to meet changing market demand. The mark-to-market procedure will consist of collecting and verifying the prices and entering them into the bank's revaluation system. The system will then calculate a value for each instrument, which will be recorded in the bank's books. The current value is also called the replacement value because it represents what the bank would have to pay if it needed to replace the transaction at current market prices. Often the system will also calculate the current risk positions generated by the instruments revalued, although this is sometimes carried out by a separate risk system.

The current value of a transaction is used for a number of purposes:

- Profit and loss calculations are made by comparing current values to original values
- Counterparty credit risk calculations are made by analyzing the current values of all deals with the same counterparty (See Chapter 3)
- Collateral calculations for OTC transactions use the current values of instruments held as collateral to ensure they are sufficient when compared to counterparty exposure
- Margin calls by futures exchanges are based on the current market value
- For cash settled instruments, the final market value is used to settle the transaction with the counterparty

6.3.9 Problems with the Mark-to-Market Process

The mark-to-market process can work well in theory but cause disasters in practice. For example, in the US energy markets in 2001, mark-to-market accounting for trades allowed Enron to overstate its earnings precisely because there were no liquid markets for some of the instruments they traded. In this case, subjective trader marks or model results (also known as mark-to-model) can end up taking the place of market quotes.

This distorts value estimates, earnings reports, and collateral requirements.

The same phenomenon occurred in 2008 during the global financial crisis. Illiquid structured debt products were marked to unverifiable mark-to-market values, triggering massive write-downs, excessive collateral and margin calls, and the demise of numerous institutions.

6.4 Managing Market Risk

For all that is written on the subject of market risk, a surprisingly large body of research is devoted to methods to estimate the value of market risk, and to describe the regulatory treatment of market risk. However, it is a daily requirement at banks to manage market risk portfolios so that they do not exceed desired limits and concurrently produce an acceptable rate of return.

There are three fundamental approaches to portfolio risk management: diversification, hedging, and synthetic portfolios.

6.4.1 Portfolio diversification approach

When managing a portfolio of long positions in financial assets, risk diversification is a matter of selecting the right portfolio components and the relative allocation to each. The principle is the same whether applied to a small sub-portfolio or to the firm-wide market risk portfolio.

There are portfolio building tools that allow a manager to construct an equally weighted portfolio (for bonds) or a market-capitalization weighted portfolio (for equities) using Markowitz mean-variance optimization. Constraints can be added in the form of minimum/maximum portfolio components, minimum/maximum volatility, minimum/maximum VaR, and so forth. The manager of the portfolio will have made an original selection of portfolio constituents and followed up with ongoing performance attribution analysis.

A conservative portfolio manager will spread positions over as many constituents as reasonable in the context of the financial instrument. For instance, a credit bond portfolio and a CDS portfolio may realistically consist of equal numbers of constituents (say, 100 or more), whereas a portfolio of FX positions will be spread over a significantly smaller number of constituents (say, 10-20).

An aggressive, or speculative, portfolio manager may reduce the diversification and select a much smaller number of assets, thereby driving up potential returns at the expense of increased market risk.

A more insightful portfolio manager will be able to use concurrent long/short positions and asset correlation data to construct portfolios that may depend less on outright directional asset performance and more on relative asset performance. A trading book with multiple types of market risk may successfully be managed this way, while simultaneously reducing the overall limit requirements and thereby capital allocation costs.

When selecting portfolio size and constraints, the manager will have transaction costs in mind. The broader the diversification in a portfolio, the smaller the value of each constituent. This in itself can lead to unattractive market prices due to small transaction size and again to even more expensive market prices due to even smaller rebalancing transaction sizes. The broader the diversification, the lower the portfolio risk and the lower its return. It is not inconceivable to think that cost of construction and rebalancing a portfolio can reach or even exceed returns.

6.4.2 Hedging approach

If diversification cannot be achieved satisfactorily, a sub-optimal portfolio of market risk may be the result. It may become either too "lumpy" or too "granular" with either too few or too many portfolio constituents. There may be an overweight of risk in one area and an underweight in another.

For instance, suppose an interest rate swaps trader has built up a customer portfolio of USD fixed/floating 10-year swaps, but the customers are all in the same direction, paying him the fixed side at the moment 10-year swap rates move up. The trader should seek out customers willing to receive the 10-year swaps and perhaps even to repeat across multiple points of the yield curve to become less dependent on a single yield curve point.

The trader/investor with an undesirable market risk portfolio will look for ways to mitigate the excess risk. He might seek out opposite customers in the market, and failing that call in prices from market makers to plug the perceived gaps in his book.

A bank trader may be slower to balance market risks in the hope of finding opposite-sided customers and thereby avoid having to pay the bid/ask spread to other traders. A hedge fund trader or long-only manager may have fewer reservations in such cases, as that trader always deals on the customer side of the spread and can therefore move faster with the market.

6.4.3 Synthetic portfolio approach

Corporate banks and passive fund managers sometimes use a synthetic portfolio approach to market risk management.

The active versus passive fund management debate currently favors passive management due to low transaction cost. The concept is simple: instead of spending expensive portfolio construction time on finding a customer-tailored equity portfolio, the passive manager will buy Treasury bills for the client funds and buy a stock index future as an overlay. The net effect is to create a perfectly diversified equity investment portfolio with no tracking error, the functional equivalent of a portfolio of long stock positions in exact proportion to the index.

Similarly, banks with large deposit volumes may at times become frustrated with the absence of good lending opportunities. In an analogous move, the bank portfolio managers may buy Treasury bills and sell CDS index positions against them. The net effect creates a long credit book for the bank, in spite of never having lent anything to the corporates specified in the CDS. JP Morgan's Chief Investment Office (CIO) conducted an example of this strategy from 2009 to the first few months of 2012.[63]

---

63 Report of JPMorgan Chase & Co. Management Task Force Regarding 2012 CIO Losses, January 16, 2013, pp21

6.5 Summary

This chapter has addressed the various trading strategies that banks follow, and the risks of those strategies.

Overview of Bank Trading Activities
- The trading strategy with the least market risk is a matched book.
- Another strategy is to manage positions in the product by executing "covering" or "hedging" deals at the discretion of the trading desk.
- A market maker will quote a buy and sell price to customers and other banks and trade on whichever price the counterparty chooses.
- To hedge their risk position, traders will take a position in a different instrument. The instrument may have different characteristics, but changes in its market value will mirror those of the original transaction.
- Hedging has many advantages but it does require careful management, as the instruments used are not identical to the original transaction. This means there will usually be some residual risk that is left uncovered and this must be measured and controlled.
- It is important to have a rigorous approval procedure for the introduction of new products that involves all the relevant departments in a bank.
- The new product checklist includes regulatory, tax, accounting, legal/documentation, IT, operational, risk reporting, pricing/valuation, funding, credit, and compliance considerations.

Bank Trading Strategies
- Basic strategies, like buying and selling, have hidden complexities, particularly short sales.
- Many bank strategies rely on leverage, which is obtained from margin loans, repo transactions, and derivatives, in addition to possibly leveraged sources of capital.
- Banks tacitly or explicitly enter carry trades, wherein they expect to profit in the long run from structural risk premiums paid in the FX, fixed income, equity, and commodity markets.
- Carry trades generally succeed, but occasionally fail dramatically, causing losses.
- Bank trading through clearinghouses has the benefits of centralized administration, position netting, lower collateral requirements, higher credit quality, and lower contracting risk.
- OTC clearing, under development in many parts of the world, has the promise of bringing these other benefits to bank trading.

External Risks in Bank Trading
- Banks have no control over some trading risks, but nevertheless need to be aware of them.
- Markets can be illiquid or lack the proper depth to execute banks' trading strategies.
- Markets may be manipulated by others, may be closed down, or may exhibit price-gapping behavior or crowded trades.
- Banks following coordinated trading styles, such as selection and timing, may find themselves holding similar risks.
- Margin requirements can be highly volatile.
- Basis hedging relationships may be unstable, leading to increasing risks rather than reducing risks.
- Option hedging strategies present special risks—model risk and tracking risk—specific to that type of trading.
- Failure of trading controls, itself an operational risk, causes unanticipated market risk.
- Mark-to-market causes many problems for bank trading particularly when markets are not transparent, and prices do not necessarily represent true value.

CHAPTER 7

Market Risk Organization and Reporting

This chapter describes how banks report their risks and manage their market risk reporting functions. This includes a description of risk governance issues, risk identification and classification, and risk reporting. We use the JPM Chase (JPM) annual report as a running example to illustrate the concepts. All materials in quotations in this chapter are taken from the 2013 Annual Report, pages 142-148. A brief overview of JP Morgan Chase is provided at the end of the chapter. Credit risk, treasury risk, and operational risk reporting are left to later chapters.

On completion of this section the reader will have an improved understanding of:

- The working definition and components of market risk
- The organization of the market risk management function
- The integration of the market risk department with other departments of a bank
- The classification and reporting of market risks
- The sources of trading risk and non-trading risk
- The different tools for measuring risk
- The users of risk management reports

7.1 Components of Market Risk

"Market risk is the potential for adverse changes in the value of the Firm's assets and liabilities resulting from changes in market variables such as interest rates, foreign exchange rates, equity prices, commodity prices, implied volatilities, or credit spreads."

—JPM 2013 Annual Report

Market risk is caused by adverse fluctuations in equity values, bond values, foreign exchange rates, and commodity prices. Furthermore, market risk can be caused by fluctuations in interest rates, including credit spreads. Changes in credit spreads may be caused by credit events or may be caused by changes in the market pricing of credit risk. Market risk also arises from the changes in relative value of very similar contracts, such as natural gas for delivery in March and April. Finally, market risk arises from option positions that have exposure to underlying market risk factors.

Sources of Market Risk
- Prices
- Price differentials (spreads)
- Interest rates
- Interest rate spreads
- Exchange rates
- Commodities
- Options

This is not the only possible definition of market risks. For example, a desk that trades inflation-indexed notes will consider changes in expected inflation to represent a market risk. Alternatively, a desk that trades catastrophe bonds will consider fluctuations in the perceived likelihood of losses to represent a market risk in trading catastrophe-linked bonds. In both of these cases, the market risk may be considered to be subsumed in the risk of fluctuations in the bond prices.

EXAMPLE

A Brazilian bank holds US corporate bonds and European equities in its investment portfolio. Because the bank holds bonds, it is exposed to changing US interest rates. It is also exposed to changes in the credit spread on the corporate bonds, and to foreign exchange volatility that affects the conversion of returns into BRL (Brazilian real), the local currency. It is exposed to European equity risk, and also to the currencies those equities trade in.

7.2 Governance of Market Risk

"Market Risk [Management] is an independent risk management function that works in close partnership with the lines of business, including Treasury and CIO within Corporate/Private Equity, to identify and monitor market risks throughout the Firm and to define market risk policies and procedures. The Market Risk function reports to the Firm's CRO. Market Risk seeks to control risk, facilitate efficient risk/return decisions, reduce volatility in operating performance, and provide transparency into the Firm's market risk profile for senior management, the Board of Directors, and regulators."
- JPM 2013 Annual Report

7.2.1 Objectives

Many students mistakenly believe that the role of market risk management is strictly to control or minimize risk. Most market risk departments do more. If a bank takes no risk, it minimizes its profit. However, the bank's ability to take risk is limited by the capital it has. Therefore, its objective is to maximize the returns it makes relative to the risks it can responsibly take.

To avoid insolvency, banks establish a maximum market risk tolerance; that number determines the maximum loss the bank is willing to take due to fluctuations in market prices and rates. While different traders and trading departments take different risks for different rewards, market risk management advises senior management on the relative returns earned for risks taken. With this information, senior managers can decide which departments should take more or less risk.

Efficient Risk-Return Decisions
When the bank can reduce volatility in operating performance without sacrificing return, it will surely do so. The challenges arise from the tradeoff between risk reduction and return reduction. This tradeoff can be measured using the RAROC concept.

In Chapter 4 in the Asset and Liability Management book in the GARP FRR Series, we study the RAROC concept in detail. RAROC is the ratio of profitability to risk for a trading portfolio or bank business unit. Simply speaking, the bank seeks to maximize its overall RAROC by controlling the absolute and relative amount of risk it takes in each of its businesses.

It would seem that a bank would maximize its RAROC by investing in the business that produced the highest individual RAROC. This is incorrect, since the bank enjoys a diversification benefit by operating many different business lines simultaneously within the bank. In some cases, a bank might even invest in an activity with a negative RAROC, provided that due to its risk reduction benefit it was able to increase the RAROC of the bank as a whole.

EXAMPLE

A bank has two businesses with zero correlation. The first business (B1) has an expected P&L of USD 50 million and a VaR of USD 100 million. The second business (B2) also has an expected P&L of USD 50 million but a VaR of USD 120 million. The RAROC of B1 is therefore 50% and the RAROC of B2 is 42%. The bank allocates its risk capital as follows:

The combined VaR (risk capital) for the bank is

$$\text{VaR combined} = \sqrt{(\text{VaR}_{B1}^2 + \text{VaR}_{B2}^2 + 2 \times \rho_{B1,B2} \times \text{VaR}_{B1} \times \text{VaR}_{B2})}$$

$$\text{VaR combined} = \sqrt{(100^2 + 120^2 + 0)} = 156.20.$$

If the bank allocated all its risk capital (156.20) to B1, it could expect to earn at best 50% of USD 156.20 million, or USD 78.10 million, compared to USD 100 million if it stays diversified. The bank should continue doing business as it has in the past.

Although risk information is ultimately used in performance assessment and capital allocation, the day-to-day primary role of the market risk management department is to report market risk accurately, clearly, and in a timely fashion to facilitate decisions and communication around risk.

Transparent Market Risk Profile
The market risk department does not control the risks, but it reports risks so that others may control them efficiently. Therefore, it is important that market risk reports be correct, as straightforward as possible, and as simple as possible without giving up important information. If senior management not only understands the major risk exposures of the bank, but also understands how those exposures relate to market risk drivers, it can make decisions as to how to alter its risk profile if necessary.

In some cases, the risk profile may be reduced by forcing line managers to reduce the size of their trades through liquidations. In other cases, management may be able to construct an overlay strategy, for example, to protect the bank's income from short-term changes in interest rates. If the risk reports are not clear and correct, the actions taken by management may be inappropriate.

7.2.2 Organization

"Market Risk is responsible for the following functions:
- *Establishment of a market risk policy framework*
- *Independent measurement, monitoring, and control of line-of-business and firm-wide market risk*
- *Definition, approval and monitoring of limits*
- *Performance of stress testing and qualitative risk assessments."*
—JPM 2013 Annual Report

Comprehensive Market Risk Policy Framework
JPMorgan's risk structure reflects that of every major bank. The Chief Risk Officer oversees market, credit, and operational risks, each of which may be headed by a different executive. The risk management policy, though proposed by the CRO, is approved by a risk management committee, the chief executive, or the board of directors.

The risk management policy usually encapsulates the bank's objectives and constraints relevant to its objectives. It also delineates limits and decision-making responsibility among traders, managers, the risk management committee, senior management, and the board. Risk management policy is chosen to be consistent with shareholder communications and objectives, and forms the basis for risk reporting, as risk reports address the bank's objectives and its constraints. The risk policy is designed to be consistent with best principles of risk management.

Independent Measurement, Monitoring, and Control
Good risk management requires the CRO function to be independent of the individual business units. This means that the CRO must not report to the head of any individual business unit, but rather to the CEO.

Furthermore, the CRO's compensation should not be directly determined by business results. In practice, it is impossible to insulate the CRO fully from the impact of business results. The ability of banks to pay bonuses to all staff, including the CRO and staff, depends on how successful the businesses are.

Definition, Approval and Monitoring of Limits
Most banks consider trading limit design, and its enforcement and reporting, to be under the direction of the CRO. In some cases, banks separate the compliance function from the reporting function, but these should both report to the CRO. In other cases, while the market risk management group

may track or report limit violations or policy violations, another group may be responsible for compliance and enforcement.

Stress Testing and Qualitative Risk Assessments
Finally, the market risk manager's job does not end with market risk and limit reporting. The market risk manager must do everything possible to ensure that risks are being identified and reported accurately. This means that when market risk reports are insufficient to capture the risk of a trading desk, the market risk manager must work with the desk to determine its exposure in extreme economic environments through stress testing. As another example, if the market risk manager suspects that a trading unit is taking risks that have not yet been quantified, it is that manager's responsibility to ensure that the risk is identified, measured, and reported.

Because the business lines generally have more specific information than the market risk manager, they are responsible for identifying and verifying risks taken in the business. Regular meetings between market risk management and the business lines ensure completeness, accuracy, and consistency of market risk reporting across the bank. Successful banks enjoy collaboration between the business units and risk management, whereas many bank failures or substantial trading losses can be traced to a lack of communication between business units and risk management. Both Barings Bank and the substantial trading losses at Allied Irish Bank in 2002 (USD 691 million) serve as excellent examples.

7.2.3 Risk Classification

JPM divides market risk reporting into "trading risk" and "non-trading risk." Other banks use the term "banking risk" for non-trading risk, but the idea is the same. At JPM, "non-trading risk includes securities and other assets held for longer-term investment, mortgage servicing rights, and securities and derivatives used to manage the firm's asset/liability exposures." This definition excludes assets in the banking book, which is exposed to credit risk. Consequently, loans that a bank holds until maturity are not included in the trading book.

Trading profits and losses fluctuate on a mark-to-market basis. Even if the gains and losses are not realized, the results are reported into net income as changes in the value of securities affect the value of the company's equity. Due to mark-to-market rules, unrealized gains and losses included in trading securities must be recognized. The fluctuations of the value of the non-traded positions have a longer-term impact on the bank, even if they are not reported to net income, but can be recognized otherwise. For this reason, it is important for the market risk management function to report both types of risk.

The risks in the banking book can be both significant and difficult to measure. Interest rates clearly drive fluctuations in value, but there are other factors.

Changes in the level and shape of market interest rate curves also may create interest rate risk, since the re-pricing characteristics of the Firm's assets do not necessarily match those of its liabilities. The Firm is also exposed to basis risk, which is the difference in the repricing characteristics of two floating rate indices, such as the prime rate and 3-month LIBOR. In addition, some of the Firm's products have embedded optionality that impact pricing and balances.

JPM probably estimates the VaR of its retained loan portfolio for internal management purposes, but does not report this figure in the annual report.

7.3 Tools Used to Measure Market Risk

JPM uses at least seven statistical and non-statistical risk reports, including:

- VaR
- Economic-value stress testing
- Non-statistical risk measures
- Loss advisories
- Profit and loss draw-downs
- Risk identification for large exposures ("RIFLEs")
- Earnings-at-risk

7.3.1 Non-statistical Risk Measures

JPM lists six non-statistical risk measures apart from stress testing. Non-statistical risk measures include sensitivities to variables used to value positions, such as credit spread sensitivities, interest rate basis point values, and market values.

"Net open positions" refers to a standard position report that is completed by every bank. Open positions are positions that were established in the past, but have never been offset by another transaction, transferred to a different legal entity, or terminated in the case of a default or bankruptcy. The net open positions report reflects the balance after identical long and short positions have been removed. Most banks include option positions as delta equivalents in this report to understand how movements in particular market prices or rates affect the bank as a whole. Many banks group similar positions into buckets, thereby approximating the risk profile in order to compute and present the risk information more quickly.

"Basis point values" refers to the changes in fixed income values for a given change in basis points. This is a risk sensitivity measure that is unique to fixed income trading and the banking book. It is used to give managers a quick estimate of how much the bank's trading and banking books will fluctuate in value for a given change in interest rates.

"Option sensitivities" refer to the Greeks discussed in Chapter 2. By aggregating option sensitivities across the firm, senior management understands how option positions respond to changes in underlying assets, volatility, interest rates, dividends, and time.

"Market values" report the change in market values of assets and positions to help management identify the changes that had the greatest impact on the bank. This indication may lead to management taking corrective action vis-à-vis those positions.

"Position concentrations" refers to unintended or unplanned concentrations of risk that have built up in the bank's overall portfolio. For example, a U.K. bank may have accumulated Australian government bonds, total return swaps on Australian corporate bonds, options on AUD, and positions in gold, which correlate to the currency value. The result of these disparate positions established in different departments can be an unexpectedly large exposure to the Australian economy.

"Position turnover" reflects how quickly traders are closing out their positions. High turnover can mean quick exit and lower risk, but it can also imply a great deal of uncertainty in knowing the position at any given point in time. Unusually high or low position turnover can be an indication to management that a trading activity may require additional scrutiny.

7.3.2 Value-at-Risk

Readers of this book are familiar with VaR, its benefits and disadvantages, as discussed in Chapter 5. However, each bank calculates VaR in a slightly different way.

> *"The Firm has one overarching VaR model framework, Risk Management VaR, used for risk management purposes across the Firm, which utilizes historical simulation based on data for the previous 12 months. The*

framework's approach assumes that historical changes in market values are representative of the distribution of potential outcomes in the immediate future. The Firm believes the use of Risk Management VaR provides a stable measure of VaR that closely aligns to the day-to-day risk management decisions made by the lines of business and provides necessary/appropriate information to respond to risk events on a daily basis.

Risk Management VaR is calculated assuming a one-day holding period and an expected tail-loss methodology that approximates a 95% confidence level. This means that, assuming current changes in market values are consistent with the historical changes used in the simulation, the Firm would expect to incur VaR "band breaks," defined as losses greater than that predicted by VaR estimates, not more than five times every 100 trading days.

Separately, the Firm calculates a daily aggregated VaR in accordance with regulatory rules ("Regulatory VaR"), which is used to derive the Firm's regulatory VaR-based capital requirements under the Basel 2.5 Market Risk Rule ("Basel 2.5"). This Regulatory VaR model framework currently assumes a 10-business-day holding period and an expected tail loss methodology that approximates a 99% confidence level. Regulatory VaR is applied to "covered" positions as defined by Basel 2.5, which may be different than the positions included in the Firm's Risk Management VaR."

– JPM 2013 Annual Report

The choice of historical simulation avoids the need for the bank to rely on parametric risk estimates such as the standard deviation. Since historical returns are not normally distributed, and correlations are neither linear nor stable, a case can be made that historical simulation is a better choice than variance-covariance analysis.[64] The use of 12 months of history emphasizes recent market movements and puts no weight on market movements over a year past. While some analysts would argue in favor of a longer timeframe, JPM prefers to conduct separate stress tests. In other words, the VaR report in this case is meant to capture typical risk, as measured by daily price changes in the last year, and stress tests are meant to identify more unusual exposures.

The one-day time horizon is usually chosen because it coincides with daily reporting of profit and loss. There are a few disadvantages with the

---

64   In some markets, this is demonstrably false if historical periods are not believed to resemble current periods from a risk perspective.

one-day timeframe, such as short-term mean-reverting return behavior, unreliable price marks in illiquid markets, and non-synchronous trading, i.e., positions that report at different times due to a 24-hour trading clock.

For example, if an emerging market bond fell 2% in a single day, was it because of a drop in value, a market over-reaction that would be corrected the next day, or simply an unrepresentative small transaction that was the only one reported? Historical VaR uses the printed price changes for the instruments and hence can be prone to these types of problems.

The Expected Tail Loss (ETL) or Expected Shortfall (ES) methodology refers to a two-step VaR calculation. The first VaR is computed to the 97th or 98th percentile confidence level. For losses above that level, the expected tail loss is determined. This expected tail loss is then compared with a VaR level as if it were chosen to be 99%.

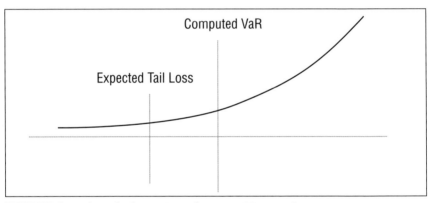

FIGURE 7.1 Left Tail of Loss Distribution, ETL, or ES

7.3.3 JPM's Value-at-Risk Report for 2013

As of or for the year ended December 31 (in millions)	2013 Avg.	2013 Min.	2013 Max.	2012 Avg.	2012 Min.	2012 Max.
CIB trading VaR by risk type						
Fixed income	$ 43 (a)	$ 23	$ 62	$ 83 (a)	$ 47	$ 131
Foreign exchange	7	5	11	10	6	22
Equities	13	9	21	21	12	35
Commodities and other	14	11	18	15	11	27
Diversification benefit to CIB trading VaR	(34) (b)	NM (c)	NM (c)	(45) (b)	NM (c)	NM (c)
CIB trading VaR	43	21	66	84	50	128
Credit portfolio VaR	13	10	18	25	16	42
Diversification benefit to CIB VaR	(9) (b)	NM (c)	NM (c)	(13) (b)	NM (c)	NM (c)
CIB VaR	47 (a)(e)	25	74	96 (a)(e)	58	142
Mortgage Banking VaR	12	4	24	17	8	43
Treasury and CIO VaR	6 (a)	3	14	92 (d)	5 (d)	196 (d)
Asset Management VaR	4	2	5	2	- (g)	5
Diversification benefit to other VaR	(8) (b)	NM (c)	NM (c)	(10) (b)	NM (c)	NM (c)
Other VaR	14	6	28	101	18	204
Diversification benefit to CIB other VaR	(9) (b)	NM (c)	NM (c)	(45) (b)	NM (c)	NM (c)
Total VaR	$ 52	$ 29	$ 87	$ 152	$ 93	$ 254

(a) On July 2, 2012, CIO transferred its synthetic credit portfolio, other than a portion aggregating approximately $12 billion notional, to CIB; CIO's retained portfolio was effectively closed out during the three months ended September 30, 2012.
(b) Average portfolio VaR and period-end portfolio VaR were less than the sum of the VaR of the components described above, which is due to portfolio diversification. The diversification effect reflects the fact that risks are not perfectly correlated.
(c) Designated as not meaningful ("NM"), because the minimum and maximum may occur on different days for distinct risk components, and hence it is not meaningful to compute a portfolio-diversification effect.
(d) The Firm restated its 2012 first quarter financial statements regarding the CIO synthetic credit portfolio. The CIO VaR amounts for 2012 were not recalculated to reflect the restatement.
(e) Effective in the fourth quarter of 2012, CIB's VaR includes the VaR of the former reportable business segments, Investment Bank and Treasury & Securities Services ("TSS"), which were combined to form the CIB business segment as a result of the reorganization of the Firm's business segments. TSS VaR was not material and was previously classified within Other VaR. Prior period VaR disclosures were not revised as a result of the business segment reorganization.
(f) The Treasury and CIO VaR includes Treasury VaR as of the third quarter of 2013.
(g) The minimum Asset Management VaR for 2012 was immaterial.

FIGURE 7.2 JPM's VaR Report for 2013—IB Trading and Credit Portfolio VaR

JPM's daily aggregate VaR varied between USD 29 million and USD 87 million with an average of USD 52 million. If positions had the same average risk through the year and returns from one day were independent of the next, then the annual VaR was USD 838 million for the combined banking and trading books.[65]

The bulk of JPM's VaR comes from its trading operations: USD 43 million. Note that the diversification benefit almost exactly offsets the VaR on the credit portfolio. Within the trading category, most stand-alone risk comes from fixed income trading, with a VaR of USD 43 million. The next largest category is commodities and other (USD 14 million), followed by equity (USD 13 million) and foreign exchange (USD 7 million). There was a USD 34 million portfolio-diversification benefit reported for the trading VaR in 2013.

Risk decreased in all categories for JPM from 2012 to 2013. This was primarily due to reduced risk in the Synthetic Credit Portfolio (CIO) and to lower market volatility across multiple asset classes. The overall risk decreased from a VaR of USD 152 million to USD 52 million.

Not all instruments are included in the VaR: See the footnotes to the table to understand the excluded assets.

RAROC

The market risk report does not report an official RAROC. However, using the Investment Bank (IB) income reported of USD 8,546 million for 2013, we could estimate a daily income, assuming 260 trading days per year, of USD 32.87 million per day. The daily RAROC is therefore an impressive 63.21%, but perhaps not accounting for other capital charges, such as the carrying charge for the Investment Bank. Also, VaR does not capture the full extent of the risks in the IB function.

Management uses risk information internally to calculate return on capital and return on risk. This information assists management in determining the relative success of each of the different business lines and the overall success of the company.

7.3.4 VaR Backtesting

Every major bank verifies the accuracy of its VaR measures over time through a process called backtesting, which was explained in Chapter 5. JPMorgan Chase assembles a histogram showing the frequency of P&L results for all levels of gains and losses.

---

65 Using JPM's statement that there were 260 trading days in 2013.

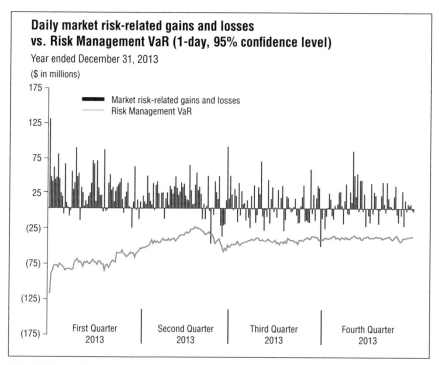

FIGURE 7.3 JPM's Daily IB Market Risk-Related Gains and Losses

In 2013, the bank had two incidents where the loss exceeded daily VaR, or about 0.8% of the 260 days. This is in line with a 99% confidence interval, as used in JPM Regulatory VaR reporting.

7.3.5 Debit Valuation Adjustment (DVA)

Recently, banks have been allowed to consider their own creditworthiness in valuing their liabilities. For example, in a swap contract, the value of the contract is commonly reduced when a counterparty's credit rating deteriorates. Symmetrically, when a bank's credit rating deteriorates, the value of its liabilities decreases, and hence swaps would generally increase in value on a mark-to-market basis. Whether or not a bank uses this accounting standard, economic analysis suggests that the value of swap liabilities will decline as a bank's credit rating falls.

JPM no longer reports DVA on a basis-point-value basis with respect to changes in its own credit spread, but records overall gains or losses in USD.

For 2013 the Firm had a DVA loss of 452 million, indicating that its main trading partners had—on average—a higher credit spread than JPM, and as a result were seen as poorer credit risks. A DVA result of zero would indicate that a bank is conducting OTC derivatives business with trading partners of approximately the same credit standing as itself.

7.3.6 Loss Advisories and Drawdowns

Like many other risk reports, these are designed to highlight major events that may warrant management attention. Loss advisories are reports of significant losses in a particular business or book. Drawdowns refer to the peak-to-trough percentage decline of an investment or fund over a defined time period. Drawdowns can be used as a complementary risk measure to VaR.

7.3.7 Economic Value Stress Testing

Most major banks do some kind of stress testing to complement their VaR analysis, and JPM is no exception. The firm stresses credit spreads, equity values, interest rates in major currencies, and key individual business segment risks that may impact the entire bank portfolio. The scenarios are reviewed and modified from time to time. Stress tests results are used not only for risk reporting, but for capital allocation purposes as well. Chapter 5 explained the concept of stress testing.

7.3.8 Earnings-at-Risk Stress Testing

Economic value stress testing shows the change in economic value of the bank's assets and liabilities. However, not all changes in assets and liabilities become part of earnings. Earnings-at-risk analysis uses the same scenario inputs, but the output is the impact of those scenarios on earnings.

JPM reports its earnings sensitivity to immediate changes in rates of +200 bp, +100 bp, −100 bp, and −200 bp. As of Dec 31, 2013, these figures were USD 4,718 million, USD 2,518 million, USD NM (not meaningful), and USD NM respectively.

The numbers show that the firm has positioned itself to gain from an interest rate increase. This may seem sensible, due to the low rates prevailing at the time. JPM does not consider an interest rate decrease meaningful as that would cause negative interest rates.

Banks gain from interest rate increases when they have short positions in fixed-income.

7.3.9 Risk Identification for Large Exposures (RIFLE)

JPM maintains records of specific, unusual events, and estimates the earnings impact of these events. The events may be a regulatory change, a political change, or another event that has the potential to damage JPM's positions. Normally, a bank will assign executive responsibility for managing large risks, and allocate some capital towards the mitigation of those risks. For example, a bank in an environment with significant regulatory risk would do well to invest in a regulatory relations department.

7.4 Risk Monitoring and Control

7.4.1 Limits

Like other banks, JPM sets aggregate risk limits based on VaR and stress tests. If management finds the firm is in violation of the limits, corrective action must be taken either to (a) reduce the size of the positions to bring them within limit or (b) revise the limit structure to reflect changes in economic conditions or risk appetite.

Similarly, individual limits are placed on business lines within the bank to ensure their risk-taking is in line with corporate expectations.

While one purpose of limits is to keep risk inside tolerable levels, the other purpose of limits is to express a risk allocation to a particular business unit. For example, a more profitable business unit may be allocated higher limits reflecting management's desire to overweight that business in its overall portfolio. Limits generally change annually to reflect changes in management attitudes about the prospects for success and risk in every one of the bank's businesses.

7.4.2 Qualitative Review

No bank should rely exclusively on numerical risk estimates. VaR estimates and historical simulation rely on historical data that do not necessarily say much about future risks. Qualitative risk assessments are important, but impossible to verify quantitatively. Therefore, banks must supplement their quantitative risk reports with qualitative assessments, and seek to understand risks that are being missed or mis-estimated.

In early 2008, correlations among commodities increased in a way that was not predicted by quantitative models. Since the models used historical correlations, many underestimated the risk of commodity positions that ended up moving together as precious metals, base metals, energy prices, and agricultural commodity prices all seemed to move more closely together.

During the European Sovereign Crisis of 2010-12, many traders and banks were operating in either "Risk On" or "Risk Off" mode, where bad news caused sell-offs in all asset classes and good news caused buy-ins. This caused asset prices in all risk classes to move in parallel, indicating very high positive correlations. It is very hard to make profits in such volatile markets.

In 2013, JPM incorporated correlation values across risk classes within the following ranges:

Interest rate correlation	−75% to +95%
Foreign exchange correlation	0% to +75%
Equity correlation	−50% to +85%
Credit correlation	+34% to +82%

7.4.3 Model Review

Banks use mathematical models for valuation and for risk assessment. Model results can be misleading for a number of reasons including:

- Errors in model specification, such as valuation drivers and the relationships between them
- Missing factors in the model
- Errors in derivation of the model
- Failure of pricing or simulation algorithms to converge
- Errors or simplifications made in programming
- Errors or simplifications in bucketing trades
- Inaccurate or inappropriate input data
- Misinterpretation of model results

An example of a simple model is interpolation between two numbers. There are several different ways of calculating an interpolation (i.e., linear, log-linear, exponential, cubic splining) and each, if applied to a yield curve, could produce a mostly correct result (cubic splining) or a wholly inadequate result (linear).

For these reasons, models must be reviewed periodically to ensure the bank has controlled its model risk as well as possible. JPM reviews new and changed models, including previously accepted models, "to assess whether there have been any changes in the product that may impact the model's validity and whether there are theoretical or competitive developments that may require reassessment of the model's adequacy."

7.5 Uses and Users of Market Risk Reports

In this chapter, we described how trading management and senior management use risk reports. The main uses of risk reports are to:

- Identify exceptional situations that require managerial attention
- Identify limit and policy violations
- Display the relative risks among different trades or business units
- Estimate the overall risk levels of the bank
- Assist in performance measurement and capital allocation

There are many other users of risk reports, including regulators, creditors, credit rating agencies, shareholders, equity analysts, and other banks.

Regulators use risk reports to verify the accuracy of a bank's risk representations and to monitor the risk-taking activity of banks. Creditors, including trade counterparties, use risk information to assess a bank's creditworthiness and to determine willingness to trade with the bank. Rating agencies use risk reports to gauge the stability of a bank's credit ratings. Shareholders and equity analysts compare a bank's performance and risk to its peer group in order to make better investment decisions. Finally, other banks look at their competitors' risk reports to ensure they themselves are following best practice and to gain an insight into the portfolios of their competition.

JPM MORGAN CHASE & CO IN FOCUS

From JPMorgan Chase's website—http://www.jpmorganchase.com

JPMorgan Chase (NYSE: JPM) is one of the oldest financial institutions in the United States. With a history dating back over 200 years, here's where we stand today:
We are a leading global financial services firm with assets of $2.4 trillion.
We operate in more than 60 countries.
We have 260,000 employees.
We serve millions of consumers, small businesses and many of the world's most prominent corporate, institutional and government clients.
We are a leader in investment banking, financial services for consumers, small business and commercial banking, financial transaction processing, asset management, and private equity.
Our stock is a component of the Dow Jones Industrial Average.

Company profile from Reuters.com—
http://www.reuters.com/finance/stocks/companyProfile?symbol=JPM

JPMorgan Chase & Co. (JPMorgan Chase), incorporated on October 28, 1968, is a financial holding company. The Company is a financial service firm and banking institution. The Firm provides investment banking; financial services for consumers and small businesses; commercial banking; financial transaction processing; asset management and private equity. The Company operates in five segments: Consumer & Community Banking, Corporate & Investment Bank, Commercial Banking, Asset Management, and Corporate/Private Equity.

JPMorgan Chase's bank subsidiaries are JPMorgan Chase Bank, National Association (JPMorgan Chase Bank, N.A.) and Chase Bank USA, National Association (Chase Bank USA, N.A.). JPMorgan Chase's principal nonbank subsidiary is J.P. Morgan Securities LLC (JPMorgan Securities). One of the Firm's principal operating subsidiaries is J.P. Morgan Securities plc.

Consumer & Community Banking

Consumer & Community Banking (CCB) serve consumers and businesses through personal service at bank branches and through automated teller machines (ATMs), online, mobile and telephone banking. CCB is organized into Consumer & Business Banking; Mortgage Banking, including Mortgage Production, Mortgage Servicing and Real Estate Portfolios, and Card, Merchant Services & Auto (Card). Consumer & Business banking offers deposit and investment products and services to consumers, and lending, deposit, and cash management and payment solutions to small businesses. Mortgage Banking includes mortgage origination and servicing activities, as well as portfolios consisting of residential mortgages and home equity loans, including the purchased credit-impaired (PCI) portfolio acquired in the Washington Mutual transaction. Card issues credit cards to consumers and small businesses, provides payment services to corporate and public sector clients through its commercial card products, offers payment-processing services to merchants, and provides auto and student loan services.

Market Risk Organization and Reporting **197**

Corporate & Investment Bank

The Corporate & Investment Bank (CIB) segment consists of Banking, and Markets and Investor Services, and offers a suite of investment banking, market-making, prime brokerage, and treasury and securities products and services to corporations, investors, financial institutions, government and municipal entities. Within Banking, the CIB offers a range of investment banking products and services in all capital markets, including advising on corporate strategy and structure, capital-raising in equity and debt markets, as well as loan origination and syndication. The Company also provides Treasury Services, which includes transaction services, consisting of cash management and liquidity solutions, and trade finance products. The Markets and Investor Services segment of the CIB is a market maker in cash securities and derivative instruments, and also offers risk management solutions, prime brokerage, and research. Markets and Investor Services also includes the Securities Services business, a global custodian, which includes custody, fund accounting and administration, and securities lending products sold principally to asset managers, insurance companies and public and private investment funds.

Commercial Banking

Commercial Banking (CB) delivers service to the United States, including corporations, municipalities, financial institutions and nonprofit entities. CB provides financing to real estate investors and owners. Partnering with the Firm's other businesses, CB provides financial solutions, including lending, treasury services, investment banking and asset management to domestic and international financial needs.

Asset Management

Asset Management (AM) provides investment and wealth management. AM clients include institutions, high-net-worth individuals and retail investors. AM offers investment management across all asset classes, including equities, fixed income, alternatives and money market funds. AM also offers multi-asset investment management, providing solutions to a range of clients' investment needs. For individual investors, AM also provides retirement products and services, brokerage and banking services including trusts and estates, loans, mortgages and deposits.

Corporate/Private Equity

The Corporate/Private Equity segment consists of Private Equity, Treasury and Chief Investment Office (CIO) and Other Corporate, which includes corporate staff units and expense that is centrally managed. Treasury and CIO are used in measuring, monitoring, reporting and managing the Firm's liquidity, funding and structural interest rate and foreign exchange risks, as well as executing the Firm's capital plan. The other corporate units include Real Estate, Central Technology, Legal, Compliance, Finance, Human Resources, Internal Audit, Risk Management, Oversight and Control, Corporate Responsibility and Other Corporate groups.

7.6 Summary

Although many of these concepts have been discussed in prior chapters, this chapter integrates market risk knowledge based on the JPM Chase annual report. Having read this chapter, the student should feel comfortable understanding every aspect of a market risk report for any major bank.

Risk Governance
- The objectives of the market risk management function are to report market risk information in a timely, accurate, and transparent manner.
- While risk management information is used to minimize risk where possible, its greater purpose is to allow the bank to take risk in the most efficient manner.
- The other responsibilities of Market Risk (management) include the establishment of a risk management framework, independent risk reporting lines, monitoring and reporting of limits, and qualitative aspects of risk management including stress testing.

Risk Tools
- JPM uses non-statistical methods to assess risk, VaR, loss advisories, drawdowns, economic value stress tests, earnings-at-risk stress tests, and RIFLE (risk identification for large exposures).
- Non-statistical reports include net open positions, basis point values, option sensitivities, market values, position concentration, and position turnover.
- VaR is measured at JPM using a historical technique that approximates a 99% confidence interval one-day VaR.

Uses and Users of Market Risk Reports
- Risk reports are used to identify exceptional situations, and policy and limit violations.
- Risk reports show the relative risk of business units and overall risk for the bank.
- Users include regulators, creditors, rating agencies, shareholders, equity analysts, and other banks.

Glossary

Amortization Amortization is the repayment of debt in regular installments over a period of time.

Arbitrage Arbitrage is a trading strategy that seeks to generate a profit by exploiting price differences of identical or similar financial instruments that are traded on different markets or in different forms.

Asian option An Asian option is a financial derivative whose final payoff is determined by the average price of the underlying asset at specific dates or during a specific pricing window.

Asset and Liability Management (ALM) The asset and liability management function in a bank typically manages the interest rate risk in the bank's banking book, the bank's liquidity risk, and the bank's overall capital position.

Asset Backed Security (ABS) An Asset Backed Security is a financial instrument backed by pools of loans or other types of securitizable, cash-flow generating assets. It is sold to investors who then receive payments based on the cash flows generated by the assets in the underlying pool.

Asset management Asset management is the management of financial assets and non-financial assets, and financial instruments to meet specified investment objectives. The term often refers to investment management.

Assets Assets are tangible or intangible claims with economic value that an individual, corporation, or other entity owns or controls with the expectation that it will provide future benefit.

Backwardation Backwardation occurs when the price of futures with longer maturities is less than prices of futures with shorter maturities. It is the opposite of contango.

Bank A bank takes deposits, makes loans, arranges payments, holds a banking license and is subject to regulatory supervision by a banking regulator.

Banking book The banking book of a bank is the portfolio of assets, primarily loans, that the bank expects to hold until maturity and typically comprises the loans the bank underwrites.

Basel Accords The Basel Accords (Basel I Accord, the Market Risk Amendment., Basel II Accord, Basel III Accord) are the cornerstones of international risk-based banking regulation, the results of a collaborative attempt by banking regulators from major developed countries to create a globally valid and widely applicable framework for banks and bank risk management.

Basel Committee on Banking Supervision The Basel Committee on Banking Supervision is a forum for regulatory cooperation between its member countries on banking supervision-related matters. It was established by the central bank governors, and consists of senior representatives of bank supervisory authorities and central banks from major economies.

Basis point A basis point is one-hundredth of one percent, or 0.0001, or 0.01%.

Basis risk Basis risk is the degree of imperfect change in the relationship between the price used to value a position and the price of the instrument used to hedge the position.

Beta Beta describes the return sensitivity of an individual stock or a portfolio of stocks to that of the market.

Bid-ask spread The bid-ask spread is the difference between the buy price or rate (bid) and sell price or rate (ask) of a financial instrument.

Black-Scholes model The Black-Scholes model is a pricing approach, initially derived by Fisher Black and Myron Scholes, used to value various types of contingent and derivative securities, such as options.

Bond A bond is a legally binding contract through which the borrower (also referred to as the issuer of the bond) borrows the principal, an amount specified in the bond, from an investor and in exchange pays a specified amount of interest (also referred as the coupon payment), usually at regular intervals, and at maturity repays the principal.

Borrower A borrower receives money by borrowing money with the promise to repay the amount borrowed, or principal, and to pay compensation for borrowing the funds, or interest, to the lender.

Bucketing Bucketing is the process of grouping similar types of exposures by type, size, kind, quality, or time period.

Calendar spread Calendar spread, a trading strategy, involves the simultaneous purchase of futures or options expiring in a particular month and the sale of the same instrument expiring in another month.

Call option A call option is a financial derivative that gives the right, but not the obligation, to buy an agreed quantity of a particular commodity or financial instrument from the seller of the option at a certain time (expiration date) for a certain price (strike price). The seller is obligated to sell the commodity or financial instrument should the buyer so decide.

Callable bond A callable bond is a bond that can be repaid at the discretion of the issuer and before the maturity of the bond, using a predetermined formula.

Capital adequacy Capital adequacy is achieved when a bank's capital ratio meets or exceeds the minimum capital ratio, which under the Basel Accords I and II is 8% of risk weighted assets. It can be satisfied with Tier 1 and Tier 2 capital. Tier 1 capital has to account for at least 4% of risk-weighted assets; the remainder can be satisfied through Tier 2 capital. National banking regulators can deviate from these minimum capital adequacy ratios. Basel III requires Core Tier 1 to be 4.5% and Total Tier 1 to be minimum 6%. However, Basel III also has a number of additional capital buffers that increase Total Capital Requirement to at least 10.5%.

Capital Asset Pricing Model (CAPM) The Capital Asset Pricing Model describes the relationship between risk and expected return and can be used to price risky securities.

Capital requirement A capital requirement determines the minimum level of capital that regulators require each bank to hold against its risk levels.

Capital Capital denotes financial assets or the financial value of assets, such as cash, or the long-term financial contribution of investors in a corporation.

Central bank A central bank is the principal monetary authority of a country, or a group of countries, and may also exercise regulatory and supervisory responsibilities over other banks, arrange payment between banks and, when needed, provide stability to the financial and banking system.

Chief Risk Officer (CRO) The Chief Risk Officer plans, leads, and manages the risk management activities of an organization.

Clearinghouse A clearinghouse guarantees the financial performance of a trade on an exchange by becoming the buyer to each seller and the seller to each buyer, and by providing clearing and settlement services for financial transactions.

Collateral Collateral is an asset pledged by a borrower to secure a loan or other credit. It acts as a guarantee to the lender in the event of the borrower's default.

Collateralized Debt Obligation (CDO) A Collateralized Debt Obligation is a type of structured asset-backed security. Its value is determined by payments derived from a specific portfolio of fixed-income generating assets or instruments.

Collateralized Mortgage Obligations (CMO) A Collateralized Mortgage Obligation is a type of structured asset-backed security. Its value is determined by payments derived from a specific portfolio of fixed-income generating assets or instruments.

Commercial bank A commercial bank offers a wide range of highly specialized loans to large businesses, acts as a middle man in raising funds, and provides specialized financial services including payment, investment, and risk management services.

Commercial paper Commercial paper is an unsecured, short-term debt security issued by a typically large, financially strong, organization that uses the proceeds to finance its operations.

Commodity A commodity is generally a physical item such as food, oil, metal, or another object with no differences in its makeup irrespective of the geographical or physical market where it is being sold.

Commodity risk Commodity risk is the potential loss from an adverse change in commodity prices.

Common risk factors Common risk factors are risk factors that may impact several obligors with similar exposures, financial instruments, or financial assets in a similar fashion at the same time.

Common Share Common shares, or common stock or common equity, typically refers to the equity in and ownership of a corporation.

Confidence Level A statistical term to specify how confident one can be of the result of a calculation. A confidence level of 99% means that statistically an outcome under the calculated value is 99% certain. Confidence levels do not explain anything above the specified percentage. The term is often used in risk management, in particular in VaR and Expected Shortfall (ES) calculations.

Contango Contango occurs when the price of futures with longer maturities are higher than prices of futures with shorter maturities. It is the opposite of backwardation.

Convertible bonds A convertible bond is a type of a bond that can be converted into an equity using a predetermined relationship. This right to convert can be exercised typically at the discretion of the bondholder.

Convexity Convexity is a measure of the nonlinear relationship between yield changes and bond price effects.

Corporate bonds A corporate bond is issued by a corporation to raise money from investors, and in return the investors receive interest payments from the corporation issuing the bonds.

Correlation Correlation is a single measure of association between two variables that establishes the strength of a statistical relationship and also forms the basis for statistical regression. Correlation ranges between 1 and −1.

Cost of credit The cost of credit is the interest rate, required return, or other compensation associated with securing and using credit.

Cost of funds The cost of funds is the interest rate, required return, or other compensation associated with securing and using capital.

Counterparty A counterparty is a party to a contract who is contractually bound and is expected to perform—deliver securities, make payments, etc.—at some time in the future.

Counterparty credit risk Counterparty credit risk is the risk that the other party to a contract or agreement will fail to perform under the terms of an agreement, and is particularly relevant for trading.

Coupon rate Coupon rate is that percentage of the principal that determines the coupon payment, which is the promised and regularly paid interest payment to the buyer of a bond or other debt security.

Covariance Covariance is a measure of association between two variables that quantifies the change between these variables.

Credit Default Swap (CDS) A credit default swap is a swap where the protection buyer makes a series of payments to the protection seller. The protection seller provides a payment if a financial instrument (such as a bond or loan), or a portfolio of financial instruments, experiences a predefined credit event.

Credit derivative A credit derivative is a contract that provides protection if a credit instrument or a portfolio of credit instruments (typically a bond or loan) experiences a credit event.

Credit event A credit event can be a default on a loan or similar exposure, or delays making full or partial interest and/or principal payments. It may also include the impact of reduced external credit rating.

Credit quality Credit quality reflects the risk associated with a loan, borrower, or facility. A higher credit quality translates to higher credit grade or credit rating.

Credit rating A credit rating identifies the relative creditworthiness of a borrower, exposure, or facility by assigning a credit grade.

Credit Rating Agency (CRA) A credit rating agency evaluates the creditworthiness of various borrowers, issuers, or credits.

Credit risk Credit risk is the risk of loss due to non-payment of a loan, bond, or other credit.

Credit risk mitigation technique A credit risk mitigation technique, such as collateral, credit default swap, insurance, and loan guarantee reduces credit risk through reduction of credit exposure.

Credit spread A credit spread is the yield differential between different securities, caused by differences in their credit quality.

CRM The Comprehensive Risk Measure (CRM) is a regulatory requirement under Basel III. It is relevant for banks with correlation trading positions in the trading book and covers not only securitization instruments (such as CDOs), but also normal correlation based trades.

Crowded trade A crowded trade is a series of simultaneous and similar trades by a larger number of market participants that follow, implement, or execute essentially the same or highly similar strategy.

CS01 Credit spread value of 1 bp: the value change of a credit related position as a result of 1 bp change in its credit spread.

Currency A currency is a generally accepted form of money—coins and bills—used in a country or a group of countries and issued by governments, central banks, or monetary authorities.

Currency futures A currency future, also FX future or foreign exchange future, is an exchange traded futures contract that conveys the right to exchange one currency for another at a specified date in the future at a predetermined exchange rate known at the purchase date.

Currency options A currency option, also FX option or foreign exchange option or forex option, is a derivative where the holder has the right but not the obligation to exchange one currency into another currency at a known exchange rate at or before a specified date.

Currency swaps A currency swap that involves the exchange of principal and interest in one currency for principal and interest in another currency. This type of swap is different from a forex swap.

CVA Credit Valuation Adjustment (CVA) is a required Basel III calculation. It is a required credit risk add-on to risk-free derivatives pricing (interest rate swaps) and must be aggregated in the trading book and reported accordingly.

Default Default is the failure to pay interest or principal according to contractual terms. It occurs when a debtor or counterparty is unable to make a timely payment or delivery.

Default risk Default risk is the potential loss due to default.

Delta Delta is the ratio of the price change of the derivative to the price change of the underlying asset.

Deposit A deposit is money entrusted to a bank for safekeeping in a bank account that allows the depositor to withdraw these funds and any interest paid by the bank on the deposit.

Derivative A (financial) derivative is a financial instrument that does not have an intrinsic value of its own, but whose value changes in response to changes in the value of a related underlying financial asset or commodity. Derivatives include swaps, options, forwards, and futures.

Disclosure Disclosure is the dissemination of otherwise internal information about the conditions, operations, and plans of an organization that allows for a proper and transparent evaluation of that organization.

Discounted Dividend Model (DDM) The Discounted Dividend Model estimates the value of a company based on the theory that the value of the company equals the sum of the discounted value of all its future dividend payments.

Dividend A dividend is the part of the earnings of a corporation that is paid out to its owners, typically either through the payment of cash or of additional shares.

Duration Duration is a measure of price sensitivity for a fixed income instrument and quantifies the sensitivity of the price of a fixed-income investment to a small incremental change in interest rates.

Economic capital Economic capital is the amount of capital a bank needs in case of loss events. It covers all risks across a bank, and is essential for the bank to survive in the long term.

Embedded options An embedded option usually provides either the bondholder or the issuer the right to take some action, as in a callable bond or convertible bond.

Equity Equity is the ownership interest in a corporation created by shareholders' contributions of capital and by retaining earnings.

Equities The plural form of Equity, Equities is the asset class representing stock or shares of corporate equities. It is often used as a catch-all when comparing risk or return of Equities to other asset classes, such as Fixed Income.

Equity risk Equity risk is the potential loss due to an adverse change in the price of stock.

Equity swap An equity swap is a financial derivative where the two counterparties exchange, at known future dates, cash flows based on the absolute or relative performance of an individual equity position, an equity portfolio, or index.

Exchange A (financial) exchange is a formal, organized physical or electronic marketplace where trades between investors follow standardized procedures.

Exchange rate An exchange rate is the price of one country's currency expressed in another country's currency, and is the rate at which one currency can be exchanged for another.

Exchange Traded Fund (ETF) An Exchange Traded Fund is a financial instrument that tracks a portfolio, a commodity, or an index, and is traded on an exchange.

Exotic instrument An exotic instrument is a financial asset or instrument with features making it more complex than simpler, plain vanilla, products.

Expected Loss (EL) Expected loss describes the size of losses that can be expected to occur.

Expected Shortfall (ES) Expected Shortfall calculates the average loss due to market risk, given that the VaR confidence interval has been breached. It is also referred to as Conditional VaR (CVaR) or Expected Tail Loss (ETL).

Exposure at Default (EAD) Exposure at Default is the maximum loss a lender or counterparty may suffer in case of a default.

Fair market price Fair market price is the price an asset would fetch if sold on the market immediately to a willing buyer.

Financial asset A financial asset derives its value from a specific contractual claim and typically includes bonds, loans, stocks, money, currency, derivatives, certain commodities, and other assets of value.

Financial instrument A financial instrument is a representation of an ownership interest claim or the contractual or contingent claim to receive or deliver cash, or another financial instrument or asset, and can either be a cash instrument (e.g., cash, securities, loans, bonds, notes, or equity) or a derivative instrument (e.g., forward, future, option, or swap).

Fixed income instrument A fixed income instrument, such as a bond, provides fixed and known periodic interest payments and the repayment of the principal at maturity.

Fixed interest rate A fixed interest rate is an interest rate that does not change over the life of a loan, bond, or other form of credit.

Fixed rate bonds A fixed rate bond is a bond where the coupon rate that determines the periodic interest rate payments does not change during the lifetime of the bond.

Floating interest rate A floating interest rate (also called variable or adjustable rate) is an interest rate other than a fixed interest rate, and may change depending on the performance of an underlying index.

Floating rate bonds A floating interest rate bond is a bond where the coupon rate on the bond is tied to an underlying index or base rate and, as a result, may change during the life of the bond.

Foreign currency cross rate A foreign currency cross rate is the exchange rate between two currencies against a third.

Foreign exchange risk Foreign exchange risk is the potential loss due to an adverse change in the value of one currency against another.

Forex swap A forex swap, is a derivative consisting of the simultaneous buying and selling of identical amounts of a currency for another currency at two different valuation dates. This type of swap is different from a currency swap.

Forward A forward contract (forward), a derivative, is a contract that defines the delivery of a specified quantity of a specified asset (e.g., commodities, currencies, bonds, or stocks), at a specified price and on a specified future date.

Forward interest rate A forward interest rate is a rate to which a borrower and lender agree for a loan to be made in the future.

Forward price A forward price is the agreed upon price of an asset in a forward contract, and can be a forward interest rate or exchange rate.

Forward Rate Agreement (FRA) A forward rate agreement is an OTC derivative contract that allows banks to take positions in forward interest rates. The contract gives the right to lend/borrow funds at a fixed rate for a specified period starting in the future.

Futures contract A futures contract (futures), a derivative, is a standardized and transferable contract traded on an exchange that defines the delivery of a specified quantity of a specified asset (e.g., commodities, currencies, bonds, or stocks), at a specified price and on a specified future date.

Gamma Gamma measures how much an option's delta changes when the underlying asset's price changes.

General or systematic market risk General, or systematic, market risk is the risk of an adverse movement in market prices that occurs across a range of financial assets, including fixed income, loans, equity, and commodities.

Governance Governance relates to the rules, processes, policies, and regulations outlining and defining the capacity, operational management, and administration of an organization, business, or other entity.

Hedging Hedging reduces risk by matching a position as closely as possible with an opposite and offsetting position in a financial instrument that tracks or mirrors the value changes in the original position.

Historical simulation Historical simulation measures risk across instruments and portfolios assuming that historical changes in market values are representative of future changes.

Historical volatility Historical volatility is the realized volatility of a financial instrument over a given time period.

Hybrid security A hybrid security is a financial instrument that has both equity and debt features.

Idiosyncratic risk Idiosyncratic risk represents risks that are particular to the conditions and circumstances of one or a defined group of individual borrowers, assets, or securities.

Implied Correlation Implied correlation is the variable that is calculated between the implied volatility of an index option and the respective implied volatilities of options on each of the index components. It is therefore a forward-looking number.

Implied volatility Implied volatility is the future volatility implied by an option's price.

Incremental Risk Charge Calculating the Incremental Risk Charge (IRC) is a Basel III regulatory requirement for banks with non-securitized positions in their trading book, e.g., bonds, equities, CDS, etc.

Index An index is a statistical composite that measures changes, performance, and risk of financial markets.

Inflation rate Inflation rate is the change in the purchasing power of money expressed as an annual percentage change.

Insolvency Insolvency occurs when liabilities exceed assets. While not synonymous with bankruptcy or illiquidity, it typically leads to either or both.

Interbank loan An interbank loan is a loan between banks.

Interbank market The interbank market is the market where banks trade with each other. It includes the interbank foreign exchange and loan market.

Interest rate An interest rate, the price of credit, is the rate charged for accessing and using borrowed funds.

Interest rate margin Interest rate margin is the difference between the interest income the bank earns on its assets and the interest expense it pays on its liabilities.

Interest rate risk Interest rate risk is the potential loss of value due to the variability of interest rates.

Interest rate risk in the banking book The interest rate risk in the banking book is caused by maturity differences between bank assets and liabilities, by differing interest rates used for pricing, and by differing repricing points.

International bank An international bank is a large commercial, investment, or merchant bank with operations in several different countries.

Investment bank An investment bank predominantly deals with corporate and institutional customers, issues financial securities in the financial and capital markets, provides advice on transactions such as mergers and acquisitions, manages investments, and trades on its own account.

ISDA The International Swap and Derivatives Association defines the standard contract terms for OTC derivatives, including the Credit Support Annex (CSA).

Issuer An issuer is a legal entity that sells financial instruments to raise funds to finance its operations. Sovereign and local governments, corporations, institutions, and other legal entities are typical issuers.

Junior bond A junior bond is subordinated to more senior bonds in case of bankruptcy, default, or a similar event, but it has priority before equity.

Kurtosis Kurtosis is a measure of "fat tails," i.e., the relative probability of extreme returns compared to usual returns.

Leverage Leverage reflects the amount or proportion of debt used in the financing structure of an organization. The higher the leverage, the more debt a company is using.

Liabilities Liabilities consist of a bank's debts, created by customer deposits and the bank's borrowings.

LIBOR (London InterBank Offered Rate) LIBOR is a daily reference rate based on the average interest rate banks in London charge other banks, on the offer side of the transaction, when borrowing and lending.

Liquidity Liquidity refers either to market (transactional) or funding (payment) liquidity.

Liquidity risk Liquidity risk can be market (transactional) liquidity risk and funding (payment) liquidity risk.

Long position A long position, the opposite of short position, represents the ownership position of an asset. When the asset's value increases, the position increases in value; when the asset's value decreases, the position decreases in value.

Loss Given Default (LGD) Loss Given Default is the actual loss suffered in the wake of a default. It is a function of the recovery rate and the exposure at default.

Macaulay duration Macaulay duration quantifies a bond's duration and approximates the percentage change in bond price for change in yield.

Margin Margin (requirement) is the amount that investors must post to their brokers and that brokers are obligated to post with the clearinghouse, and is determined by various considerations including the different types of instruments the broker trades on the exchange, the risk of the instrument, and the overall trading volume.

Market liquidity risk Market liquidity risk refers to conditions when trading—buying and selling—assets significantly affects their transaction price, or when trading can be only be executed at significant price concessions.

Market risk Market risk is defined as the risk of losses in on- and off-balance-sheet positions arising from movements in market prices. It typically encompasses the risks pertaining to interest rate related instruments and equities in the trading book, and foreign exchange risk and commodities risk throughout the bank.

Market Risk Amendment The Market Risk Amendment of 1996 required banks to maintain regulatory minimum capital against their positions in various market-traded financial assets such as foreign exchange, fixed income, equity, commodities, and derivatives. It is now superseded by The Basel II Accord, which incorporated significant proportions of the amendment.

Market risk capital Market risk capital is capital allocated against possible market losses.

Mark-to-market Mark-to-market (accounting) assigns a value to an asset that reflects its current market value.

Maturity Maturity is the time period until a loan, bond, or other credit is repaid fully.

Modified Duration (MD) Modified duration is one approach to quantifying a bond's duration and approximates the percentage change in bond price for a 1% change in yield.

Mortgage A mortgage is a loan that finances the purchase of real estate with the real estate serving as collateral for the financing.

Netting Netting is the settlement of mutual obligations by cancelling out mutual debts. Settlement is based on net exposure and not gross exposure.

Nonstatistical risk measure Nonstatistical risk measure is a tool that quantifies market risk and includes measuring net open positions, basis point values, option sensitivities, market values, position concentrations, position turnover, and stress testing.

Off-balance-sheet activity An off-balance-sheet activity is not recorded on the balance sheet, and includes asset, debt, or financing related activities such as derivatives or loan commitments and other contingent exposures that could pose a risk to the bank.

Operational risk Operational risk is the risk of loss resulting from inadequate or failed internal processes, people, or systems, or from external events. This definition includes legal risk, but excludes strategic and reputational risk.

Option An option conveys certain rights to the buyer of an option. The two main types of options are a call option and a put option.

Option price An option price is the price the buyer of the option contract pays for the right to buy or sell a security at a specified price in the future.

Over-the-Counter (OTC) Market The over-the-counter market is a decentralized market without a physical marketplace, where both standardized and non-standardized securities and other financial instruments are traded.

Paid-in capital Paid-in capital is the (equity) capital that owners have invested in a corporation.

Payment system A payment system is the infrastructure that settles financial and other transactions or transfers funds between financial institutions using established procedures and protocols.

Plain vanilla Plain vanilla is the standard type of a financial asset or instrument.

Portfolio A portfolio is a collection of investments, such as stocks, bonds and cash equivalents, held by an institution or a private individual.

Position A position is the amount of a security either owned (which constitutes a long position) or borrowed (which constitutes a short position) by an individual or by a dealer.

Preferred share A preferred share has properties of both equity and debt, and is senior to common stock, but is subordinated to bonds. Usually preferred shares do not carry any voting rights.

Present value Present value, the discounted value of future payments, adjusts values to reflect the time value of money and to make these values comparable.

Prime lending rate The prime lending rate or prime rate is the rate the banks typically charge their best customers.

Principal The principal is the amount borrowed on credit and excludes interest or other charges.

Private offering A private offering raises capital by selling new securities to a selected group of individuals, but not to the public.

Probability of Default (PD) The probability of default is the likelihood that a loan will not be repaid and will fall into default.

Project finance Project finance provides funds for the completion of large-scale industrial or infrastructure projects where the assets of the project are pledged as collateral for the loan and the realized income or cash flow once the project is completed is expected to repay the loan.

Provision for loan loss Provision for loan loss represents funds set aside to absorb anticipated loan losses.

Public borrower A public borrower is typically a sovereign state, or a provincial, county, municipal, or local government, including their sub-entities or agencies.

Public offering A public offering raises capital by selling new securities to the public.

Purchasing Power Parity (PPP) Purchasing Power Parity is a theory of long-term equilibrium of exchange rates where the relative value of two currencies is determined solely on the relative differences between price levels of two countries.

Put option A put option is a financial derivative that gives its buyer the right, but not the obligation, to sell an agreed quantity of a particular commodity or financial instrument to the seller of the option at a certain time (expiration date) for a certain price (strike price). The seller of the option is obligated to buy the commodity or financial instrument should the holder of the option decide to sell.

Recovery rate (RR) The recovery rate is that fraction of a defaulted obligation that can be recovered.

Regulatory capital requirement A regulatory capital requirement specifies the minimum capital that a bank must hold to guard against the various risks it takes, such as market risk, credit risk, and operational risk.

Repurchase agreement or "repo" A repurchase agreement or "repo" is a contract between two parties in which one party sells the other a security at a specified price and with the obligation to buy the security back at a later date at another specified price. Repos are widely used by central banks to provide support for a bank's short-term liquidity.

Reputational risk Reputational, or headline, risk is the potential loss resulting from a decrease in standing in public opinion.

Reserve requirement The reserve requirement, in a fractional reserve banking system, is the proportion of cash a bank must keep on hand to fulfill regulatory requirements. It limits the amount of money an initial deposit could potentially create through the multiplier effect.

Retained earnings Retained earnings are the part of corporate earnings not returned to the owners as dividends.

Rho Rho is the sensitivity of the option price to changes in the risk-free rate.

Risk appetite Risk appetite is the level of risk exposure an investor is willing to assume in exchange for the potential for a profit.

Risk factor mapping Risk factor mapping is a process that tells us how to convert selected risk factors into combinations of other risk factors.

Risk management Risk management is a structured approach to monitoring, measuring, and managing exposures to reduce the potential impact an uncertain event happening.

Risk policy A risk policy outlines the risk management framework of an organization in relationship to its objectives. It varies across and within industries and firms based on the ability to absorb losses and the rate of return sought from operations.

Risk transfer Risk transfer is the assumption of specific risk for a fee, or premium.

Risk-adjusted Return on Capital (RAROC) Risk-Adjusted Return on Capital adjusts the return generated by an asset for the inherent risk assumed by the project, making it easier to compare and contrast projects with different risk profiles.

Risk-free rate The risk-free rate is the rate of return from an investment that is completely free from all types of risks.

Rogue trader A rogue trader typically violates trading controls or manipulates reporting systems to hide unsanctioned trading activity.

Scenario analysis Scenario analysis, or "what-if" analysis, assesses the potential outcome of various scenarios by setting up several possible situations and analyzing the potential outcomes of each situation.

Securitization Securitization is a process where illiquid cash flow producing assets (such as mortgages, credit cards, and loans) are pooled into a portfolio; the purchase of the assets in the portfolio is financed by securities issued to investors, who then share the cash flows generated by the portfolio.

Security A (financial) security is a fungible financial instrument.

Senior bond A senior bond has priority over all other more junior and subordinated bonds in case of bankruptcy, default, or a similar event.

Settlement risk Settlement or "Herstatt" risk is the risk that a counterparty fails to perform as agreed and does not deliver a security, or its value, after the other counterparty has already delivered on the same transaction.

Shareholder A shareholder, stockholder, or equity holder is one of the owners of a corporation, with the right to elect the board of directors, decide corporate matters, and receive dividends.

Short position A short position, the opposite of long position, is the result of selling of a borrowed asset, writing an option, or selling a futures position. When the asset's value increases, the position declines in value and when the asset's value declines, the position increases in value.

Solvency Solvency denotes the financial condition of a firm when assets exceed the liabilities.

Specific, non-systematic, firm-specific, unique risk Specific, non-systematic, firm-specific, unique risk is the risk of an adverse movement in the price of one individual security or financial asset due to factors specific to that particular security or issuer.

Speculation Speculation involves the buying (long position), holding, selling, and short selling (short position) of financial assets, commodities, foreign exchange, or derivatives, in the expectation that price fluctuations will generate a profit. It also denotes a position that is not hedged. Speculation is the opposite of hedging.

Standard deviation Standard deviation is a measure of risk, and quantifies the dispersion of the data from its mean. It is also the square root of variance.

Standardized Approach The Standardized Approach to calculate the bank's credit and market risk capital is the simplest approach outlined in the Basel II Accord for these risks. For operational risk, this is an intermediate level approach.

Stop-loss order A stop-loss order instructs a broker to buy or sell a security at the best available price when a certain, stated price is reached.

Stress testing Stress testing assesses the potential outcome of specific changes that are fundamental, material, and adverse.

Stressed VaR (SVaR) Computing Stressed VaR (SVaR) is a regulatory requirement under Basel III. It tests how a given portfolio performs during a hypothetical period of stress. The portfolio is stressed with a data series from a volatile market. It is commonly assumed to mean market data from the 2008 Credit Crisis, but in reality banks are free to choose a stressed period of their own.

Strike price The strike price is a fixed and known price at which an option can be exercised.

Swap A swap is a derivative that enables two counterparties to exchange streams of future cash flows with each other.

Systemic risk Systemic risk is the risk of a system-wide breakdown in the banking or financial system.

Theta Theta measures the expected decline in option value with the passage of time.

Total Return Swap (TRS) A Total Return Swap is an equity swap where the receiver receives a payment equal to the total return—capital gains plus dividends—of a stock over a fixed period of time, usually a calendar quarter.

Trading book The trading book of a bank is the portfolio of various positions in financial assets, instruments, and commodities that a bank holds with the intention to invest, to trade, or to hedge other positions in the trading book.

Transaction cost Transaction cost is an expense incurred in buying or selling a security, including commissions, markups, markdowns, fees, and any direct taxes as well as the potential cost of executing the trade in the market due to widening spreads and liquidity considerations.

Underlying assets An underlying asset is the asset that the price of a derivative depends on.

Unexpected loss An unexpected loss describes a loss that is in excess of the expected loss. It is expressed with a certain confidence level.

Value-at-Risk (VaR) Value-at-Risk, a measure of risk, estimates the potential loss at a specified confidence level using statistical analysis.

Vega Vega, a measure of sensitivity to volatility, is the first derivative of the option value with respect to the volatility of the asset or instrument underlying the option.

Volatility Volatility, or conditional standard deviation, quantifies the risk of a financial instrument over a specified time horizon.

Yield curve A yield curve illustrates the relationship between prevailing interest rates based on the time remaining to maturity.

Zero-coupon bonds A zero-coupon bond is a type of fixed income instrument that makes only one payment at maturity, including both interest accrued and the repayment of principal. It is traded at a deep discount from its stated principal value.

Index

Amortization 74, 83
Arbitrage 29, 169
Asian options 43, 97
Asset-liability management (ALM) 7, 68
Asset management 197

Backwardation 95-96
Banking book 68, 154, 184, 185, 186
Banking risk 165, 184
Bank risk management 1
Bank's trading book 7
Bank trading 151,163
Basis point 48, 63
Basis risk 74, 98, 131, 170-171, 185
Beta 84
Bond issuers 57
Bonds 55-56, 59, 63
  - Government 60
  - Junior 56
  - Senior 56
  - Zero-coupon bonds 57
Bucketing 128, 130, 132
Business lines 182, 184, 193

Callable bonds 57
Call option 34, 89
Capital 3, 55, 84, 157
Capital Asset Pricing Model (CAPM) 84
Central banks 25, 59, 66, 93
Chicago mercantile exchange 31
Chief risk officer 13, 183

Clearinghouse 32, 163, 164
Collateral 54, 72, 164
Collateral 164, 173
Collateralized Debt Obligations, or CDO 75
Collateralized Mortgage Obligations (CMOS) 74
Commercial banking 197
Commodities 32, 90, 92-93, 133
Commodity markets 90-91, 92, 95, 97, 167
Commodity prices 92-93, 96
Commodity trading 91
Contango 95
Convertible bonds 57
Convexity 65
Corporate bonds 56
Correlation 43, 125, 100, 128-129, 187
Cost of credit 61
Counterparty 33, 72, 163, 164, 173, 176
Covariance 126, 137
Credit quality 56
Credit risk 7, 32, 52, 54 ,179
Crowded trades 168, 177
Currency positions 30
Currency swaps 33, 71

Debit Valuation Adjustment (DVA) 191
Delta 39
Delta-gamma method 134
Delta-normal method 134

217

Derivatives 3, 27, 59, 69, 155, 162
Discount rate 66
Dividend 83, 86, 87
Drivers of equity values 83
Duration 64, 65, 68

Embedded bond options 57, 75
Equity 79, 81-83, 90, 84, 132
Equity risk drivers 83
Exchange rates for major currencies 23
Exchange traded funds (etfs) 82
Exotic 44
Exotic options 42
Exotic risk 44
Exotics 73, 75

Failure of trading controls 171
False risk reporting 9
Fixed income instruments 48, 51, 54, 63, 75, 77
Fixed rate 53
Fixed rate bond 66, 72
Floating interest rate bonds 66-68, 72-73
Foreign exchange 22, 28, 30, 33, 36, 132
Foreign exchange market 19, 27, 30, 153
Foreign exchange rates 23-24
Foreign exchange risk 20, 23
Foreign exchange trading 31
Forward 32, 41
Forward foreign exchange 28
Forward interest rate 33, 69
Forward positions 87-88, 98-99, 132
Forward price 87, 93-94, 99

Forward rate 28, 30
Forward Rate Agreements (FRAS) 69
Forwards 86
Futures contract 31, 87, 173

Gamma 39
Gapping markets 171

Hedging 6, 39, 41, 70, 89, 99, 154-155, 157, 169, 171
Historical simulation 124-125, 130, 136, 187
Historical volatility 116, 120, 123, 136
Historical volatility method 147

Interbank market 51, 59, 70
Interest rate markets 77
Interest rate risk 3, 30, 32, 54, 67-68, 71, 72, 74, 132, 154, 157, 185
Interest rates 51, 63, 69
Issuer 55, -56 62

Kurtosis 117, 118, 119

Leverage 160, 162
LIBOR rate 52, 70
Liquidity positions 52, 55
Loans 51, 54, 55, 61, 75, 184
Long futures position 162
Long position 157, 160
Long-term rates 59, 60, 66

Macaulay duration 64
Margin 85, 88, 173
Marketable loans 54
Market price 123, 166

Index

Market prices 96, 123, 151-152, 154, 170, 186
Market risk 7, 38, 53, 151, 154, 179, 180, 183-184
Market risk factors 136
Market risk management 181
Market risk reports 182, 184, 190
Market value 173, 186
Market variables 179
Mark-to-market 172, 174
Modified duration 63, 67
Mortgages 74

Netting 163
Non-statistical risk measures 185

Open positions 186
Operational risk 5, 7, 171
Option positions 41, 179, 133, 186
Option price 35-37, 38, 41
Option risk 39, 41, 106, 171
Option value 35-36, 40, 133
Over-the-Counter (OTC) Market 27

Portfolio 53, 65, 67, 74, 114, 156, 186
Portfolio risks 106
Preferred shares 82, 86
Present value 57, 63-64, 83
Profit 173
Purchasing Power Parity (PPP) 24
RAROC 3, 181, 190
Rates 58-59
Real interest rate 45
Required market interest rate 57
Rho 40
Risk-adjusted rate 84
Risk factor mapping 130

Risk factors 20, 105, 129
Risk-free interest rates 85, 87-89, 90, 106
Risk Identification For Large Exposures (RIFLE) 193
Risk information 5, 182
Risk models 5, 29, 130, 133, 137
Risk reports 6, 163, 183, 192, 195
Rogue traders 172

Securitization 54
Short selling 92, 159-160
Standard deviation 113, 114, 117
Stop-loss orders 168
Stress testing 192
Swaps 30, 69, 71, 72

Term structure 60, 64
Theta 40
Total return swap (trs) 88
Trading activities 152, 155, 157, 172
Transaction costs 39, 41

Underlying assets 39, 42, 44, 69, 89
Underlying instruments 27, 32, 34, 41, 58, 89

Value-at-Risk (VaR) 112, 143, 186
Vega 40, 41
Volatility 36, 38, 40, 41, 114, 123, 181

Yield curve 57-58, 65

Zero correlation 126